23 Days in Korea

An American at the World Cup

Andy Gustafson

Order this book online at www.trafford.com
or email orders@trafford.com

Most Trafford titles are also available at major online book retailers.

Print information available on the last page.

ISBN: 978-1-4120-0325-4 (sc)

Trafford rev. 10/09/2018

 www.trafford.com

North America & international
toll-free: 1 888 232 4444 (USA & Canada)
fax: 812 355 4082

To Ivy
The perfect girl
The perfect wife
I would not have finished
This book without you
Stuff Forever

To the players
And coaches of the
U.S. National Team
Whose outstanding efforts
Brought us so much joy
And earned the respect
Of the world

To the fans of U.S. Soccer
Who made the long trip
You made those
23 Days in Korea
So very special
I will never forget
The times we had

Preface

This book is a collection of my daily reflections on my experiences at the 2002 World Cup in South Korea. Each chapter details the events of the day, as well as my thoughts on the both the past and the future. The games played by the United States are written in the present tense for dramatic effect.

As this book is written predominately for an American audience, please forgive me for not using traditional terminology. Though a match of football is played on a pitch by footballers and watched by supporters, we still think that a game of soccer is played on a field by players and watched by fans.

I also realize that Korea is not a single country but that North Korea and South Korea are two separate nations. In this book, I use "Korea" for simplicity. When "Korea" is used, it refers to South Korea, one of the host nations.

Acknowledgements

I want to thank all the fans and my friends who offered encouraging words about this project. Each of them inspired me to keep writing when I only wanted to play Championship Manager.

Thanks to my friends who helped with the editing: Mark, Wells, Jimmy, Sarah, Rod, and Ivy. Your aid, corrections, and criticism were invaluable. The book is infinitely better because of you.

Thanks to John. Without your computer expertise, none of this would have even made it to the publisher.

Thanks to everyone at Verizon for allowing me to take the month of June off so I could travel to the Cup.

Ivy, your encouragement, support, research, and many types of help were invaluable. This book is as much yours as it is mine.

Introduction

"It is with regret that we are unable to provide you with . . ." With those words the focus of this book was drastically changed. My original intent was to write a book chronicling the U.S. Men's National team during the 2002 World Cup. I am a big fan of this kind of book, as it takes the reader inside the team. It often provides a view that the average fan never sees. One can get to know the players through not so much interviews, but real conversations. Anecdotes abound, generally adding humor and showing these superstars as normal, living, breathing human beings.

I was hoping to take the reader to the practices as the U.S. prepared for the most important tournament in sports. My vision was to give insight to Coach Bruce Arena's tactics, line-ups, player evaluation, and overall strategy. Perhaps I could have even been able to have a player give me a first hand account of what was said in the locker room, as the team was about to take the field. I had visions of reporting on Knute Rockne-like speeches that swept the team into a swarming frenzy and convinced them they were world-beaters. In my wildest dreams, I would have earned the trust of the staff and would have been welcomed into that sacred getaway known as the locker room, to hear for myself what happens during halftime. What fountain of soccer knowledge spews from the all-knowing coaches that if followed by the players would guarantee victory? Maybe I'd even hang around for meals with the players. That way I would be sharing with you all the nutritional secrets that are available only to the world's finest athletes.

I was planning on featuring four or five players and telling the story of the 2002 Cup through their eyes. I would have spent a lot of time with Jeff Agoos as he prepared to take the field for his long awaited debut on this highest stage. What a story. Goose was the last player cut in 1994. Then, although starting most of the qualifiers for 1998, found himself in Coach Steve Samson's Marmaduke-sized doghouse and never saw the pitch. Finally, I wanted to capture his emotions as he suited up after nearly a decade.

I was planning to tell this story without including myself. My ego struggled with this decision, but I had decided to tell it as if I was a bug on the wall. It was to be a story on the team and that was it. However, with that letter from U.S. Soccer, my hopes were crushed. "It is with regret that we are unable to provide you with an accreditation form for the 2002 FIFA World Cup in Korea/Japan."

Though a major setback (how can I tell who polishes the boots in the locker room if I can't even get into the stadium?), it was not at all unexpected. Sure, I held out hope that I would obtain the coveted passes, but deep down, I knew it was a long shot. I did have a lot going for me. I host, along with my good friend Mark Bushman, a somewhat weekly television show, *This Week in Soccer*. Unfortunately, US Soccer must have realized that it is only seen in two small Virginia counties. I truly believe it is as good as any soccer show in America. It is the kind of show I would love to have the opportunity to see. However, being that this is America and we are talking about soccer (the World's game, America's joke) to see Mark and I, you need to live in Stafford or Spotsylvania County and subscribe to Adelphia Cable.

If you are among those lucky 800, you are able to see Mark and I report from such exotic locations as University of Richmond Stadium and Courtland High School. Mark has built a tremendous relationship with the Richmond Kickers and many others in the A-League. In fact, he is considered by many to be the A-League expert. They love the attention he brings the team and the league. In return, he is treated like a king. He has the access that I have dreamed about. Forget the locker room, he travels to away games on the teams state of the art bus! He is privy to all sorts of inside stuff.

Mark is also the driving force behind the show. It was his show from the start, and needing help, he invited me along for the ride. I live in Northern Virginia, which suits me best to cover D.C. United. That is fine with me as I have always been a sucker for the major leagues. However, as far as perks go, MLS could do a lot better. We journalists are given food before the game; usually it is pretty good. We also get bottled water and soft drinks. At halftime there are cookies, though I miss out on them as I am usually running from the press box to our cameraman who is typically situated behind one of the goals. Of course, it is great going to the press conference after the game and then into the locker room. Talking to players is fascinating and great fun for someone who is such a huge fan, but usually there is not much being said. Everyone crowds around the goal scorers. I usually talk to the defensemen or new players that are not attracting much attention.

It was no surprise that I was rejected for credentials for the World Cup. Sure, U.S. Soccer realized I worked for a small local show with no budget, but I thought I still had a card to play. Through our vast networking efforts, Mark and I met Jimmy LaRoue. Jimmy had recently launched a website devoted to soccer in the Mid-Atlantic region. He asked if we would like to help him. Mark had been writing columns for a number of sites, but nothing steady. I was hoping to do so myself.

Though we both have good, well paying, if not boring jobs, Mark and I are always trying to figure out ways to make a living on soccer. Although there is not much demand, there is a shortage of soccer journalists in America. Of course neither Mark nor I have a journalism degree, but we do not see why a silly little thing like that should stop us. So we try to do as much as possible and hope that someday this great sport catches fire. Then we would be in demand. For a while we were members of John Dyson's *The Soccer Show,* which is a weekly Internet based radio show. While doing this, we anointed ourselves Kings of All Soccer Media! We had our TV show, we were writing on the web, and we were on the radio. What more could anyone ask? Well, some money would be nice, or even a bit of recognition. But that is something we are still working at.

Now that we were writing for Jimmy's site *Onthesidelines.org,* I hoped that would push the pubahs at U.S. Soccer over the edge and give me the credentials that would allow me to write this book. But again, U.S. Soccer outsmarted us by actually going to the site. Although it is, in my biased opinion, one of the better soccer sites in America, it was in its infancy. It was not at all pretty to look at and we were getting fewer hits than an American League pitcher.

I had also dropped hints that a book was in the works. Alas, it all was for not. In the meantime, Jimmy had decided that he should go to Korea as well. This was fine with me, as I really was not looking forward to a trip to the other side of the world alone. We submitted our credential application together and were rejected together.

We went to plan B. We had entered into FIFA's draw for tickets. That left us with a dilemma, what tickets to try to get. Of course we ordered the US first round matches, but what about beyond that? The way FIFA set it up, you could either choose the game in the second round and beyond in one of two ways. The first was contingent on the U.S. making it that far. Basically, we would pay for the games and if the U.S. did not make it that far, we get our money back. The other option was to order the tickets, regardless of who would be playing. We decided on this option, through the quarterfinals. We assumed this would be a safe choice, as we did not see the U.S. advancing beyond that stage. We also thought it would be a good idea to have tickets to perhaps sell if we decided to come home early. We also put ourselves on the list for two other games, not involving the U.S.

Being newly acquainted, Jimmy and I were not sure if we would be able to stand each other for long. We also decided that since we had no idea how much anything would cost, we would stay until our money ran out. As long as we had the funds, we could stick around through the quarterfinals, unless the Korean lifestyle did not sit well with us. Then we would be on the first plane home as soon as the Americans were finished.

Jimmy was planning on reporting on the web site daily from Korea. I told him I would be happy to do the same. Thus, our readers would really get a feel of the atmosphere at the Cup. However, the whole book idea was bothering me. It has always been a goal of mine to write a book. I have started two novels and have a great screenplay in mind, however, like most would be authors, my motivation seems to disappear about one chapter in.

I had proposed to my girlfriend sometime back and did feel somewhat guilty about leaving her for nearly a month to go watch soccer. She has been a great supporter of mine and actually now enjoys the game. I felt the need to do something more than write a few columns for the web site on this trip. Therefore, I made the momentous decision to write the book anyway. This way I could better justify leaving her only four months before our wedding. Also, as I am always hoping for a job in the sport; having written a book could not hurt. I secretly fancied myself an up and coming writer of books in the John Feinstein mold.

Now that the book was back on, I needed to decide how to do it. It would be very difficult to give an inside look at the team if I was not allowed in. If I have no access to the players, how can I tell stories of their innermost thoughts? If I can't get into the locker room, how can I quote Arena's speeches verbatim? If I can't sit down and talk with the players, how can I tell of their fears or expectations? Clearly, my book would need to change.

Now my ego was able to force itself to the forefront. The book would no longer be about the team; it would be about me! All about me! Well, the ego didn't win all that. The book is still about the team, only they have been pushed back a bit. The book became sort of an adventure story, *Two Americans in Seoul.* Certainly it is an exotic location, one that is not on most American's itineraries. We were sure to meet colorful characters and see strange things. We would also be attending one of the world's biggest parties, the World Cup! So most of all, this book would be about soccer. Soccer and the adventure of two young men in a strange land. Soccer and the adventure of two young men in a strange land surrounded by people from all over the world. And parties. And people and soccer. And the U.S. National Team.

So there it is. Soccer and the adventure of two young men in a strange land surrounded by exotic characters partying and watching soccer and the U.S. National Team.

Before Korea

When France and Senegal kicked off to start the 2002 World Cup, I was as far away both mentally and physically as anyone in the world. As I arrived at work that Friday morning, it was hard for me to believe that in three days I would be in that same city, Seoul, over half way around the world. I imagine that when Pape Bouba Diop scored that now famous goal, my mind was on nothing more than surviving my last day at work for a month. It was not until my fiancée, Ivy, called me sometime after halftime to tell me that Senegal was winning 1-0 that I entered the World Cup Zone.

For the rest of my workday, the game to which I had paid so little attention, occupied my mind. I could concentrate on nothing except what Senegal must be going through in trying to prevent what was in my mind the greatest team in the world from equalizing. A call from my friend, Mark Bushman, alerted me that it was still 1-0 in the 70th minute. My mind raced faster. I imagined people in Senegal crowding around a small television set in a nameless village hanging on every pass, willing their countrymen to hold on. I thought of the crowd watching a giant screen outside *L'Hotel de la Ville* in Paris trying to come to terms with what they were seeing as their mighty heroes were being humbled by their former colony. Then I cursed my situation, as I was not able to watch the dramatic upset along with the rest of the world.

Mark called once more, this time to confirm that it was over and Senegal had stunned the defending champions. My mind went back to the opening match in 1990 when Cameroon had done the same to Argentina. I remembered ESPN's Sports Center leading with that story and thinking, "Why are they so worked up over a first round match?" As a college sophomore, I was in my soccer infancy. Now, 12 years and countless matches, books, magazine stories, and interviews later, I understood the full gravity of what had just happened. Although Argentina had gone on to the final game in 1990, their defeat in the first game has been hailed as the moment that African football arrived. By 2002 Africa had won two Olympic Gold medals but were still waiting on a team to advance to the semi-finals in the World Cup. But for the moment, none of that mattered.

I sensed that an entire nation, if not a continent, was celebrating. I have always found it heart-warming watching a people come together to celebrate. It is an experience I feel Americans truly miss out on, singing and dancing in the streets in patriotic joy. I was thinking that of anyplace in the world I could be, Dakar would be the place on this day. Though their team was supposed to be happy just playing on the world's stage for the first time, their players came together, shocked the world, and gave their fellow citizens a night of celebrations that would be remembered for a lifetime. One match in and the Cup was already making dreams come true.

The rest of the day was a blur. I listened to Tony Kornheiser and his guests trying to put this game into perspective. It was great to listen to people on the radio talk about soccer, but as none of them were fans, they came up very short.

I remember thinking that in every tournament there is one great upset. This did not bode well for the U.S. as they prepared to play a Portugal team that was favored by some as potential champions. I was on record having written that there was no way we could beat them on June 5th in both their and my first game of the Cup. With Senegal's victory, it made me feel that anything was possible, though still very unlikely.

I was to get off work at 3:45 P.M. but by 3:00 I was clearly done. I spent the next 45 minutes walking around the office, saying goodbye to everyone and imploring them to watch some games. "Be sure to look for me on Tuesday morning when we play Portugal. "I will be in the 2nd row, right behind the goal," I told them.

I had received the tickets just three days earlier, a fact that had nearly scared me to death. I was witness to what has been a well-documented FIFA fiasco. Apparently, FIFA hired a very small and inexperienced company with very good connections to handle the ticketing for the games. This company proved the adage, "It's not what you know, it's who you know," true. They knew the who but not the what. Tickets were to have been delivered by early May, but I spoke with many who left for Korea in early June without their tickets! Fortunately for me, mine had arrived with four days to spare.

Finally 3:45 came and I was out of the office like a shot. I made it home quickly and rather than packing (the plane did not leave until Sunday morning at 7:30), I called Jimmy to find his answer to a question that would drastically affect my trip.

Jimmy and I had spent hours planning the trip. We went through a number of scenarios for traveling to Korea and back, the most ridiculous of which had us leaving on Thursday May 30th and driving to San Francisco with Ivy. We would leave the car with her sister who lived there and fly to Korea. Upon returning, we would pick up the car and drive to Las Vegas where we would meet up with Mark Bushman who would be vacationing in Sin City. I would usually never turn down a trip to Vegas, but fortunately, we came to our senses and avoided the longest drive of our lives piggybacked on the longest flight.

Jimmy and I also debated what tickets to buy, where to stay, and how we would travel in Korea. We bought and paid for both airline and game tickets and were very excited about the grand adventure. Then it nearly fell apart.

It was a Wednesday in early May, four weeks to the day when the U.S. would take the field in Suwon to face the mighty Portuguese. Bushman and I had traveled to Raleigh where the U.S. team had recently opened their training camp, to see them scrimmage against the Richmond Kickers. After the U.S. had been lucky to salvage a 2-2 draw, we called Jimmy, who was stuck at work, to tell him about the shocking result. But, it was he who dropped the bomb. "We had a big problem at work. I might not be able to go." I could hear from the disappointment in his voice that he was serious.

Over the next three and a half weeks I called Jimmy daily, if not hourly. His answer was usually the same. "I still don't know. I am still preparing to go, but I don't know when I'll know." For the first week or so, that answer was fine, however it soon got old. I was having a difficult time preparing to spend three weeks on the other side of the planet when I did not know if I would be traveling alone.

I began to press Jimmy. "What are the odds?" I would ask.

He was as frustrated as I was, and my incessant questioning was not helping. "I don't know. Probably 50-50." I was pressing for an answer that Jimmy did not have and was lucky that Jimmy is a very patient and all around great guy.

As the departure day grew near, we came up with a plan for the airport. Even though neither of us knew if Jimmy would be making the trip, we planned as if he would. We decided that Jimmy would leave his car at his work, and I would pick him up there on Saturday, June 1st. I would invite some friends over and we would play poker until the games began at 1:30 A.M. Then we would watch the games until it was time to head to the airport at 5:00 the next morning.

All the plans were coming into place, and yet less than two days before the plane was to leave, I still did not know if Jimmy was going. As I arrived home after my last day of work that Friday afternoon, I knew that Jimmy would have the answer. Nearly all of my friends who knew the story were telling me Jimmy would not end up going, but I held out hope. I have to say that I was a bit nervous when I called him that day. I have never traveled alone before and though I was sure I would be fine, I was not looking forward to it.

Jimmy answered his phone, and I casually asked him what was up. "Nothing much," he answered, his voice giving me no clue as to which way he was leaning, so I asked if he had any news. "Yeah, I decided I am going," he answered nonchalantly.

"Alright!" I nearly yelled into the phone with a great sense of relief.

"I decided there is no way I can miss this. It's a once in a lifetime trip, and my boss understands. We should be okay at work, so I'm going."

We made a few more plans for leaving and then hung up without much small talk, which is rare with Jimmy. He is a big talker, so much in fact that there was some concern that his gift of gab would cause friction between us. After all, we would be spending nearly a month together, and sometimes I just need some quiet. With new vigor, I jumped back in my car and headed to Summer's Restaurant to catch the replay of the by now famous match.

The previous Friday I had met with a few other D.C. area residents who were making the trip. We had met through the Yanks in Korea, Yahoo group that someone with great foresight had set up. It was invaluable for me in making plans as 341 of us exchanged ideas, information, and itineraries. A little over a week before the Cup, I sent out a message for all those in my area and found that there was a good number of D.C. area fans heading over. We decided to gather at the Brickskeller, a famous D.C. pub with an outstanding beer collection. There I met six others, Dave and Mark, two dark haired guys who were about the same age as I. Geta, an Ethiopian, and Vladimir, a Dynamo fan from Moscow, would be supporting the U.S. as if they had been here all their lives. The last two, a newly wed couple, were heading to Korea after a week in New Zealand.

As I left the Brickskeller, Mark said he would be at Summer's to see the replay. Summer's is a soccer themed sports bar and restaurant in Arlington, VA that is well known in the soccer mad community of America. Many fans make the pilgrimage when they come to town for U.S. National Team games. Whether at 8:00 on a Saturday morning for Premier League matches from England or at 4:00 in the morning for an Olympic match, Summer's is the place to be for soccer in the D.C. area. It was therefore no surprise that when I showed up about a half hour before the replay was to begin that it was quickly filling. Soon I noticed both Geta and Vladimir arriving. Mark joined them during the first half.

Those three informed me that they would be lodging together in Korea, though not traveling all together. Mark was leaving in the morning, a day before I. He had found a direct flight to Seoul. Vlad and Geta were not leaving until Monday, which would put them in Seoul Tuesday night, the eve of the match with Portugal. They said they would see me at Nashville.

Nashville was the first of the curiously named pubs where we Yanks would gather in Korea. A few members of the Yanks in Korea group who were familiar with Seoul had suggested we hold a rally there the night before the Portugal match. It was said to be a spacious, western type sports bar. I thought it a great idea to get together and get to know each other. I also admired Vlad and Geta's will for guaranteeing they would be there, coming directly from the airport!

Watching the replay, I thought France was unlucky not to score as they were denied by both the bar and the keeper. However, Senegal was not intimidated and deserved the three points. Though I knew the outcome, it was a great feeling watching it unfold. After the game, I wished my three new friends bon voyage and promised to meet them at Nashville in Seoul, South Korea.

Ivy and I headed home, and I prepared to watch the late games or actually those from Day 2, hoping they would be as dramatic as the first.

Day 1
Sunday, June 2

Airplanes

I am calling this "Day 1", though technically Jimmy and I would not arrive in Korea until Monday evening. As Saturday turned to Sunday, I was playing poker and avoiding drinking beer. In preparation for a 19-hour flight, I was determined to completely hydrate myself with water to stave off the effects of jetlag as much as possible.

It had been a good evening as a few of my friends showed up to say farewell and to help me stay up until the games started at 1:30 A.M. The guys were playing a very low limit poker game and the girls were doing something in the next room. I was having a great time, but was feeling uneasy about still needing to pack. Finally when midnight hit, I had to get up and start packing. As the big game, Argentina v. Nigeria, began in 90 minutes, and I needed to leave for the airport at 5:00, I realized that this was my only time to pack and not miss any of the games. There would be four games in a row, but I would miss the last two while on the plane. I really hated missing the England v Sweden match, but I had no choice.

Ivy pitched in a big hand and basically did my packing for me. With her help the packing was easy and I was back downstairs with my friends just before 1:00 A.M. One couple said their goodbyes and left, thus ending the poker game. I was hanging with my good friend Rob until he announced that he and his wife needed to leave. He absolutely hates soccer; at least he says he does, though I am not sure he has ever seen a game. He has never taken me up on my numerous offers of free tickets to D.C. United games. I knew he was anxious to leave before the games started, so we shook hands and I told him I'd see him in a month.

Then Ivy and I made a quick trip to 7-11. This was the last time Ivy and I would be alone for over three weeks, and she was struggling with it. We had been engaged less than a year and had only recently purchased a house. While she was excited for me, she was apprehensive about my being so far away at such a big event while the world has been in such turmoil since September 11th. I assured her that everything would be fine, but she was not completely convinced.

We returned home just before kickoff. As I am a huge England fan, I was hoping for a draw, but the Argies made sure to further my agony that night by scoring in the second half. Curiously, the referee blew the final whistle as Nigeria had a corner kick.

After the game, I went upstairs to lie down with Ivy, who was sleeping. I was only there a short while because I did not want to wake her and the Paraguay-South Africa game was starting. I was not really looking forward to this match, as they were not the most glamorous of teams, however it proved to be entertaining. Paraguay scored on a beautiful volley and South Africa wasted their chances.

9

At around 4:30 Ivy woke up and came downstairs. The game was at the half, and I was writing her an e-mail that I was hoping would surprise her when she arrived at work on Monday. However, as we were leaving in a half hour, Ivy was not pleased to see me on the computer. She ever so kindly suggested that it would be a good idea for me to get off the computer and spend the last few minutes with her.

I was able to put her off long enough to quickly finish the note. We spent about 20 minutes snuggling on the couch. As I sat there with her in my arms, I felt guilty and sad. Guilty because I was leaving her. Since meeting we had never spent even a week apart, and now I was going a long way away to watch soccer, leaving her behind. I felt sad because for the first time, I actually realized how much I would miss her. Leading up to this moment it was all excitement and planning. Now it was real. I would not hold her like this for a long time. Sadly, the clock moved very quickly, and soon we were out the door.

That early on a Sunday morning, even the infamous Beltway was empty, and we made the 30-minute trip to Dullas Airport in 20 minutes. Soon we were in front of the Air Canada entrance. This was the moment I feared, the moment when I would leave Ivy. She cries easily at the lamest of movies, and I did not want to walk away while she was crying. Luckily for me, she was her usual fabulous self. After unloading our bags, she hugged me, gave me an amazing but quick kiss, said "I love you," turned and left. I, too, quickly walked away and breathed a sigh of relief. I could not have planned a better drop off.

Jimmy and I found the counter and after a short wait, were given our boarding passes. We also were told that this was their inaugural flight to Vancouver.

I spent the flight to the Canadian city with my forehead pressed against the window. I watched my country pass below and did very little talking or even thinking. I simply enjoyed the view.

In Vancouver we switched planes and met up with some other Yanks heading over. That raised the excitement level and for the first time, it seemed real. I was going to the World Cup!

On the plane, I again took the window seat, which allowed Jimmy to stretch his long legs. I looked out the window and marveled at the snow-covered mountains.

As we flew over the North Pacific, I set aside the excitement of the upcoming month and reflected on what it took to reach this point. More specifically, the qualification process and the games I had attended. It occurred to me that it was odd that I was traveling to Asia to see the U.S. play three games (hopefully more) when I had only attended that same number of qualifying matches. But the three I saw were big ones. The three I attended defined the struggle the team faced.

The games I attended were Guatemala at RFK Stadium in the second round, Mexico in Columbus the first game of the hexagonal, and later Honduras in RFK. I witnessed these three games in three very different settings.

The Guatemala match proved to be a war of attrition. It was a brutally hot and humid day in our nations capital. Both teams were desperate for a win. On Big

Soccer, there was an amazing build-up as fans organized themselves into what was deemed Project Mayhem. For the first time American supporters set out to give a Central American team the same sort of treatment that our boys receive when they play down there. A few of the leaders booked rooms in the Guatemalan's hotel. They spent the night before the match running through the halls with loud noisemakers.

Yes, it was a far cry to the all night blaring radio remotes set up just outside the hotel while fire alarms are being pulled inside the hotel, but it was a start.

As for me, I was doubly excited. Not only was I going to see this important match, but also I would witness it from field level. Mark Bushman and I had only been doing the show for a few months, and I had found it a wonderful experience to watch D.C. United games standing on the field behind the goal. The noise down there is deafening, but it is the speed of the game that always takes hold of me. For the first time, I got a sense of just how fast these athletes run, how quickly they cut, and how hard they kick the ball.

I had spent a few months in MLS, now it was time to get my feet wet in International play. About thirty minutes before the match, my cameraman, Luis, and I stepped down from the stands and onto the field. Luis set the camera up only a few feet to the left of the 18-yard box. ESPN's Jack Edwards and Ty Keough were walking the field. I noticed that they were looking closely at some soggy patches from an earlier rain. The Guatemalan's fans were already inside the stadium, singing loudly in their blue and white shirts. Americans were beginning to trickle in, and more than a few had received the word to wear red.

As game time neared, the stadium was full and noisy. I would love to report that I could understand songs and chants, but in reality all I heard was noise and a lot of it. Unlike the D.C. United games, the end line was packed. There were hundreds of photographers jockeying for position, and I was relegated to stand behind them.

The noise was deafening for most of the first half as the U.S. attacked the goal where I was standing. Despite a lot of possession and a few great chances, they failed to score. At halftime, Luis and I moved to the opposite side of the field, keeping the U.S. goal nearest us. We wanted a good shot of the goal we were sure to score.

This side was as crowded as the other, however, due to the low stands, I was forced to kneel so the fans behind me could see. I was hot and sweaty, and I sensed our players were wilting as well. Things looked bad when Eddie Lewis was sent off for throwing an elbow. However, Cobi Jones provided a spark off the bench and sent a beautiful cross to Brian McBride who put the ball in the net. He was perhaps 20 feet from me and from my vantage point I thought it had been a diving header, it had happened so fast. As I jumped to my feet, McBride lay on the field in what I assumed to be ecstasy.

After the game, which we won 1-0, I asked him if he had lay on the field due to fatigue. He responded by lifting his leg and pointing to a golf ball sized not on his shin. "No, I was in pain," he said and then, "the collision broke my shin guards." Upon seeing the replay, I realized he had reached with his right leg for the ball, rather than with his head. Just as he met it, the goalkeeper, also leading with his feet, slammed into him.

We had won a hard fought game and McBride had proven, once again, how brave a player he is. Few players have the ability to ignore any potential damage a play may cause their body. This trait makes McBride a valuable player and a key striker for us.

In total contrast to the humidity of D.C. was the freezing weather in Columbus. Again, I held a press pass that entitled me to stand on the field, but I did not want a repeat of the difficulty I had finding a place to stand, so I joined a few friends of mine standing in the Sam's Army section. I was also able to combat the cold by downing a few beers, which I am pretty sure I would not have been able to do on the field.

Again, the game got off to a rocky start as both McBride and Reyna were substituted out with injuries in the first half. At halftime, I called Mark Bushman, who was watching at home. He told me that McBride now sported a golf ball sized knot on his head!

The second half was incredible. First Clint Mathis sent a long ball that Josh Wolff beat Mexican goalkeeper, Jorge Campos, to and finished into an open net. We in the Army went nuts! We did so a second time when Wolff split two defenders in the corner and laid off a nice pass that Earnie Stewart who sent the frozen army into delirium.

After the match I fought my way down to the first row and holding my credentials up, jumped the fence and made my way to the players tunnel. As I reached it, I realized someone had joined me for the walk. It was the man of the match, Josh Wolff. Being that I am not really a journalist, but a fan, I heaped the praise on the young forward. "Great game! You were awesome!"

"Thanks," Wolff said with a wide grin. I could tell he was basking in the victory. I continued with the superlatives and he looked me right in the eye and said again, "Thanks."

The final qualifying match I saw was again at RFK Stadium. This time I sat in an auxiliary press box. It was a key match against Honduras. We got off to a great start, but Honduras stormed back to the delight of their many fans. The atmosphere was as good as I had ever seen, and I actually had goose bumps listening to the two sets of supporters trying to outdo each other. Though I had a great view and comfortable seat, I missed standing in the Army and screaming support. It made me somewhat grateful that I had not received passes to the Cup matches. In Korea, I would be a fan! I would act, party, and dress like a fan and not like a journalist.

The Honduras game turned into a fiasco as they ran wild. We were lucky to have only lost 3-2. Afterwards, I was sick; our qualification was in jeopardy. I wrote that I felt gutted. The date was September 1, 2001. Ten days later I was forced to redefine my definition of gutted.

Fortunately, things worked out well on the field, and we qualified with a game to spare. It had been a long, emotional process, but that is what qualifying is all about. Now, I was headed to Korea!

Day 2
Monday, June 3

World Cup Fever

Once again, I am not sure when this day began. Neither Jimmy nor I had a watch, which made the 12-hour flight from Vancouver even more disorienting. I was very glad when the plane began descending, though I doubt I was alone. As usual, my forehead was glued to the window.

It somehow seemed odd to me that from the air, Korea did not look any different than parts of the United States. There were mountains and cities. There seemed to be good roads leading just about everywhere. When the plane was significantly lower than its cruising altitude, I saw a soccer stadium. I nudged Jimmy and he strained to look out the window. I could tell that he saw the stadium as well. We exchanged a look that said, "Here we go."

Soon the plane was banking to the right and I looked out over what I assumed was the Yellow Sea. This looked like nothing I have seen in America, but was what I pictured Asia to be. There were a few small, green islands that rose straight out of the sea. I think these types of islands are shown in all the promotional pictures of Thailand. They are both remote and inviting. The kind of place that you can get away from it all, yet still have your favorite rum drink served on the beach. For a moment, I hoped to make it out to an island sometime during the next three weeks, though I knew that it was highly unlikely.

As I was admiring the islands, the plane dropped even lower and soon we were passing just above a road. Seconds later we touched down. The flight was over! We taxied past many exotic airlines and a number of Air Korea jets and pulled to the gate.

Jimmy and I easily made our way through customs, though we did have to fill out a card while in line because for some reason we were not given one on the plane. Perhaps we were mistaken for Koreans. We found and retrieved our luggage with no problems. At that point, we stopped and looked at one another.

"What do we do now?" asked Jimmy.

It was a valid question. For over 20 hours someone else had scripted everything we did for us. Leave for the airport at this time. Stand in this line. Board now. Eat this. Get off the plane. Go through this gate. Pick up the luggage. We were now on our own and it felt strange. Not scary or intimidating, just odd that we had no one to guide us through this strange place.

Of course, we had discussed what to do at this point. From that wonderful Yanks in Korea Yahoo Group, I had become acquainted with an American who for the past six years had been in Korea teaching English at a university in Gwangju, a World Cup venue in the southwest part of the country. Chuck had been a Godsend. He arranged rooms for us that were less than half expensive as any I had found on the internet. He had answered nearly every question I asked, and in doing so, set my mind at ease. He advised that no medical precautions were needed although he did say to not drink the water from the tap. He told us that we would find ATMs whenever we needed money. Most importantly, he assured us that Korea was a very safe place.

Chuck had given us a plan for making it from the airport to the hotel. His instructions were simple: take the KAL Bus to Seoul Station. From there, get a cab to Seoul Hotel, which he advised all cab drivers would know. Our hotel was next door to the Seoul Hotel. This sounded pretty simple, though I was a bit apprehensive, wondering aloud, "How do we find the KAL Bus." I was also praying that there would be an ATM in the airport. Jimmy and I had so trusted Chuck that neither of us had bothered to exchange any dollars to *won*.

We were tired from the trip, so we decided to take it slowly, keeping in mind that although it seemed like it, we were not on the *Amazing Race*, a reality program where pairs race around the world. We had made our way to the front of the airport when I saw a new, wide-screen TV with a few rows of benches set up in front of it. Better still, it was showing what looked to be the beginning of a soccer game! Without consulting Jimmy, I made directly for it and dropped all of my luggage in front of a bench and sat down. Sure enough, it was Mexico and Croatia and they were about to kickoff. The TV was beautiful, large with bright colors. Remembering that I once put quarters in small black and white TVs in the Roanoke Airport, I thought that I must be in the greatest airport in the world.

Jimmy joined me on the bench and we watched the first few minutes of the game. Though I considered this a key match in Group G and one that interested me as Mexico is our biggest rival and a team I am familiar with, I felt like I should be doing something more productive than watching it.

I told Jimmy I was going to walk around a bit. I did not go more than 50 feet when I saw an ATM. I took out my bankcard and nervously stuck it in the machine. I was delighted as it asked me, "Foreign Card?" After a few moments, I realized I needed to touch the screen where it said "YES". I was then presented with a choice of denominations that I suspect are options only on Bill Gates' private ATM. 10,000; 20,000; 50,000; 100,000; 150,000; or 200,000. This took be aback. I tried to do some quick math in my head. Chuck had advised me that there were about 1,200 *won* in a dollar. Although I only received a C in Math for Liberal Arts, I was able to do some rudimentary calculations that went like this.

"If 1,200 are in a dollar, there are 120,000 in $100. That means there are 240,000 *won* in $200. I guess that means there is between $100 and $200 in 200,000 *won*." Thinking that I needed to buy bus tickets, pay for a taxi and hotel, and eat without knowing when I would next see an ATM, I went for it all! "I'll have 200,000, please," I said to myself as I pushed the button for, by far, the largest number I have ever considered in relations to cash for me. A moment later, out slid 200,000 *won*, in 10,000 *won* bills! Twenty of them, quite a wad! They were larger than our money, but not huge. There was a Korean guy on them, but they were clearly marked as 10,000. Interestingly enough they said "Bank of Korea" in English.

I returned to Jimmy and told him how easy the transaction had been. He got up to get some cash himself, but I told him that he also needed to find the bus. "I found the ATM, you get the bus." He could not argue with that, so off he went. I watched as he spent quite awhile at the ATM before pulling out a stack equally as thick as mine. He then walked off only to return minutes later.

"The ticket counter is right there," he said, pointing towards the ATM. "It's 10,000."

That sounded great to me as I quickly did some more calculations in my head, coming to the conclusion that for the purpose of this trip, 10,000 *won* was $8.00. I told Jimmy that I would like to watch the game until halftime and then get on the bus. He was fine with that.

Our plan now agreed upon and with a pocket full of *won*, I decided to check out the little convenience store that was nearby. It seemed very similar to a 7-11, and my first purchase in Asia was very simple, a Coke and a Snickers Bar. The Snickers looked exactly like one in the U.S., same size and wrapper. The Coke, on the other hand, was in a skinny can, as tall as a normal one, but probably less than one half the circumference. It did have the familiar Coca-Cola script, but the rest of the can showed the World Cup trophy and featured Korean writing. The year before I had gone to London and found most things there to be similar to the U.S., but just a little bit different. Thus I was surprised to find that both treats tasted just like they did back home.

Halftime came, and Jimmy and I made our way to the KLM Bus counter. I went first and said, "Seoul Station." To my amazement the clerk handed me a ticket! They do speak English! I was thrilled. And it only cost me one of the bills. Jimmy purchased one as well and we were pointed out the nearby doors.

Outside the airport for the first time some confusion set in. There were numerous KLM stops, but no sign said Seoul Station. Jimmy and I began walking, hoping to see some familiar words. After passing a few of the stops, a Korean guy with a funny looking vest asked for our tickets. We showed him and he said, "Seoul Station?" We answered positively and he pointed to the stop right in front of us. He then took our bags and set them right on the curb.

This worried me somewhat as I was not even sure this guy was with KLM so Jimmy and I stood with them, but shortly another passenger left their bags next to ours and sat down on a bench back away from the road. The guy in the vest motioned for us to sit down saying something to the effect of it would be a few minutes. The two of us obliged, but kept an eye on our bags.

As it turned out, there was nothing to fear because after about 15 minutes, a bus pulled up. The driver got out and loaded our bags and took our tickets. We boarded the bus, which fortunately had a working air conditioner. It was cool and comfortable. The seats were large and leather. There were two seats on one side of the aisle and one on the other. Jimmy and I sat on opposite sides of the aisle and I stretched my body. I was amazed at how comfortable the bus was. The nearly empty bus soon pulled out and a recorded voice told us the trip would last about an hour.

Just as on the plane, I stared out the window. We passed a lot of rice paddies along the way. I recognized the low, water covered land with rows and rows of small green plants from watching many Vietnam War movies.

Before long the rice paddies gave way to high-rise apartments and I suspected I was having my first look at Seoul. There were many identical apartments, most white stone and at least 15 stories high. They all looked the same, and it made the former pizza delivery boy in me shudder. It also gave a sense of the huge population of Seoul.

Minutes later a river came into view and we crossed it over a very old looking steel bridge, one that reminds me of Pennsylvania, with girders forming a half circle above the road. As we made our way over the bridge, I saw a water ferry shooting a stream of water high into the air, much like they do when a cruise ship is pulling out of port. It was a welcoming sight, as it seemed to be the promise of an incredible journey.

Once across the river, the streets became busier, and I realized it must have been rush hour, as the time was between 4:00 and 5:00 in the afternoon. The streets were lined with the flags of the World Cup teams and it was not long before I saw our flag. As someone who was raised to be and has always considered himself to be patriotic, it warmed my heart to see Old Glory there on some random street in Seoul. I was also proud that our team was there, to compete with the rest of the World, and I was filled with a sense of duty; that I was representing our nation, as well. Right then and there on that bus, I made two pledges to myself. The first was to not be the typical "ugly American." The second was to do everything in my power to let the rest of the world know I am here, representing the colors. I wanted our fans to show the type of support for our team that other, more traditional soccer countries do. I wanted people in England to say, "Wow, listen to those Yanks. Sounds like they know what they are doing." I vowed to be heard at the games.

As the bus rolled on, I thought about the upcoming games and counted the flags. Passing certain flags, I would silently cheer for those whose teams I support, such as England, Ireland, and Costa Rica and would boo those I do not, Germany, Argentina, and Mexico. I was so wrapped up in this game that I did not notice we were pulling into the station, but soon enough, Jimmy and I were off, bags in hand, looking for a taxi. We saw, in English, the words "Taxi Stand" and headed towards them. There was no crowd but we realized we had to get in line anyway. I was so anxious to get in one of the many waiting cabs, I did not realize I entered the Deluxe Taxi line. We had both read that these cabs were a more luxurious than a regular cab and also more expensive. Most tour books recommended avoiding them.

Jimmy was more aware than I and pointed out we were in the Deluxe line, but I had no intention of turning around to retrace my steps and pressed forward, telling Jimmy to "Come on." Being there was no line, we were greeted at the gate by a few different drivers. I told the first one, "Seoul Hotel."

He just looked back at me with a blank look on his face. Again, I said, "Seoul Hotel." Still no response.

The next time I said, "Seoul Hotel" I showed him the instructions from Chuck that I had printed. This may not have been the best idea because the instructions were written in English and all they really said was "Seoul Hotel."

The situation became serious as the driver who was holding Chuck's instructions shook his head and gave them back to me. Before we had time to panic, however, another driver took the paper out of my hand. He gave it a quick look over, nodded, and pointed us to his car.

Jimmy and I rode in the back and after a few minutes the driver turned on the radio. Although it was in Korean, it sounded somewhat like a game, though not exactly. In any case, it made me wonder who had won the Mexico game. I tried to think of a way to ask, but we had already determined the driver spoke no English. He did, however, soon surprise us with a bit of World Cup news.

He struggled for a moment to say Brazil and Turkey, pronouncing "Brassila" and "TukaHee." We nodded and did our best to assure him that we knew what he was saying, repeating, "Brazil and Turkey."

He responded saying, "Game off. Brassila and Tukahee, game off."

To me that meant the game was over and I tried to ask him who won, but he continued saying the same thing about the game being "off". After repeating his phrase about five times, he quickly changed the radio station and appeared to be caught up in the talk show that had come on.

Shortly, he made a right turn off of what seemed to me a main street onto what, for lack of a better term, I would describe as an alley. If it was an alley, and I am sure Koreans have a name for this type of street, it was unlike one I have seen anywhere else. Alley came to mind because of its width. There was just enough room for the taxi to squeeze by the pedestrians, who were forced to quickly move out of our way.

The road was as wide as a typical alley in the U.S., but that is where the similarities ended. It was bustling. There were shops lining both sides of the road and there were people everywhere. Most of the shops seemed to be restaurants, which excited my desire to eat all sorts of exotic food. I thought that it might even be possible to find some dog to eat here. I just wanted to sample it, if only to say that I did.

The road had a colorful, market-like atmosphere that got my adrenaline going. I was fearful that our hotel might be located far from anything else. This fear was dispelled the moment we turned onto this carnival of an alley.

After about a block, the narrow path widened a bit and the driver steered sharply to the left and stopped. We were directly in front of a nine or ten story, tan brick building that said in red neon letters, "Seoul Hotel." I quickly summoned up from memory the directions Chuck had sent. "Next to the Seoul Hotel is a chicken restaurant, go down the alley between the two, and the *Dong-Il* will be the first door on the right."

I surveyed the area and did in fact see a chicken restaurant with, not really what I would call an alley, but more like a path or walkway leading between the two. Relieved and very happy, I said to Jimmy, "This is it; we're here."

As I gave assurances to Jimmy, the driver had popped the trunk and before we could do anything, a bellman from the Seoul Hotel had our bags and was heading for the front door. Jimmy was first out of the taxi to stop him and was easily able to convince him that we were not staying at the nice, expensive Seoul Hotel. I paid the driver with a 5,000 *won* bill I had been given as change when I bought the Coke and Snickers bar and turned before he could give me change. Four dollars for a ten-minute cab ride seemed like a good deal to me.

We scooped up our luggage and made our way about 40 feet between the two buildings, to the first door in the right. Now was the moment of truth. The entire goal of the last two days was to find the *Dong-Il* and get to our rooms. Chuck had said it was a small, family run *yeogwan.* He said they do not take reservations, but that he had told them we were coming and it would not be a problem. This concerned me, particularly when he had added that they do not speak English, but he said he had one of his students write them a note for us.

I went up the two steps first, and there was a small office on the right. When I looked in, I saw two women in their late 40's sitting on the floor, watching a small TV. They jumped to attention and began speaking Korean. Chuck had mentioned that he was very tall and for some reason I started telling the two women that Chuck sent us, all the while holding my hand up high, describing a tall person. Amazingly, the nodded as if the understood me. One of them started upstairs, beckoning us to follow.

The stairway was dark, and the stairs were covered with a thin red carpet and were of different sizes. I might have to step up a foot and a half one step and then only ten inches the next! I worried that this may not bode well for me on a drunken night.

Fortunately, I only went up one flight. I followed her to the end of the hall, passing three other rooms, before she motioned me into Room 206 and Jimmy into the one right across the hall.

The Ritz, it was not. In fact I would say, Motel 6, it was not, but it would suit me fine. The room was small, perhaps 10x12. A bed that was maybe just smaller than a double sat low on the floor with two pillows. Against the wall was a long wooden item that had a couple of drawers. An 18-inch television set rested on top of it and next to that was a small refrigerator, much like the one I had in my dorm room in college. The room was small, very basic, but clean.

A door led from my room to my bathroom, which was perplexing. There was a sink, and a toilet, just like in a normal bathroom. There was also a shower, but curiously, there was no shower stall! A plastic bucket rested underneath the shower spigot and there was a drain in the middle of the floor, just in front of the toilet. I also noticed that the only towel was small and thin; one that I would not use even to dry dishes.

I was thrilled! I had a private room with a bathroom. The refrigerator, which was stocked with bottled water, was a nice surprise, and Chuck had said that it was only 30,000 a night. After spending a few nights on the internet looking for rooms in Korea, I was absolutely delighted to be paying just $24.00 a night. Most I had found were in the 100,000 to 120,000 range for a double, which broke down to about $40 a night to share. Yes, the *Dong-Il* would do nicely. Thank you, Chuck.

After surveying our rooms, we met up in the hallway. Jimmy was also happy with his room and we gave the lady a "thumbs up" sign. She led us back down to the office where she produced a calculator and punched in some numbers. She turned it to show us and we gathered that it was the price of the room. Again, I was pleasantly surprised to read not 30,000, but 28,000. We immediately reached into our wad of cash and handed her three 10,000 *won* bills, and she gave us each two 1,000 bills in change.

I saw a large calendar on the wall and ran my finger over the next three weeks, saying "Seoul, Seoul, Seoul," until I reached the 24th and then said, "Bye-bye." Again, they understood and I was fairly sure they understood we would be staying with them for the next twenty-three days.

The other lady then pointed to the next day, June 4th on the calendar and said, "Poh-lend."

"Poland. Yes, Korea plays Poland tomorrow." I said slowly and she nodded. I then pointed to the following day, the 5th and said, "USA, Portugal."

She responded by pointing out the next two Korea matches, one of which was against us. I was amazed that she knew the dates and times of their matches.

I next pointed to our game days and said, from memory, the city where they would be played. She seemed impressed and surprised that Jimmy and I would be going to them all.

As I was enjoying playing Calendar with my new friend, Jimmy asked if I wanted to walk around. Of course I did, and we made our way back up the steps to our rooms. The innkeeper chased us down and presented us with our room keys. These were the type of keys that you use to open a bathroom door in a gas station in North Carolina. The key was a normal key, but attached to it was a brick sized piece of hard plastic with Korean letters and the room number.

I ducked into my room and grabbed my red ACC Basketball cap. I was planning to wear it to all the games and after almost a day on a plane, thought it wise to wear out. I locked the door and waited in the hall a few moments for Jimmy.

Now, I must tell you about the floor plan of the rooms. The main door led to a small, square foyer. The foyer had two other doors, one to the bathroom and the other to the bedroom. I had simply locked the main door and was waiting when I heard Jimmy curse. He came out of his main door and said, "You can't lock the inner door."

"That's cool," I said, a bit slow on the uptake.

"I just locked it. I can't get in the room. I locked the wrong one," he admitted.

I took his key, and as expected, it would not open the door to his bedroom. "What do we do? I have no idea how to tell them," I said, but Jimmy reminded me that I had a phrase book.

We went into my room and found the book in my suitcase. I went through the pages, looking for the words for, "I locked the wrong door." However, the publishers apparently had never run into this problem, and the closest we came was "I've locked myself out."

We went back to the office and Jimmy bravely tried his best to use the phonetic approach. His effort was met with blank stairs. My friend quickly caved and handed them the book, pointing to the phrase in Korean. Surely they read that he locked himself out. They spoke back and forth, certainly wondering amongst themselves if Americans use keys because clearly Jimmy was holding his like a baton in his hand.

They felt a demonstration would clear things up. Against our protests, the two women retrieved a key from the office and slowly showed us how to first insert the key into the lock and then to turn it. After the show, they looked at us to see if we had understood. At this point, I was cracking up, but Jimmy was growing frustrated and was looking at me for help, as if I knew what to tell them.

Sensing he still did not understand the proper use of a key, they took Jimmy's from his hand and this time simply pantomimed unlocking a door. Jimmy was saying that he understood, but it did not unlock the inner door. Finally, he pushed his way by the two and took hold of the inner door of the room they had been using for the demonstration and pretended it was locked. He took his key and acted like he was trying to open it. I was trying not to laugh out loud, but his acting worked as some quick chatter between them gave the sense of understanding. One of the ladies returned to the office, took a key that did not have a block attached to it, and led Jimmy back up the stairs. After a few moments he was back down, confirming that all was well.

We were finally free to explore our neighborhood and were headed out the door, when we were stopped by the ladies, who took our keys and sat them in a box just inside the door to the office. It was obvious to us that we were to leave them there and though I was uneasy about leaving the key to my room just sitting there, I was even happier that I would not have to carry it all over the country.

Walking around the neighborhood was exhilarating and made it easy to shake off any tiredness we had from the flight. Chuck had told us we would be in central Seoul, and though I had no idea what that meant, it turned out to be the equivalent to Times Square. Walking the area, we saw that every shop, be it a small office, a restaurant, or even a street vendor, had a TV that was tuned to the World Cup. Brazil was playing Turkey, and I realized that I had completely misunderstood what the cabbie had been telling us. It was quite a sight, seeing World Cup fever; every set had people crowded around it. I was not sure if it was the lure of Brazil and their Beautiful Game or if everyone was into the tournament. In any case, it announced to us that we were here, where the games were played, and everyone seemed to welcome both it and us.

I had suggested to Jimmy that we eat Korean on this first night here, just to fully get into our surroundings and he agreed. It would have been easy to eat more familiar food. Jimmy and I exited our alley after a short block and suddenly found ourselves on a wide and busy street. In order not to get lost, we turned left, and continued doing so until we were back at the *Dong-Il*. In doing so, we passed such well-known restaurants as McDonalds, Popeye's, Subway, Pizza Hut, and even a Starbucks. This left us much more at ease. Although I love to try new and exotic foods, it was reassuring to know a Quarter Pounder was just a few minutes away.

Tonight, however, we were set on some local cuisine and though a few factors intervened to thwart us, we were not going to let anything stop us from eating something we had never seen before. The first thing that got in our way was nerves. It was intimidating looking in the myriad of eateries. In some, there were people waiting in line at counters. In others, the diners were sitting on the floor. We were completely unsure of what to do once we were inside, and thus, we chickened out more than once before entering an establishment. Another thing we noticed was that no place really had anything written in English. I guess this was to be expected, but it caught us off guard nonetheless.

We had gone around the block almost twice when I decided that it was ridiculous that we were scared to get some food. I announced that we would go into the next place. The next place was only a few steps away and when we looked in, everyone was sitting on the floor. Frustrated, I said, "Here is the deal, the next place where the game is on and nobody is on the floor, we go in. Let's not worry about the menu, somebody will speak English."

Jimmy agreed and said that he thought most people would speak English; that we would be fine.

In seconds, we were in front of another Korean place. Peering through the large open window, we saw people sitting at tables. A television was tuned to the game. There was no turning back. In we went, and a young lady with an apron on pointed to a table so we took our seats to await the menu, hoping that it would be in

English. Before we had time to acclimate ourselves, a waitress arrived and said something that was clearly a question.

"Speak English?" I replied. From the look on her face, it was clear she did not. "Anyone speak English?" I asked, waving my hands hoping she would know another waitress who did. Again I was answered with a confused look, but this time, she pointed to the wall behind us.

It was a white wall with large red Korean letters. We could tell that it was the menu as there were prices, which ranged from W3,000 to W8,000, on every line.

Panic was about to set in, when we heard a recognizable sound. "Excuse me," a man's voice said with a thick Korean accent. "I recommend..." we could not make out what he recommended because he said it in Korean, but he was now standing over us, pointing at the top of the wall. "Very good. You will like."

He was wearing an apron like all the waitresses, but had a shirt and tie on underneath. I sensed he was the owner. I also realized that he was pointing to the most expensive item on the wall, something that cost W8,000. "Of course," I thought. "What owner does not recommend the priciest thing?" I shot a quick look at Jimmy and he was nodding. I was more than happy to go along, and soon Jimmy and I were shaking our heads to the waitress and holding up two fingers. She said something to the owner and left.

"Thank you," Jimmy said to the man who returned to a seat by the door where he sat with another man in a similar outfit. He was grinning and bowing and also saying "Thank you." Soon we were all saying "Thank you."

In no time at all, small dishes were set in front of us, each containing a different sort of food. I recognized one to be *kim' chi*, the staple of Korean food, I had read in both of my travel guides. I had had it on a few occasions at the Korean restaurant near my home and was slowly developing a taste for the cabbage, which was marinated in a spicy red sauce. Another of the dishes contained red sauce; others held onions, a clear, yellowish sauce, bean sprouts, and other unrecognizable foods. There were six small servings in front of each of us.

From the kitchen, our waitress appeared with a sort of pan, which was placed on a burner that was built into the table between Jimmy and I. It reminded me of a fondue restaurant, but was much larger. The fire was lit, and a large plate of raw beef strips was set on the table. Jimmy and I had no idea what was going on, but our waitress was attentive and understood our dilemma. She cut the strips into bite-sized pieces with scissors and dropped them on the grill.

After cutting 20-30 pieces she went to the kitchen and quickly returned with a large plate of lettuce leaves. When the beef was through cooking, she instructed us on how to eat. First she held a piece of lettuce in her left hand. She spread red sauce on it and added onions and a few round white things that turned out to be raw cloves of garlic. Finally she topped it off with the beef, rolled it up like a burrito and handed it to me.

Wow! It was hot. Both hot hot and spicy hot, and it had a lot of flavor. It was also dripping all over me. Jimmy made one for himself and agreed that it was delicious. It was truly a flavor that I had never tasted. The red spice did not seem to be tomato based. The garlic was fantastic and very spicy. The beef had an unusual marinade. Combined, I enjoyed it immensely.

The taste was good, and I like spicy food, so that did not bother me, but I desperately needed something to drink. Our waitress had left a pitcher of water on the table, but all the guidebooks, as well as Chuck, had warned against drinking the water. In fact, it was a bit unsettling just sitting there. Something that would make me sick has no business on a table next to good food. Jimmy and I both ordered a Coke, and she returned with a glass bottle of Coke and two small glasses. From the way he gulped his glass, I could tell that Jimmy's mouth was as hot as mine!

As we were enjoying our meal, we were also taking note of the game. Though I was hoping Costa Rica would advance out of their group, Group C, which in addition to the two teams playing also included China, I was pulling for Turkey. I was aware that Costa Rica would more than likely battle Turkey for second place, but for some reason, I like the Turks. Maybe it is because I enjoy rooting for underdogs and was hoping for another upset. On the other hand, maybe it is because I like the way they shook up the European establishment by winning the UAEFA Cup and showing so well at the European Championships in 2000. Perhaps it was that I just like to say Galatassary and Fenerbache, but whatever it was, it was driving me to pull for the boys in red.

They were up a goal at halftime, and I was thinking how great it would be for them to stun Brazil. Over my beef in lettuce I imagined the streets of Istanbul and how they would be alive should their countrymen pull this one off. Surely, that would be the place to be if the score held.

However, Ronaldo, who had just begun playing his first serious soccer in years, would have none of it and equalized just after halftime. It was a cracking match and seemed to be headed for a deserved tie when the referee stepped to the forefront.

A Brazilian, Luizao, was streaking in on goal, when a Turkish defender pulled him down from behind before he reached the penalty box. I immediately thought that it was a great play, but then saw the ref pointing to the spot.

"No way!" I said loud enough for the other patrons to turn and look at me. Jimmy had just ordered another Coke and had missed the incident, so I filled him in on the fact that the ref was giving a bad penalty. As I was ripping the ref to Jimmy, his eyes got big and he pointed back to the screen.

"Red Card," he said.

"What? To who?" I asked, more upset than I should have been. Sure enough, it was shown to Alpay, the Turkish defender. In hindsight, the red card was the right call, but not the penalty. The ref was right to send him off as he was the last defender and did pull the man down. The penalty was just wrong; there is no way the ref, who was Korean, could have seen it clearly as it was outside the box.

Once the protesting Turks were shooed away, Rivaldo put the spot kick home and Turkey was screwed out of a crucial point. However, all was not finished. Not only was I was still a bit angry with the referee, but the tension from the fans in the stadium, as well as the Turkish players, was palpable. As I was making another wrap, I saw out of the corner of my eye, Rivaldo, who was about to take a corner, go down, holding his head.

"Oh!" I almost yelled. "Somebody threw something that hit Rivaldo in the head! A fan hit Rivaldo!" I was shocked to see a player as great as the Brazilian become the victim of an over zealous fan. I knew the Turks were upset, but this was not right. "They're showing the replay," I said to Jimmy as if he was not watching.

What I saw was as shocking and disturbing as what I had thought had happened. A Turkish defender kicked the ball a bit harder than he should have at Rivaldo, who was clearly wasting time. The ball struck him in the thigh. For a brief moment the Number 10 looked up in astonishment, and then quickly fell to the ground holding his head. There had been no missile, as the British say, thrown. He was taking the most ridiculous dive I had ever seen.

"The nerve of him," Jimmy said.

"Yeah, and FIFA had warned against diving. They should throw him out," I was really into this game, and though I have always marveled at his skill, I could not believe what he had tried to do. After a few moments, we saw the Turks arguing with the referee. "Good," I thought, "at least book him."

Now let me say that the whole scene was quite confusing as the announcers were speaking Korean and that I had spilled the entire contents of a lettuce burrito on my lap. Thus, it took me a little while before I realized that the referee had pulled out a red card, only instead of sending off the cynical Rivaldo, he had brandished it to Haken Unsal, the defender who had kicked the ball, out of which Rivaldo had made such a meal.

The Turks were furious, and I was left with a feeling that once FIFA reviewed the tape, Rivaldo himself would be suspended. As I had mentioned, FIFA had warned the players that they had instructed referees to punish them for diving. "What a great message this will be to send," I told Jimmy. "Suspending one of the biggest stars. It should really clean up that sort of business for the rest of the tournament."

The game ended shortly and the waitress brought our check. All it said was W20,000. As we stood to leave, the man who had helped us order approached and said that his friend would like to buy us a beer. I looked to Jimmy, just to make sure he wanted to go and he nodded. "Sure. It sounds great," I said. I left W2,000 on the table. It felt strange to leave that little, but all the books said not to tip at all. I felt the waitress deserved something for all her help.

Jimmy and I paid at the cash register by the door and as we turned to leave, the waitress ran to us and extended her hand. In it was the W2,000 I had left. I tried to tell her it was for her, but she had none of it. As great as it seems to not have to tip, it felt very strange.

The two Korean men were in front of us and led us out and to the left, which was towards our hotel. We only went about 20 feet before the owner asked if the bar there was all right. I had no objections and we found a table on a long porch

I had thought that tonight should be low key as tomorrow we were going to meet up with many other Americans in, what was described to us as the "Foreign Zone", Itaewon at a bar called The Nashville. However I am not one to turn down a beer, particularly when a native in a foreign land offers it. I viewed this as a possible adventure. One never knows when opportunities will present themselves.

Jimmy, on the other hand, was full of doubt. For reasons that are not clear to me, Jimmy does not drink. I was curious as to what he would do, but he told me that he would have one. I was happy that he was opening his mind, but then thought that if his mouth opened too much, I might have to baby sit him.

As we sat, we made our introductions. The owner was Mr. Hyun and his friend was Mr. Joung. I have no idea why they did not give us their first name, particularly when we later discovered that all four of us were 32 years old. Mr. Joung asked what kind of beer we wanted. Of course Jimmy had no idea, and he told them that he had never had a beer. They seemed honored that he would have his first with them.

A month earlier, I had asked for a Korean beer at a Korean restaurant Ivy and I frequent near our house. They had brought me an OB, which was pretty good, and so I said that an OB would be good. The Misters ordered four of them, as well as some type of food.

While waiting, I asked Mr. Hyun if he was the owner of the restaurant where we had just eaten. To my surprise he said "No. I am Salary man." This news surprised me, but I simply thanked him for recommending such good food. It quickly became apparent that although Mr. Hyun did not speak great English, his was much better than Mr. Joung's.

As the waiter arrived with four OBs, we were learning that Mr. Hyun had spent two years living in Minnesota and somehow Mr. Joung's limited command of the English language had seen him survive a year in Melbourne, Australia. We knocked our large bottles together in a trans-Pacific toast and I watched as Jimmy took his first swig of beer.

"How is it?" I asked.

"Not bad," answered my tall friend.

"I am happy to meet you," Mr. Joung stated for the sixth time in five minutes. Though he said some other words, this was by far the phrase with which he was most comfortable.

The waiter returned with a large round plate that had cafeteria-like sections. Each of the eight sections was filled with dried food. Mr. Hyun explained what the travel guides had advised. "At bars in Korea, you are to order food with beer." I nodded to show that I was aware of this. It seems that pubs do not make much money on beer and thus it is tradition to order some sort of food, usually something simple, like chips. The same question was now in my head that I had when I first read of this strange tradition, "Do we really have to order snacks?"

The snacks were good, for the most part. There was familiar food, peanuts and raisins and then there was the exotic, seaweed and dried squid. I did not like the dried seaweed and really did not like the squid. It was nothing like the calamari that I love back home. It, like everything else on the platter, was dried. It was very chewy and tasted of the ocean; very fishy. Jimmy would not touch it. There were a few other things, one of which was very good, that I was unable to identify.

We talked about the Cup, but did not get very far because the two Koreans were not soccer fans. I asked if they ever wanted to have Korea unified. Neither hesitated, and I learned that it was not even a question for them. Absolutely, they wanted one Korea. They both felt that it was inevitable and would happen in their lifetime. I was somewhat amazed to learn that it is virtually impossible for them to travel to North Korea. The DMZ is very much like the Berlin wall. Of course I was aware of the divide, but I had assumed that there was an exchange; that students would visit their estranged countrymen. However, my two new friends assured me that the only way to visit is to sneak in and that is nothing that anyone wanted a part of.

This revelation saddened me. How terrible for Koreans to not have any contact with another group of Koreans. The situation is almost the opposite of Ireland. My sister married and Irishman and on a trip to meet his family, I was stunned to hear that Ireland wants nothing at all to do with Northern Ireland. Of course, they may travel there, but for those in the Republic, a unified Ireland is out of the question. Here in Korea, the separation is not religion, but that scourge to many common men, the pride of government.

Halfway through the beer, Mr. Joung was able to get out that his favorite beer was Cass. The waiter came by and I ordered three Cass. Jimmy had advised that his drinking for the evening was done. I suspected that he might have just had the only beer he will ever drink, poor guy.

The Cass arrived in bottles equally as large as the OB. They were larger than pint size, probably 20 ounces, I guessed. As I pulled down my first taste of Cass, I took a moment to reflect. There I was somewhere in Seoul discussing politics, sports, and religion with two guys I had just met, eating crazy food and drinking half 40s! What a trip this already was.

We had one more round; my third was an OB that I liked better. As the effects of the beer were felt, our group grew louder, and we were now toasting on nearly every sip. Mr. Joung, in particular, loved to knock glasses. After every statement, he crashed his bottle against mine. These were not the sort of "love taps" we exchange when saying "Cheers." No, these were collisions. I was actually worried that Mr. Joung was going to break the bottles as hard as he was hitting them.

"I am happy to meet you!" Ching!!!

Jimmy was amused watching me try to protect my beer against Mr. Joung's wild swings. Somehow, I was able to finish the OB with the bottle intact and not wanting to face an even drunker Mr. Joung, we told the two Koreans that we had an early morning and should get going.

They agreed, as they both had to work the next day, and they had already had more than anticipated. They gave us their cards and told us to call if we needed any help at all. We thanked them and made off, but not before I said, "I am happy to meet you."

Back at the *Dong-Il*, sleep came easily. In fact, I dozed off, woke up an hour or so later, dragged myself to the bathroom to brush my teeth with the bottled water from my refrigerator and was soon back asleep.

Day 3
Tuesday, June 4

Nashville

I woke up feeling great at 7:30 in the morning and killed time watching TV. They replayed the Italy-Ecuador match and I was happy with the result . . . not so much that Italy won, but for the fact that there was no refereeing controversy

The game had been officiated by Brian Hall of the U.S. Most MLS fans are familiar with him and realize he is capable of ruining a game. There is an old adage that the best referee is the one who is not noticed. It was my fear that he would leave his stamp on this game. If he blew it, there would be two results. First it would embarrass U.S. Soccer and we certainly do not need any more of that. However, as bad as another blow to our international reputation would be, the second result could be much worse.

If Brain Hall made a bad call that angered Ecuador, the favor may be returned. The referee for the U.S.-Portugal match was from Ecuador. No one I spoke with had any doubts that there would be payback for any mistake. This is the reality of international competition; referees hold grudges.

Therefore, it was with great delight and relief that I scarcely noticed Hall as Italy went on to win comfortably and without controversy, 2-0.

After the game, Jimmy knocked on the door and announced he was ready to go. We had decided to have some breakfast in our neighborhood and then make our way to Itaewon. We would spend the day there and hit Nashville that evening for the big party with the other Americans. I was looking forward to meeting those with the passion to travel to Korea for soccer. Being a soccer fan can be lonely so when you are with another fan, you must revel in the conversation. That evening I would meet a few hundred passionate U.S. fans and was very excited at the prospect. In particular, I was looking forward to meeting Big Dog.

Big Dog runs much of the Sam's Army website and is known around the U.S. Soccer community as a passionate and vocal supporter. Both Jimmy and I had written some stories for him and his site, and for a while, we had talked about staying together in Korea. Those plans changed when Big Dog and his travel partner, Monty, decided to do a Home Stay. He tried to sell me on the benefits, low cost, someone to show you around and feed you. However, I was worried that it might curtail the freedom I felt I needed.

In any case, we made hotel reservations together in two of the away cities, and I was looking forward to meeting and getting to know the Big Dog.

Out on the main street, Jimmy and I found a PC Bang, the Korean term for an Internet café. We sent some e-mails home and then went to read some news when a shockingly bad story took me by surprise. It reported that both Clint Mathis and Claudio Reyna were doubtful for the match the next day.

I was stunned and disheartened. Mathis was set to be the American who used this Cup as a launching pad to a major club in Europe. Rumors were already in that Bayern Munich had offered $5 million for him. Other clubs were said to be in the chase. The Metro Star forward was poised to become the first superstar of American soccer, now it looked like he would not play in the first match.

If Mathis was the flashy goal scorer, Reyna was our gritty heart and soul. He wore the number 10 of the playmaker, but that was not particularly his forte, it was just that he was better at it than anyone else we had. He was not only our captain, but also our best technical player. Before the Cup I said that if there is one player we cannot win without, it is Reyna. Although the U.S. had looked good beating Uruguay a few weeks earlier without him, generally a game without the captain is not one the U.S. expects to win.

I felt that with a completely healthy squad, we would be fortunate to hold the Porto's to a draw. At that Uruguay match we had lost the important defensive midfielder, Chris Armas. Now we were set to lose both Mathis and Reyna. Oh well, I thought, it is the other two games that hold the key for us. It is South Korea and Poland that we need to beat out, not Portugal.

I decided not to dwell on the doom that was going to befall us the next day, but rather to focus my attention on a happier subject, a great party.

Jimmy and I decided on Starbucks for breakfast and I enjoyed café mocha and a dry cinnamon roll. This small meal cost W4,500 or about $4.00 and probably the same it would have cost back home. Jimmy and I decided that all we ate the night before for just over twice as much had been a much better deal and that we should avoid western places when possible.

Outside the Starbucks was a subway station, and nervously Jimmy and I made our way down the stairs, past an old man selling a very cheap looking plastic toy train that was going around and around a small circular track. The station was busy, and we sensed that this was an important stop in Seoul. Soon we found a map and had just about figured out which trains we needed to take when an old man asked if we needed help. The man did not speak much English and did more to confuse than help, however we were soon rescued by a young girl who pointed out the trains and showed us where to go.

The guidebooks said that a subway ticket was W800 and advised purchasing a W10,000 ticket, as they add an extra W2,000 to it. Armed with this information and determined to not only save money but to act as if I know what is going on, I approached the ticket window.

"Ten thousand," I said as I handed over the bill. To my dismay he gave me W9,000 change and a ticket clearly marked W1,000. "Oh well, no big deal," I thought, "No point in telling him his mistake, he does not seem to speak English."

Jimmy did not learn from whatever mistake I had made and was given the same in return for his W10,000 bill as I had received.

"We'll have to try that one again," he said. I was sure we would have many more of these miscues over the next three weeks.

Jimmy and I easily found our train. All the signs were both in Korean and English and I wondered why that was. I assume it is because of the war. During the 1950's many Koreans learned English to help with our military. It is either a custom from the past or a new attempt to teach the young our language to help with business.

Whatever the case, we were grateful. We stood near the door, which gave us a view of the map above it. We quickly identified the station where we were to change trains, which we did with no problem. Soon we were exiting the station at Itaewon.

From the travel guides we had read that Itaewon is the foreign zone of Seoul. It caters mainly to American Servicemen and to a lesser extent, Chinese and Japanese tourists. During the Cup, it was the place to be. We also read that it was a place to buy anything at all. Some on the Yanks in Korea Yahoo list advised buying a custom made suit. Shoes and other clothes were also recommended.

Jimmy and I emerged from the underground station and were hit with a blast of hot, humid air, which was in severe contrast to the cool subway station. Catching our eye were the bright colors of the three story buildings that lined the four-lane street. We did not know where we were in relation to Nashville, but quickly realized we were in the heart of Itaewon.

We moved slowly, taking in the exciting scene. The sidewalks were crowded with people who were forced to walk close to the buildings by the vendors who set up shop just on the curb. The first thing I saw for sale was a table of sunglasses, which we passed by without a second glance, when Jimmy exclaimed, "Here it is!"

I looked up and there was a sign that announced "Nashville." "That was easy," I said, wondering how to spend the rest of the day. I had thought it would take at least an hour or two to stumble onto the site of the gathering, but we had found it in less than a minute.

As we were staring up, it occupied the second and third floors of the building, I heard a voice asking if we were looking for Nashville. I turned to see four dark haired guys wearing U.S.A. shirts and jerseys.

"Yeah, this is it, huh?" I answered.

"Yeah, there is a party here tonight," one of them informed me.

"We know, we were just trying to see where it was." We began introductions but they were cut short by the arrival of a bus.

"Sorry, we gotta run, we're taking this tour. See you tonight," one of them said and they were quickly aboard and gone.

Jimmy and I continued to walk down the sidewalk, past people wearing jerseys of many teams. I was in my Washington Redskins t-Shirt, which I hoped would identify me as an American, at least to other Yanks.

We had not gone far before we were following an older man in a nice suit down a narrow stairwell that led to a clothing store. He assured me that he made the best suits in Korea and preceded to show me his large collection of fabrics.

I had considered getting a suit and thus humored him for a while, saying I liked this fabric and that. He then asked me how many suits I wanted. "Just one," I assured him.

"Special price for you. $220," he said which led me to cynically wonder what I did to deserve a "special price." "We measure you now." He was moving way too quickly for me.

"No, no, I don't really want a suit. I am just looking."

"OK, how about $200?"

"I don't want one today. I just got here." That was the truth. If I bought a suit, I was not going to buy from the first shop I visited. I was also unsure if I needed one. I have a suit and do not need it for work. Yes, it would be nice to have a second one, but I needed to see how my money would hold out over the length of the trip before I decided on this luxury.

"Bottom price, $180." This guy was easy...easy and desperate. I told him no again and we left after he gave me his card.

Over the next two blocks, we were solicited to buy a custom made suit at least five times. Other aggressive merchants were hawking watches and leather goods, all in fluent English. I enjoyed the scene because it reminded me of the flea markets of Fort Lauderdale I had visited has a youth. A few stores had some very colorful Hawaiian shirts, many featuring the trendy Spiderman.

Jimmy and I soon reached the end of the commercial area so we crossed the street and headed back on the other side. Much to our surprise this side was very different. Like the craziness opposite us, it was crowded with vendors, however, unlike the permanent shops that had called us, this was the World Cup side. Most of the stores were selling soccer related items. From shirts and key chains to clocks and balls, everything was World Cup related. The street vendors were here for the Cup as well. We first passed the food tents. Each of these featured food from a different country. Smells of exotic foods filled the air. We passed tents featuring goodies from Indonesia, Japan, Mexico, India, Pakistan, and Turkey. Then we came to the Italian tent, and I had to wonder at the authenticity. I was expecting a nice bowl of pasta with loads of tomato sauce. What I saw was small English muffin sized pizzas. I am not sure these have ever been seen in Italy! I did not care, though, for when I got hungry, I wanted to sample the kabobs and other foods that I do not see every day. Jimmy looked like he wanted the pizza.

After passing a number of vendors selling scarves, we were back across from Nashville. Before crossing back over, however, I ducked into an indoor market. This provided a nice relief from the heat. The first thing I saw was what looked like a jewelry store.

One of the things Ivy had asked for was jade which she had been told was easily found in Korea. This proved to be true, as even I was able to recognize the beautiful green stones. A pretty young Korean lady behind the counter asked me if I liked the jade and for whom was I shopping. I told her I did like it, and it was for my fiancée.

She immediately pointed to a necklace that had a picture of two swans in gold and told me that they represented "Love forever."

"Well, that would be the one," I said, happy to find a nice gift so easily.

"It is W45,000."

"Thanks," I said, "but not now." I turned and walked away, but was disappointed that she did not try to stop me. I was hoping she would come down in price, like the suit salesman had. I did some quick math in my head, "W45,000. That is 4 times 8 which is 32, plus half of 8, 4 is 36, $36.00. That's not bad." I thought that I could certainly afford $36.00 for a jade necklace for Ivy. I soon had another chance.

Not far from the first counter was a nearly identical one. It had the same necklace with the two swans. "You like? It means love forever," the saleswoman informed me, and I began to see a pattern.

"It's very nice," I politely answered.

She took out a calculator and punched in some numbers, which she showed me as she said, "This much." The numbers said "W25,000"!

"What a windfall," I thought. "That's almost half price; it's like 20 bucks!" I almost bought it right there, but for some reason, I walked away again.

Before I knew it I was bargaining over a unique chess set. The pieces were Korean figures carved in marble. I have wanted a nice chess set to display for a long time and thought this would be perfect. I had talked the lady down from W120,000 to W75,000, but she would go no lower, and I was not ready to spend that kind of money this early in the trip. In addition, I was still in a sort of sticker shock just talking in terms of 100,000, even if it was *won*.

Jimmy found me and looked anxious to leave. As we were walking out, I passed yet another jewelry counter. I got right to the point, "How much for the one with the swans?"

Another calculator showed me the same W25,000 price, and I was very happy I did not spend W45,000 at the first place but was, for some reason, still not yet ready.

"I have 20,000," I said.

"W20,000? No. Mmmmm...how about W22,000? Lowest price," came the reply from another young lady.

"Nope, W20,000." I held firm. Generally I do not enjoy this type of bargaining, but for some reason, I was enjoying this. Perhaps I felt I had the language advantage.

"Sorry, W22,000. Lowest price," she said, and I turned to walk away. When I was far enough away that I knew she was not going to call me back, I turned and handed over the W22,000. To my surprise, she put it in a very nice jewelry bag with a Korean design stitched on it. It was something I probably would have paid extra for if they had asked me.

All in all, I was happy with the purchase and relieved that no matter what else happened, Ivy would get a jade necklace.

Back out in the heat on the busy main drag, I literally bumped into Mark, the guy I had first met at the Brickskeller back in D.C. The three of us went over our first few days in Korea while still standing on the sidewalk. After about fifteen minutes, I commented on the heat, and Mark suggested we simply head on over to Nashville. This sounded like a great idea to me, but first, Mark wanted to run down to his hotel, so Jimmy and I tagged along.

Mark was staying at the Crown Hotel, which was at the other end of the main road and then to the left, down a long hill. By the time we reached it, I was very hot and thirsty. Mark had just checked into the room as he had spent his first few days in a smaller place. His three roommates, two of whom I had also met back home, Vladimir and Geta, were arriving that night.

The first thing I thought when I saw his room was, "Thank goodness for the *Dong-Il*." There was nothing wrong with his room. It was clean and Western; it would not have been out of place in America. However, as nice as it may have been, it only had two twin beds and was not very large. The two who slept on the floor would not have much space. I cringed when I thought of four people sharing this space. What's more, they were each paying more than I was for my private room.

I, for the by now countless time, thanked Chuck for all he had done for me. I was looking forward to meeting him but would have to wait until tomorrow because he was not coming to the party at The Nashville. He had said something about having to give an exam to his class the morning of the U.S.-Portugal match and would catch a train to Suwon early that afternoon.

Mark took care of whatever business that led us to his hotel quickly, and we headed off to Nashville. It was early afternoon, and Mark was excited about getting a good seat to watch the day's games which began at 3:30 with China and Costa Rica.

By the time we reached the club, I was dying for a beer. Upon entering The Nashville, we realized that they also had a nice restaurant downstairs. But it was not good food that we wanted. We wanted a sports bar, a place full of TV's that would offer everyone a great view of all the action and keg upon keg of cold beer. Well, we got one out of two.

We had been told that Nashville was the best sports bar in Seoul. If so, their standards are not quite up to ours. They had the beer side of the equation and people would need to drink a lot, because watching the games was going to be difficult for everyone except us. We were so very early that we had our pick of tables, and for obvious reasons, we chose the one in front of the only television! I immediately decided that this was a fine spot to spend the next 10-12 hours.

The bar itself was nice; everything was wooden and there seemed to be an Old West theme. A waitress arrived at our table, and Mark and I ordered a pitcher of OB, and Jimmy asked for a Coke. I then selected a cheeseburger and fries. The beer was soon on the table, and thankfully, it was very cold. I was somewhat hesitant about drinking that early in the day, but when I saw the small size of Jimmy's Coke, I knew I would not be ordering any soft drinks.

As we were finishing the first pitcher and a very good burger, the Costa Rica match began. This time I was able to fully support our regional rival and both Mark and Jimmy cheered along the Ticos. We all hoped that they would advance to the second round, which could only help increase respect for CONCACAF on the world stage.

Throughout the first half, a number of Americans popped in to make sure this was to be the site of the nights gathering, but only three stayed. Tom and his wife Ellen collapsed onto a couch (yes couch) with their five-month-old baby girl! They had been walking all day and were as ready to settle down as we had been earlier.

Tom is a lawyer in Chicago and a prolific poster on Big Soccer. He is also a very vocal supporter of the team. He and Ellen told me they had some very patriotic outfits to wear to the matches.

I showed Ellen the jade I had bought for Ivy and was relieved to have a woman say that it was a great gift. She also told me that she had not seen any leather bags that were worth purchasing. That had been another thing on Ivy's wish list, but I decided that if Ellen could not find a nice purse, chances were slim that I could do better.

By the time Costa Rica had cruised to an easy 2-0 win, other Americans were settling in. The first group I met was the N.Y. Crew. They were loud and rip roaringly funny. These MetroStars fans certainly got the party started, singing some hilarious, original songs at the top of their lungs. After the first few songs, I had to introduce myself and soon ended up throwing darts with one of them.

Joe, or MetroTard on Big Soccer, is an Irishman who had stopped in Japan to attend the *Bhoys* in Green's first match. I was thinking that I was being setup as we played a game of cricket for a beer, but I came out on top, even though I had not thrown in a year. Joe is a great guy, and I enjoyed our match and the beer he poured for me afterward.

Joe rejoined his other two mates, and they sang "In the Lisbon Slums", a song directed at the World Player of the Year and our most dangerous opponent, Luis Figo. They then broke into *I'd Rather Have Clint Mathis than Figo*, which was sung to the tune of *She'll be Coming 'Round the Mountain When She Comes*. This insinuation was so outlandish that I immediately loved it. The three New Yorkers, Joe, Brent, a very loud and confident Filipino, and Leo, a normal looking white guy if you can overlook his dyed red crew cut, told me they had written many similar songs. I promised to sing loudly with them at the games.

The crowd continued to fill in during the Japan-Belgium match that provided some great play, as well as a mistake by the referee that prevented the home side from winning, and it finished 2-2. At about the time the game ended, I ordered yet another pitcher and was told it was W8,000. I asked Mark for the time and he informed me that it was 8:05 and thus we realized we had just perpetrated one of the worst cases of clock management in history. The first few pitchers were W8,000. Then we were advised that happy hour was from 6:00 until 8:00 and for those two hours, a pitcher was only W6,500. Somehow, during these two hours we had only ordered one pitcher. Now, I must say, that others were generously sharing their beer with us, filling my mug when it was empty. But it was disheartening to realize we had worked the clock like a second-string freshman quarterback who throws a short one down the middle, only to have the whistle blow before the field goal team can run onto the field.

By the time the home team, Korea kicked off against Poland at 8:30, Nashville was full of Americans. This match was important for the U.S., and many crowded around the TV. I discussed this match with many others, and most everyone agreed that a tie would be the best result for us. Everyone thought along the same lines as I; that Portugal would advance, leaving the U.S. and the two sides playing to battle it out for the other spot. Each of them earning just one point was better for us than one of them taking the full three.

Korea looked shaky at the start but soon settled down. The crowd at the stadium looked amazing. They were all in red and were synchronized in their cheering. I got chills thinking of our game with them, just six days away. I was a bit apprehensive about crowd control, but was excited about the atmosphere that would make for an awesome experience.

The Koreans gave their fanatical supporters something to really cheer for in the 26th minute as Hwang Sun-Hong scored a very nice goal. I swear I heard an explosion outside and it seemed that noise was coming in from everywhere. There were a few Koreans in the bar with us, and they were delighted.

I was suddenly aware of a number of camera crews. Evidently someone had tipped off the press off about our gathering and they had come to see how the Yanks were partying.

At some point someone introduced me to Big Dog. He was as I imagined...very large, but also with a baby face. He had just arrived after a long flight and was drinking some mixed drink. I was surprised to hear that he did not drink beer. Big Dog introduced me to his travel buddy, Monty, who is an Indian from Boston. They told me they were spending the night in Seoul and would head to Suwon in the morning to meet their host family. Jimmy and I agreed to meet them and another pair at Seoul Station and ride the train together.

The other pair was two brothers from Seattle, Scott and Neil. Scott was a huge sports fan who worked for a radio station where he hosts a sports show. Neil, the younger and taller of the two, sported a crazy, bleached blond hairstyle that would have been considered an Afro were it not for the visor he wore to keep it in line. They were also participating in a Home Stay, which Big Dog had helped them with, however theirs came with a twist.

Koreans were proud of their land and loved to show it off to the world. They were eager to see how Americans found and enjoyed their country. Capitalizing on this, a television show decided to follow two Americans around, to film them non-stop for a few days in order to show the whole country exactly how two Americans coped with and felt about their culture.

Scott and Neil were asked if they would be interested in being the subjects, and they agreed, thinking it to be cool to be followed by a camera crew, much like on *The Real World* or *Survivor*. They were more than happy to be stars of their own reality series.

I thought that it would be interesting to see for myself if you can actually forget about the cameras and act normally, knowing that you are on television. While meeting and getting to know them, I was acutely aware of the cameras on me.

Korea added another goal to crush the Poles 2-0, thus setting up a showdown with us. For the moment this looked to be the most important game of the group. If everything else went as planned, the US-Korea game would decide which team would advance along with Portugal.

However, I was feeling too good to worry about the game with Korea at this time. I was having a ball. I did not really watch much of the match, just enough to see that Korea played very well, Poland was crap, and Liverpool and Poland's goalkeeper, Jerzy Dudek, had a nightmare of a game.

I was mingling and meeting as many of my countrymen as possible. From reading Big Soccer, I was able to put many faces with names, or at least screen names. Big Dog introduced me to Anthony who runs a company most soccer fans are familiar with, Soccer Vacations. Although I had never used them, I had considered taking trips with them since they take groups to all U.S. away matches, as well as a good number of important international and league matches around the world.

I asked him about the European Championships in 2004 to be held in Portugal. Ivy and I had talked of going, and at the moment I was considering booking with Soccer Vacations. I was hearing nothing but good things about his company. He did drop a bomb, though, saying that FIFA was very unhappy with Portugal's preparations and were going to announce soon that they were going to move the tournament. I thought that was stunning news. As he had great connections, I had no choice but to believe him, however I was somewhat skeptical that a move would be made just two years before the tournament.

I found Jimmy, and he was still talking to a good-looking young American reporter. Earlier that evening he introduced me to Daniella. She was a student at Princeton and was interning at an English language newspaper in Korea. She interviewed me, and then returned to Jimmy. I was shocked that he was still working her.

As I was having a laugh at Jimmy, I saw a familiar face enter the bar. It was Ethan Zohn, the winner of *Survivor-Africa*. Ivy and I love that show, and I knew that she would be excited to hear I met Ethan. Ethan was a goalkeeper in college and played in the minor leagues in the U.S., as well as in the Zimbabwean League.

The million-dollar winner had a cameraman with him and was interviewing people. I soon heard that he was working with U.S. Soccer's website during the Cup. I had consumed a number of beers and was feeling very good when I decided it was time to introduce myself, however each time I approached, he would ask someone else for an interview. This happened a few times, and I decided not to worry about it. I would certainly catch up with him at some point.

I was downing yet another OB when a few loud Yanks began singing the National Anthem. It was a great scene as the entire bar stopped what they were doing and joined in. There were probably 250 people belting out the anthem. My right hand was over my heart, and my left hand held a mug, and I was singing as loudly and as badly as everyone else when I glanced to my left and saw Ethan right next to me singing along.

When the song finished, there was the predictable chant of U!S!A!, U!S!A! When that calmed down, I quickly introduced myself to Ethan, and we talked for quite awhile. At some point he told me that he needed to interview me and did so. During the interview, I noticed Jimmy snapping pictures of us with my camera. He then joined us along with another fan and we discussed *Survivor*.

Ethan was a great guy and very candid about the show. He told us of his website, www.grassrootsoccer.org, which is devoted to helping AIDS in Africa. He had been genuinely touched by his experience there and had made it his goal to do as much as he could to bring awareness and help to that often overlooked continent.

I spent the next hour or so talking with Big Dog, Scott, and Neil, but Jimmy had other ideas and was seen talking with a cute blond. She was Amanda and was serving in the Army. She was from Tampa, like Ivy, and when Jimmy introduced us, we talked of Cuban sandwiches, which she said she missed more than anything in Korea.

By this time it was late, and my head was foggy, but I was able to catch the eye of another familiar face, Vladimir. The Russian had just arrived after the long flight. His Ethiopian friend, Geta, was right behind him. They were both exhausted but very happy to finally be here. A short time later they left with Mark to head to the hotel. Soon, Big Dog and his crew, Monty, Scott, and Neil, were leaving as well.

The crowd at The Nashville was thinning out, and I was in the mood to return to the *Dong-Il* for a good night's sleep. I could tell that I was probably a bit beyond my limit, and the last thing I wanted was to be hung over tomorrow for the U.S.-Portugal match. It is funny that with age I am able to recognize my limit, which I could never do in my 20s. But now, in my early 30s, I am susceptible to terrible hangovers.

I may have been ready to leave in order to preserve myself, but Jimmy was in full stride. Not drinking had enabled him to have a great conversation with Amanda, and I could tell he was not even thinking about leaving. I killed some time chatting up a few other Yanks, while hoping Jimmy would soon want to leave, but then something caught my eye. It was a Portuguese jersey. There were a few of them sitting at the bar.

This was an opportunity I could not resist. Without a moment's hesitancy or a single thought of potential trouble, I went straight up to them. There were six of them and they had just ordered a pitcher of beer. Luckily, three of them spoke English, one of them almost perfectly. They ended up being great guys.

They were shocked I was staying in Korea for three weeks. Their trip was a bit shorter, tomorrow's game would be their only one, they were here for only two days. I was stunned that anyone would fly that far for a single match, but they said they did it for "the team."

We gave each other information on our team, likely starting lineups, injuries, and omissions. They knew very little about our team. For example, I would say, "Our captain is Claudio Reyna." They shrugged. I said, "He plays for Sunderland but just transferred from Rangers." Again, blank stares. I was thinking, "How can these guys who know so much about soccer know so little about Reyna." Flabbergasted, I asked if they followed the English Premier League.

"No," came the simple answer.

"What leagues do you follow?" I asked.

"Portugal, of course. Spain and Italy, a little."

"Why don't you watch England?" This was killing me. I thought everyone in the world followed the Premier league and its famous clubs.

"Why should we?"

"Because it is the best" I really did not know what to say and my mind was buzzing, so I was not able to express myself as well as I would have liked.

"It is not better than Spain or Italy," the main talker informed me. I was in no mood or condition to argue this point, and with the Spanish clubs' performance in the last few Champions League tournaments; there really was no argument. I took another direction.

"Do you know who David Beckham is," I asked.

"Of course."

"How about Paul Scholes?"

"No," they said, and that about summed up all I needed to know about the soccer they follow.

At this point, I was really talking only to the one who spoke the best English. Those who spoke no English were never really involved in our conversation. The others who did eventually joined their countrymen, leaving me and the one to talk.

He was a Porto fan and told me a lot about the Portuguese League. I surprised him by naming a few of the clubs, of course, the big ones: Benfica, Sporting Lisbon, and his beloved Porto. I told him of my earlier conversation with Anthony and how he said FIFA was going to move Euro2004. My new friend scoffed at this saying there was not a chance it would happen. He said Portugal had invested a lot, building new and rebuilding old stadiums.

I told him Ivy and I were planning to attend and was happy to hear him say that we would have a great time. I was really enjoying the conversation and I ordered two pitchers for the group. As I did so, the bartender advised that it was last call. The rest of the Portos were happy with the beer I provided and all toasted me.

One of them had a Portugal scarf around his neck and I asked to see it. It was a typical soccer scarf except that I had a lot of small words around the frame. They explained that it was a song. Whether of not it was their national anthem or just a sort of fight song, I do not know. However, they took the time to translate it. The translation was going along fine until they came to the word "Armas."

Now, you must remember that at this point I had drunk a lot. When I saw this word, I got very excited, and told them, very loudly, that that was one of our players.

"Armas! He plays for us! Chris Armas!" I was yelling. "He was a starter but just got hurt, so he's not here."

They acknowledged me, but really wanted to continue the translation. "Yes, it means arms, like weapons," they patiently explained.

"No! He was our defensive mid! He plays for us!" I was off my barstool and gesturing wildly. "You're lucky he got hurt cause he is really good. You've got our players name on your scarf!" Once again, they tried to translate, but I was having none of it, and they realized further explanation was futile.

By then the pitchers were empty, and the staff was about to ask us to leave. Even Jimmy was ready to go. We were all up and shaking hands. "Wait, wait," I said. "What is your prediction?" I asked the Porto fan.

"4-0."

"No, come on. Not that many. Not with our guy in your song and on your scarf." I was taken aback at his total lack of respect.

"What do you say?" he asked me.

"2-0. You will win, but it won't be that easy." We were walking down the steps and were soon on the now deserted streets on Itaewon. The six Portos were looking for another bar and a passerby pointed about a block up and said it would be open much later.

"Come on," the guy told me and I really wanted to, but Jimmy was already hailing a cab and the two of us told the six that we would see them tomorrow in Suwon.

As I stumbled up the stairs back at the *Dong-Il*, I saw a clock on the wall that said 3:00. I was out the moment my head hit the brick-like pillow.

Day 4
Wednesday, June 5

What's Going On?

I woke up with a sick feeling that began in my stomach and was quickly traveling to my head. I slowly made my way to the small refrigerator and took a long drink of the cold, bottled water that the two ladies of the *Dong-Il* provided. The water brought temporary relief, but I still cursed myself for allowing this hangover. How could I have been so foolish, feeling rough on the day of the long anticipated U.S-Portugal match?

To make matters worse, Jimmy and I had to meet Big Dog, Monty, Scott, and Neil at Seoul Station at 9:30. These plans would prevent me from enjoying any more sleep. At least, that is what I thought, but really had no idea as my room did not have a clock. I was worried that it may have already been too late. So, as I tried to ignore the pounding in my head, I pulled on some shorts and a t-shirt and stumbled into the hall. I cursed a second time upon seeing the clock. It said, 8:00...too early to leave right away, too late to go back to sleep.

I knocked on Jimmy's door and woke him up. Then I showered, dressed, and watched a few minutes of TV, all the while downing another bottle of water. I was determined to be at 100 percent for the game. I had waited all my life to watch the U.S. in a World Cup match, and I would be damned if I would let a hangover keep me down.

At 9:00 Jimmy and I headed out to the subway and caught a train for the short ride to Seoul Station. We were to meet them at the information booth, however when we arrived a few minutes before the meeting time, we found no information booth. We decided Jimmy would wait outside, above ground, while I would stay in the subway tunnel.

Before I could worry that we would not meet them, I saw the four making their way towards me with Scott and Neil's camera crew in tow. They were some sight, all wearing red and waving the flag, drawing stares from the local commuters. We quickly identified the train we would need to board for Suwon and then made our way to the main train station to buy tickets to Daegu for the game with Korea. We had heard rumors that the tickets had been snapped up quickly and may already be gone.

Nervously, we approached the ticket counter, but the soccer gods were with us, and we were able to purchase the tickets we wanted. Perhaps with this worry gone or maybe it was the excitement of the day, maybe even mind over matter, but whatever it was made me feel better. My queasy stomach and headache were replaced with hunger.

I had seen a sort of lunch counter that seemed to be serving noodle soup in the underground station. Though it was early, I was craving it, hoping for a sort of chicken soup fixer upper. Jimmy wanted the soup as well, but Big Dog and Monty were not as adventurous and said they would hit Dunkin' Donuts which was in the train station. Scott and Neil volunteered to watch all our luggage.

At the lunch counter, Jimmy and I found no one that spoke English, so we pointed to the soup that the only customer at the small counter was eating. The old woman behind the counter nodded and in moments placed a large bowl of very hot soup in front of us. It had long noodles similar to those found in Oodles of Noodles, that cheap staple of dormitory life, and was very good. There was *kim' chi* in it, and I was beginning to believe that they ate it with everything. The only thing I did not like about it was a small pile of seaweed that floated on top of the steaming, brown broth. I have never liked the taste of seaweed, as I have always found it to have a fishy flavor. In the case of this soup, it was easily avoidable, and when I was finished, all that remained was a small glob of the green stuff. Big Dog and Monty had rejoined us, and I got up feeling much better. My stomach was filled, and it had only cost W2,000 or $1.60. I thought that if money ran low, I could easily survive on this soup.

The four of us collected Scott and Neil, who were guarding our large pile of luggage. Our four new friends were all taking advantage of the Home Stay program that the city of Suwon had organized. They were to meet their host families for the first time when we arrived in Suwon.

As we made off for the subway train, we had a disagreement on which way to go. I looked to the two Koreans, the cameraman and director, for some guidance, but they just stared back, offering no help. I asked Scott if they could help, and he said that when they first met at the airport, they had freely offered advice. Then a third person, the producer, had told them not to do so, and ever since, they had been no help at all. It was as if they were not there at all.

Once on the train, the six of us had a good time, telling stories and trading jokes. It was as if we had been friends for a long time. All the while, the camera crew filmed us, and I found that after about fifteen minutes, I was no longer conscious of them.

The ride lasted about an hour with probably twenty stops. I had read that Suwon was a suburb of Seoul, but on the ride, it looked to be just one huge city as the urban sprawl never stopped. When we got off the train, we saw the New York Crew getting off about five cars ahead of us. Living up to their billing, they were loudly singing. The six of us, followed by the cameras, rushed to join them.

The platform was covered and made for great acoustics as we sang, "Ohhhhhh, Oh-Ohhh, Oh-Ohhh, Oh-Ohhh, Oh-Ohhh, Oh-Ohh-Ohhhh, Oh-Ohh-Ohhhh, Oh-Oh-Oh, O-O-O, U!S!A!" We, again, drew stares from the locals, many of who cheered and clapped along with us. Most of us wore red, the color that Sam's Army asks all U.S. fans to wear to games, making us easily recognizable. Probably half of us, including myself, had the flag tied around our necks like a cape. I was wearing a

42

red Sam's Army T-shirt, and the only red baseball cap I own, one that says, "ACC Basketball."

Both Big Dog and Monty, who were also wearing Sam's Army T-shirts, and Scott and Neil found their host family with no problems and were soon off to their new homes, leaving Jimmy and I with the NY Crew. It was another hot day, and shortly after leaving the train station, we were looking for a cool place to kill a couple of hours. At Nashville someone had advised that a bar called Sante Fe would be a good place to gather before the game. Everyone was planning on meeting there around 2:00.

In no time we found a PC Bang, and our red, white, and blue group went in and logged on. We spent time e-mailing home and reading news and soccer message boards. While we were on-line, the Carolina Hurricanes scored an overtime goal to shock all hockey fans by taking Game One from the Redwings in the Stanley Cup Finals.

It was cool in the PC Bang and we were content to spend quality time in there. We talked about the evenings match and I spent most of the time trying to convince the others not to be upset when we lose. I maintained, once again, that it was the other two games that really mattered.

Joe, the guy I had beaten in darts the night before, told me that he had left Nashville to watch the Korea-Poland game on a large screen set up in the streets. He said that the atmosphere was amazing, that the Koreans were great fans, singing and chanting the whole game, before going nuts at the final whistle. They marched, sang, and shot off fireworks for hours afterwards. Even though he hated leaving the party at Nashville, he said he would not have missed being on the streets for anything.

He made me realize that I had missed out on a big part of this experience, celebrating with the home team. I had no idea the Koreans were so passionate about their team. I lamented the fact that I would not get the chance to watch them play from the streets. For their next game I would be in the stadium rooting against them, and we would be playing Poland at the same time they played Portugal.

After an hour or so in the PC Bang, we left in search of food and were soon entering a McDonalds. The vocal leader of the NY Crew, Brent, was good enough to buy my combo meal. Again, the burger, fries, and Coke were very similar to what we were served at home.

While eating, I read the preview of our game in the English language newspaper, *The Korean Herald*. It offered nothing significant until the final paragraph, which simply stated, "Korea has barred 6,515 known terrorists and 2,689 hooligans from today's U.S.-Portugal game." This led me to wonder if these 6,515 terrorists were welcomed to the other games!? And if so, was our government aware of them? Did the FBI have this list? Was Bin Laden allowed to go to the Brazil-Turkey match? There were no answers to these questions, so I simply put my trust in the South Korean government. Surely, they would keep me safe.

After eating, we decided it was time to head to Sante Fe, which was only a block away. We went up the steps to the second floor bar and entered through a door, which announced, in English, that they served "Spainish food." Inside, there were about 20 Yanks, sitting around tables on couches. Many were in red, and there were more flags on display. I saw Scott and Neil and Jimmy, and I sat with them. On the table was a bowl of corn. Not popcorn or corn off the cob, but dried and salty corn.

In no time, Brent and the NY Crew started singing. One of the songs was "Da-da-da, da-da, da-da-da, da-da, da-da-da, da-da, da-da-da, Figo Sucks!" I was sure that after this game, the "Figo Sucks" will simply be replaced with "U.S.A."

While the singing continued, I tried to get a beer, but Neil said it might take a while. I noticed their camera crew had collapsed in a booth. They looked pretty tired from chasing the two Seattle brothers all over Korea. Scott said the meeting with their host family went well, and they were excited about their stay.

It seemed that there was only one waiter on duty, and people were grumbling about the lack of service. In an effort to outsmart everyone, I went into the other room where the bar was. There I saw the one waiter and the bartender. They were busy tying a napkin in some intricate design around the bottle tops of the beers that had been ordered.

I tried to order a beer, but they motioned me to go back to the main room, saying they would get to me. As I left, they were still perfecting their origami. When I made it back to the table, I heard someone say they had ordered a beer 20 minutes ago. People began talking of finding another bar. Not only was the service slow, but there was no TV on which to watch the early game.

About twelve of us left for a better watering hole. We continued singing as we made our way through the hot, bustling streets of Suwon. When I first got off the train, my first impression of Suwon was that it reminded me of Coruscant, the planet in Star Wars that is one large city. Everywhere I looked, there was development. Buildings were all at least three stories tall and many were six. There were no amazingly, tall buildings to draw my attention, just large, low buildings separated from each other by narrow roads for as far as I could see.

Shopkeepers emerged from their ground floor markets and joined with the street vendors and pedestrians, cheering us as we passed. It was a good feeling, being cheered in a foreign land. I am not sure if it was because we were Americans or if they were simply caught up in the excitement of the moment and would be cheering the Portos when they walked by. I had heard that there is a lot of anti-American sentiment in Korea but had not experienced any of it yet. There was no doubting we were Americans, as at least half of our group carried Old Glory, but there was not a single frown from anyone we passed.

We rounded a corner and were met with a spectacular site. The road we turned onto was narrow, maybe a lane and a half wide. It was straight and seemed to go on forever. What was amazing was the colors. Nearly every shop had a brightly colored sign, in Korean. It was something out of a kung-fu movie where the bad guy disappears down a crowded Hong Kong street, the language on the signs only adding to the confusion.

We easily found a bar called Orgasm, which advertised World Cup matches on TV. I was sweating and craving a beer. Without hesitation, we all went in and headed downstairs to the bar. It was dark and cool...a great place to chill before leaving for the match. There was just one problem. They were not opening for another hour! We tried to convince them, saying that we would be on the bus to the stadium by then, but it was no use.

Back outside in the heat someone went in the next bar to check it out, only to come out and say simply, "No."

"What's going on?" I asked to no one in particular. "How can we not get a beer?"

During the walk, Jimmy, Scott, Neil, and I had begun talking with a married couple, Doug and Tonya. Tonya was five months pregnant with their first child, a daughter, but had not given traveling here a second thought. I admired not only her determination, but also her attitude, as she did not complain about the heat. Frustrated, the six of us decided to break away from the larger group and just head to the stadium. Tonya said that we would be able to get food and drink there.

Along the short walk to the shuttle bus stop, I bought a Coke from a vendor, which did wonders to quench my thirst. Soon we were on the bus and about fifteen minutes later were dropped off a few blocks from the stadium.

The stadium was a magnificent site. It was clearly modern in design with its sloped, rounded covering that would provide shelter from the sun for those on the sidelines. Perched on a small hilltop, the first glimpse of it really got my soccer juices flowing.

As soon as we were off the bus, we headed toward the stadium. Along the way, many Koreans handing out small trinkets greeted us. I was surprised to see that most of these gifts had a Bible verse printed on them. At the stadium, there was no sign of any food or drink, a fact I noted often to Tonya. We were away from the hustle of downtown Suwon and were now out into the neighborhoods and there was not much there. In fact, I was shocked that there was nothing going on at the stadium.

We decided to make our way up a long walk up a hill to one entrance of the stadium where there were a lot of people in blue, waving American flags. We did so without Scott and Neil who left to meet up with their host family on the other side of the stadium.

At the top of the walkway, we saw a strange thing. There were twenty or so Koreans, mostly over the age of, I would guess, sixty. There were wearing a slightly darker shade of Carolina Blue. To our astonishment, they were rhythmically waving American flags. Just as stunning, they were led by two very good-looking, skimpily dressed, young ladies. They were acting as a sort of bandleader or head cheerleader.

As we watched this spectacle, many Koreans greeted us and asked us to pose for pictures with them. We were celebrities, sporting our U.S. clothes and flags. For a while, there was even a line of them waiting to pose with us.

After about twenty or so pictures, we decided to move away from the pep squad, disappointing a few who were still waiting for pictures. While we were walking, a pretty, redheaded girl joined us. Kaela lives in Boston and is a huge soccer fan. I was surprised that she had also traveled to France for the 1998 World Cup. What a great girl!

The heat was getting to us, and we were desperate to find refreshment but were not having any luck finding anything, not even a soda machine or a street vendor. From time to time we were stopped to pose for more pictures. The young Koreans were able to ask for a photo, but their English was not good enough to point us to refreshment.

We did see the occasional Yank, but it was still early, and the grounds were filled with mostly Koreans. At one point, a group of Americans made their way towards us. They said they were with Soccer Vacations, but more importantly, a few of them were carrying beers. They were good enough to give a can to Kaela, Jimmy, and I. Of course, Jimmy passed his to Doug and the three of us enjoyed a cold Cass.

Invigorated by the beer, we decided to go to the far side of the stadium, the only side we had not yet seen. Along the way, a television camera crew stopped us. Before I knew it, I was being interviewed.

"What will be the score and who will score the goals?" the pretty Korean reporter asked in passable English.

Although I was convinced we had no chance, there was no way I was going on Korean TV predicting we would lose, so I said, "2-1, USA. Goals scored by…" This was tough, as I had not considered we would score. "…Clint Mathis," I calmly stated (I was still holding out hope he would play, that the whole thing was one of Bruce Arena's ruses) "and Eddie Pope. And, I guess, Figo might get one in for them."

"Oh, OK. Are you going to the game U.S.A. against Korea?" she asked.

"Of course."

"What do you think the score will be?"

Had I answered truthfully, I would have said something like 2-1 or 1-1, but I thought that as long as I was lying, there was no need to stop just yet. "4 to 0."

Not only did the reporter act as if she was hit by lightening, but I noticed the cameraman almost dropped the camera! They were stunned. Finally the reporter incredulously choked out, "4 to 0 for U.S.A.?"

"At least four, maybe five," I said looking directly into the camera.

"OK, thanks." And just like that the interview was over, as the rest of our group laughed at the stunned reporter.

My interview had apparently caught the eye of another camera crew, and they immediately pounced on us, but rather than a one on one interview, this reporter simply asked us to cheer.

Perhaps it was the heat or the one beer or maybe it was simply the moment, but I did something I would never do back home. I yelled my head off for no reason, other than the presence of a camera. The reporter then asked us to sing a song. I looked at the others and we agreed on one.

On cue, the five of us broke into, "Oh I'd rather have Clint Mathis than Figo! Oh I'd rather have Clint Mathis than Figo! Oh I'd rather have Clint Mathis, rather have Clint Mathis, rather have Clint Mathis than Figo!"

When we finished, the reporter thanked us, but before we could leave, the other camera crew asked us to sing for them. This was the same reporter to whom I had made my outrageous predictions, so to further her misery; I suggested we sing Jingle Bells.

She did not flinch as we belted out the Christmas favorite, though we got some looks from some other Yanks passing by. When we finished with a loud "Hey!", we thought we were through with this crew, but for some reason they requested one more song. I have no idea why, but we did one more for them. It was an original I put together a week earlier. It is sung to the tune of *Old MacDonald Had a Farm* and goes like this:

> Bruce Arena had a team.
> E-I-E-I-O
> And on this team he has a Wolff.
> E-I-E-I-O
> With a goal, goal here
> And a goal, goal there.
> Here a goal, there a goal
> Everywhere a goal, goal.
>
> Bruce Arena has a team.
> E-I-E-I-O
> And on this team he has a Goose.
> E-I-E-I-O
> With a stop, stop here
> And a stop, stop there.
> Here a stop, there a stop
> Every where a stop, stop.
>
> Bruce Arena has a team
> E-I-E-I-O

Finally, the television folks were through with us and we were back on the march. Our number one priority was finding food and drink, but I was also searching for Chuck, the English teacher who had helped me plan the trip. He had told me he was tall and would be wearing a red, Ohio State shirt. Since the moment we got off the bus at the stadium, Jimmy and I had been looking for someone fitting that bill.

Having walked the length of the stadium along a wide sidewalk next to a wide road, which was virtually free of traffic, we made a right turn and began up a hill to the one corner of the complex we had yet to see. Of course since this was the last stop on our 90-minute search for some activity, we finally saw what we had been seeking.

I do not know the official name for this area, but it was defiantly the World Cup Zone. There were thousands of people around. Music blasted from speakers. There were games for kids, such as kicking a ball to a target, having a kick timed, and so forth. There was a huge, two-story high, soccer ball that people were signing. A car company was displaying their latest model, complete with Price-Is-Right-style girls in tight clothes.

We quickly identified and made our way to the refreshment stand. It was a mirage-like sight for someone as hot and thirsty as I. Three selections caught my eye, Budweiser, Coke, and Power Aid. As my hangover was long gone, my first thought was to grab a Bud, but I wanted my head as clear as possible for the match, so I bought a Power Aid. The vendor pulled it out of a cooler filled with ice. Kaela had a Bud and was happy it was only W2,500 or $2.00. What a great price for a beer at a game, quite different from back home where it is generally around $6.00.

Our group took a seat on a brick ledge near the drink stand. After chugging half of the cold Power Aid, I mentioned to everyone to be on the lookout for Chuck in a red Ohio State shirt. At this point, Jimmy, unbelievably, told me he just saw a guy in a Buckeye jersey.

"What? Why didn't you tell me," I asked. Not only was I anxious to meet the man who had helped me so much, but he was planning on returning to Seoul with us and spending the next day showing Jimmy and I around the large city.

I looked at him incredulously when he answered, "You said a Ohio State shirt, not a jersey."

"You didn't think to point him out because he had on a jersey, not a shirt? I don't know, he just said an OSU shirt. When did you see him?"

"About two minutes ago. He walked off that way." Jimmy pointed toward a stage that was obviously going to host some sort of concert. There were a lot of people that way, but I headed off in that direction, telling Jimmy and the others to wait for me.

I walked around for a short time, taking in the scene. I saw many other Americans posing for pictures with Koreans. A few times, I was waived in to join a group for a photo. The Koreans were extremely nice and polite, and I enjoyed these meetings. It was as if I was a celebrity.

Celebrity or not, I saw no tall American in an Ohio State jersey and after a few minutes, I headed back to where the group was sitting. As I approached them, I noticed them talking to someone who had to be Chuck! He was tall and was wearing the elusive Buckeye jersey. I introduced myself, and it seemed Chuck was as excited about meeting me, as I was he. We had a lot of correspondence over e-mail, and I had also brought a few things over for him; in particular a Sam's Army T-Shirt and the new Jimmy Buffet CD.

The first thing I realized about Chuck was that he talked, a lot. He told a few stories of the other games he had attended, notably the opener. About an hour before game time, we decided to head into the stadium, just to insure we did not miss anything.

We had to wait in a slow moving line that went through an airport-like metal detector. Security guards patted us down and we wondered if every game was like this or if there was special precaution for the United States. I made it through with no problem, but Jimmy was carrying a backpack and had to empty it before he could pass.

We were in! The excitement was really hitting me now. In less than an hour, I would witness the U.S. play a World Cup match against one of the best teams in the world, Portugal, and all their famous players. Our group split up and Jimmy and I hurried to our seats, followed by Chuck, who announced he would stand with us.

Our seats were amazing! Second row, behind and just to the right of the goal. We were about 15 feet above the field, so the vantage point was not too bad for the far end. The U.S. players were warming up right in front of us. As our section quickly filled with Americans, we began singing for the players. At one point, I saw Assistant Coach Dave Sarachan working out some players. I had seen him do this before and knew that these had to be the starters.

There had been much speculation on who they would be. For some, back in the States with the Internet at their fingertips, the line-up may not have been a surprise. For me, even with the warnings about Mathis and Reyna, it was shocking.

I was happy and relieved to see Brad Freidel in the goal. The defenders were Tony Sanneh, Eddie Pope, Jeff Agoos, and Frankie Hedjuk. Hedjuk was on the left, taking the place of David Regis. Most fans feel right back is our weakest position. Tonight we were starting two of them, one on the left side.

I was very happy for Jeff Agoos. He is the consummate professional. He has often been criticized for making a big mistake, however having watched him for years at D.C. United, I have always felt that he is as solid a defender as we have. I have always been confident with him in the back. Though not the fastest player, he makes up for it with superior positioning. He is a leader on and off the field, something fans in San Jose learned as he led them to the MLS Cup in his first year after leaving D.C. United.

Despite his steady play and leadership, Agoos had never played in the World Cup. In 1994, he was one of the last players cut. After hearing the disappointing news, he burned his practice uniform in the parking lot. He rebounded from this setback when he was allocated to D.C. United when MLS began in 1996 and was one of the best defenders in the league. New National Team coach Steve Sampson called him the "first name I wrote on the line-up card" during qualifying. However, shortly before the 1998 Cup in France, Sampson, in as curious a move as has been seen in sports, re-evaluated the team that had qualified. He cut his captain, John Harkes. He called in a few young, inexperienced players. He changed the tactical formation with which the team had been successful. Though Agoos was on the team, these changes saw him on the bench the entire tournament. Today, Agoos would play in the World Cup.

The starting midfield saw three youngsters, DeMarkus Beasley, John O'Brien, and Pablo Mastroeni and one veteran, Earnie Stewart. I was hopeful that Beasley's speed would cause trouble for the Portuguese but worried that the experienced Europeans would shut down the moves that worked so well in MLS. I was happy to see Mastroeni starting. It was Chris Armas' position, but I have always thought the dread locked one to be a great defender. If Arena had confidence in him in the midfield, that was fine with me.

The forwards were Brian McBride and the exciting, young Landon Donovan.

With three key players not starting, Armas, Reyna, and Mathis, and with Hedjuk at left back, had I stopped to think about it, I would have said we had no chance. If you had told me this would be our line-up three weeks ago, I would have said, "You're crazy," and would have thought that we are in a lot of trouble.

However, I was caught up in the excitement and never considered our chances. For over six months I have told everyone who would listen that we could not win this match. Portugal is just too good. Maybe we could tie, but we should not be disappointed with a loss here. However, now our boys were on the field and there is a reason they play the game. I looked across to the far side and saw the Portuguese in their reddish-maroon shirts and green shorts. I saw Luis Figo and watched him warm up and found myself not in awe as I thought I might be, seeing the best player on the planet.

The stadium was filling up and the noise was growing. In our section, there were many U.S. flags. In most others, Koreans were waving Portuguese flags. This upset Chuck, who seemed suspicious of Koreans, but seemed fair to me. For them to advance they had to beat us, so, of course they would support Portugal, just as we will do in Portugal's other two games.

In front of me were some Yanks wearing wings of eagles on their head. To my left was an Asian looking man wearing a blue U.S.A. shirt. The noise was rising. Behind me, a drummer was playing Led Zeppelin's, *Immigrant Song*, with our section singing along "USAaaaaaaaaa Aaaay! USAaaaaaaaaa Aaaay!"

***

The teams are now walking out onto the pitch, the U.S. led by captain Stewart, the Portos by Figo. In the far corner of the stadium, the Portuguese supporters are unfurling a giant maroon uniform and the Koreans are responding with

50

cheers. I am as nervous as if I were playing, perhaps more so. I am nearly hoarse but continue shouting and singing. When I am not singing, I always yell the same thing. "Come on boys!" I do not know why I scream that or when I started, but for as long as I can remember, that is what I yell before the game starts.

It is now time for the anthem. I take off my red ACC Basketball cap and hold it over my heart with my right hand. In my left hand, I hold a small U.S. flag on a stick that was handed out to everyone in our section by stadium volunteers. I think they gave everyone else Portuguese flags. Everyone around me belted out the words. As I sing, I watch the screen at the far side of the field. It shows the faces of all of our players as a cameraman walks in front of them. Suddenly, after our team and Bruce Arena are shown, I am on the huge scoreboard. Not a shot of a lot of fans that included me, but just me! I am up there for probably three of four seconds and the whole time, I never stop singing. When I am finally removed from the screen, I look down and see a cameraman turning away. I wonder if that feed went to the TV as well. If so, I was just seen representing the U.S. all over the world.

Everything is happening very fast. We sing *Oh When the Yanks Go Marching In* as the players run to their positions. The U.S. comes to our end. Just before kickoff, Guus Hiddink, the coach of Korea is shown on the scoreboard and the crowd erupts. He is a hero here after last night. The Koreans are still on cloud nine after their historic victory.

Now the world's eyes turn to Suwon to watch the U.S. play Portugal. I am honored to be there and fell proud of our team. Thirty other teams had already played in this Cup, now it is our turn. Flash bulbs explode with the referee's whistle and the game is underway. It is as electric a start as I can remember for a sporting event. Caught up in it as I am, anything seemed possible, even a win by our team.

That optimism soon fades. As we sing *Ole, Ole, Ole, Ole* Portugal works the ball around and attacks. It feels like forever before we get a touch on the ball, but when we do, we nervously turn it over. All the action is at the far end. After a tense two minutes, we win a goal kick. Friedel sends it long and McBride is fouled as he goes for the header. It is not deep enough for a shot, but is close enough to be served into the box.

As Earnie Stewart stands over the ball, I suddenly think of one of the best threads I ever read on Big Soccer. Leading up to the Cup, this one asked, "What should the U.S. do if they were to get an early goal against Portugal?" Responses ranged from attack and try to build on it to defend with all eleven. Personally, I was torn. If you attack, Portugal could run rampant and quickly come back. However, to defend for most of the game is very difficult. You would like to think that you would only surrender a single goal, thus earning an important tie. I read these responses over and over and had no idea how I would handle it as a coach. There was one thing I was sure of and that was that Arena would not be fazed and would know exactly what to do. He would not alter his game plan. Whatever he was doing, he would continue to do, be that attacking, countering, or defending. Arena is one of the most thoroughly prepared coaches I have ever seen in any sport. Again, I was confident he would know what to do.

The captain serves the ball in towards Sanneh and a defender leaps to deflect the ball out for a corner. There seems to be some confusion in the Portuguese defense. For some reason, I am more nervous now than I was before kickoff. At least the players can run around. I can only watch the action, which is so close that I can look into McBride's steely brown eyes.

"Come on boys!" I yell as Stewart swings in the ball from the corner to my right. There is some pinball action as the ball seems to hit everyone in the box. I cannot discern what is happening. Things suddenly appear to move in slow motion, and I see the action as clearly as I have ever seen anything in my life. The ball falls to O'Brien just a few feet from the left side of the goal. The keeper is on the ground with a few other bodies. O'Brien is looking straight at me as he drills the ball into the net. Had the net not been there, I believe the ball would have come straight to me. Even before he applied the finish, I saw the goal. By the time it did, in fact, hit the net, I was higher off the ground than at anytime since that day back in high school when, for the first and only time, I touched the rim.

When my feet hit the cement, there is bedlam. I am jumping up and down and screaming simply, "Yes! Yes!" and then "Oh my God! Oh my God!" After the second or third "Yes!" something clicks in my throat and my voice is suddenly very high, like I had been sucking helium or was a chipmunk. I find myself hugging the guy next to me in the blue shirt, a man to whom I had not yet introduced myself.

The whole section is going absolutely bonkers. It is one of the most happily stunning things I have ever seen. It is so unexpected. I think we are all caught off guard, and the suddenness of it only serves to intensify our celebration. I have been in a crowd for some great moments but nothing like this. All over, people are hugging each other. Not the usual high fives or quick hugs, no, these are long, tight, squeeze the breath out of each other hugs. And we are all strangers. I cannot stop screaming "Oh my God!" over and over in my high-pitched voice. I should say that I am a Christian, and I do not take the Lord's name in vain. I do hope He takes no offense in my celebratory shouts, as I really do not think I am choosing to say this.

Our out of control euphoria lasts a minute or two. I am not aware of the kickoff and only regain my senses as a replay is shown on the scoreboard. We see McBride power a header, and the goalkeeper makes a great play to keep the ball out of the goal, but it falls right to OB. We cheer the replay and a few others from different angles. They all show the world the same thing. The United States, the team laughed at for four years since finishing last in 1998, is beating mighty Portugal.

When the replays stop, I calm down and take stock of the situation. People are chanting "U!S!A! U!S!A!" I hold off for a moment as I notice that I am shaking, really shaking. I cannot control my hands and they are moving alarmingly fast. I try to alert Jimmy, to show him, but with my voice the way it is, he cannot hear me over the din.

We have that early lead and I know the players, under Bruce's control, will remain composed, even as I turn to Jell-O only a few feet from the pitch.

We attack again and Beasley's speed shows as he is fouled just outside the box. Stewart puts this one on frame and the keeper parries it right onto the feet of Donovan who is just outside of the goal box. Unfortunately, it happens too quickly for him to react, and the ball caroms off his feet and rolls across the goalmouth. I see Eddie Pope streaking towards it and in those few seconds, every goal I have ever seen Pope score flashes through my mind. "He will finish this one," I think to myself. But, by the time he reaches the ball, the angle is too great and his shot only finds the side netting.

For only a moment I lament a near miss, but then I realize that Portugal is in disarray. They did not expect this and are not responding well. I now think we have a chance, although we are only some six minutes in.

The game is exciting as Portugal tries to attack. The Korean crowd comes to life, and I hold my breath every time Figo gets the ball. However, he finds little room, thanks to Hejduk and Mastroeni. There are a few tense moments, but a defender is always there to challenge the forwards who are looking to equalize.

Then there is a misplay by a Portuguese defender that almost sends in Beasley and forces the goalkeeper, Baia, to clear with his feet.

Our confidence leads to louder singing. "You'll never, beat, the U.S.," we half sing, half chant. We boo as it looks to us like the Portuguese dive time and time again.

"We are the U.S. The mighty might U.S.," we sing.

There are other shaky moments for Portugal, and as they seem to wilt, we grow in both confidence and composure. It is clear that Arena is not going to defend his one goal lead.

About twenty minutes in McBride wins yet another header, and Donovan fires a shot from the left side of the goal (our left, his right). The shot is high, and wide, but it sails into the first row near me. A fan catches it, and I push my way over and put my hand on it. I finally have a touch, and as with most players, it steadies my nerves somewhat. My hands stop shaking, but I still sound like Alvin, Simon, and Theodore, much to Jimmy's delight.

In case the Portuguese cannot understand us, we chant "*Estados Unidos*!" At least I think they can understand that rudimentary Spanish. There is some intrigue in the stands that I am not paying much attention to, but am aware of. Though our section is mostly American, it is probably ten percent foreign. There are about ten Brazilians partying it up with us. There is also a good number of Bangladeshis, who have a large banner to announce themselves. Anyway, one of them commandeers the ball that Donovan had shot into us. There is a security guard looking for it, but they are keeping quiet and we are all to focused on the game to give them up.

I am glad I was watching because for the second time I have the perfect angle for a U.S. goal. Donovan and Sanneh pressure the ball in the left corner. It looks

53

like the Portos had it out, but it deflects right to Donovan who aims a cross to McBride, but it takes a deflection off a defender and heads for the goal. As it is all in front of me, I can see that Baia has come out for the cross. I can also see the ball is goal-bound. I am shocked, 2-0! But then, before the ball is in the net, Baia recovers, and I hold my breath as he gets a hand to it. Much to our delight, he is only able to put it onto the post and from there it ricochets into the goal. Again, we jump around like fools, but with not quite the intensity of the first one.

We are delighted to be up 2-0, but with a few near misses and the disorganization of the Portuguese defense, it was almost inevitable. There is none of the hugging of strangers. Nonetheless, we are all beside ourselves with joy. Not even on Big Soccer, the bastion of all outlandish rumors, trash-talk, and dreams, did anyone suggest a 2-0 lead.

As we watch the replay, we are treated to the sight of someone else who is stunned. It is Coach Dave Sarachan. The camera is focused on Arena, but his trusty assistant is holding onto him as they edge forward, their eyes following the flight of the ball. At the moment it must have crossed the goal line, Sarachan releases Arena and grabs his head with both hands, his mouth agape as if he cannot believe what he is seeing. A split second later, it registers. As Arena triumphantly raises his right arm, Sarachan loses whatever traces of stoicism that remained on his face, and he becomes one of us, a fervent fan looking for someone to hug.

We in the cheap seats organize ourselves quickly and begin the one chant that I do not like. "Overrated…overrated!" Everyone chants in unison. I do not like this because while it does disparage the opponent, it also takes away from what our team is doing. I do not want to think Portugal is overrated; I want to believe they are one of the best teams in the world, and we are kicking their ass in front of the entire planet! Hell no, they are not overrated, we are taking it to them and you better watch out because we can do it to you to. Yeah, you, France and England and Germany and Italy and the rest of you Euro-snobs who look down your nose at our soccer and dismiss us! Look at what we are doing to one of you.

Maybe I am a bit fired up, but WOW, we are beating Portugal 2-0 in the World Cup! Then Donovan steals the ball and sends a cross to an awaiting McBride. Baia makes a diving save just in time, and we are delirious. It seems that Arena will not defend a two-goal lead!

A few moments later the referee books one of their guys for diving! This referee is not putting up with their desperate attempts to get back into the game. So far, I think he has done a good job. Now Stewart is volleying the ball on frame, but Baia, again, makes a shaky save.

I decide it is time to get out my camera and snap a few shots before halftime. We are chanting, "Let's go U.S. Let's go U.S.," and I see Tony Sanneh coming down his wing, preparing for a cross. I see McBride streaking in to receive it, and I think, "This will make a good picture." As Sanneh flights in the ball, I steady my aim, but suddenly I have a feeling that this is no ordinary cross. I quickly look up, away from the camera and see that McBride has some space and is zeroing in on the ball!

With the camera above my head, I snap a shot just as the tall striker heads the ball . . .into the net! "Yes!" I scream as pandemonium once again reigns behind Baia's goal. I am jumping with all my might, though with an $800.00 camera in my hand, I am as careful as possible under these extraordinary circumstances. Thus, I am not in such a frazzle that I am unaware what is taking place on the pitch. I am able to see the goal scorer right in front of me with an elated Beasley jumping into his arms. I am able to take a few shots of the celebration on the field.

As the players make their way back to their side of the pitch, we break into the famous, "U!S!A! U!S!A!" chant. We are loud, but have nowhere the intensity we had after the first goal. I think we are all a bit stunned. Never did anyone think we would be up 3-0 before halftime.

As Portugal sets up for a corner, I say to Jimmy and Chuck, "If we can go into halftime with this lead, we will win!" They both nodded their agreement. On the corner, I see the ball bouncing in the far end and it is directed right to Beto who hammers it past Friedel. "Damn it." I swear as the stadium erupts.

I fear that now the Portuguese will feel that the floodgates will open. Momentum is one of the greatest forces in sports, and now they have it. I think that if we can hold them until halftime, we will be ecstatic with a 3-1 lead. But should they get another before the break, it will be devastating. They will be back in the game, and we will feel it slipping away.

The replay shows O'Brien making a poor clearance and Beto displaying quick feet to one time the ball into the net. For a moment, I am upset that Beto goes over Agoos, fouling him to win the header, which went to OB and then right back to the Porto. But, no, it is not that bad.

Six minutes plus before the half. We must hold on. There is now noise everywhere. We are yelling encouragement. The Portuguese supporters are chanting, urging their heroes on. The Koreans are cheering excitedly as well. The atmosphere is fantastic. Portugal seems to recognize my fears and set their stall to attack. There are some tense moments as the Maroon shirts crash the goal some 120 yards from me. Crosses are sent in from both sides, and Figo looks as if he is ready to do what superstars do, take over the game.

In the central defense, we have Pope and Agoos. The two former teammates at D.C. United hold firm. Their understanding of one another proves very useful as they thwart numerous attacks. Mastroeni dogs Figo, and Beasley tracks back to lend support. About two minutes into injury time, moments after a terrifying series that begins with a Figo cross, a collision between Agoos and Friedel, the ball at an attacker's feet with the U.S. defense scrambling, and finally concludes with a clearance by Hejduk, the referee mercifully blows the whistle.

We have held onto the 3-1 lead. Portugal had been the aggressor the last ten minutes or so, but we weathered the storm and lead 3-1. The entire section breathes a huge sigh of relief, takes a brief moment to collect itself, and then cheers the boys off the field. Once they are in the locker room, I turn around and see a mass of exhausted Americans. There are people with stars and stripes painted on their face waving flags. Some are holding a scarf above their sweat-drenched heads. Others are simply staring into the Suwon night. All wear grins that seem to stretch from here all the way back home.

Then everyone begins talking. We are recapping the incredible half we have just witnessed. Jimmy says, "I am scared that I'm dreaming." Then, to punctuate the statement, he asks someone to pinch him.

This may not have been the best choice of words and those around us give him a good ribbing. We all agree we should ask to be punched and not pinched, if we doubt the reality of the situation. Soon, everyone is punching each other! Good solid shots to the bicep that hurt enough to announce, "Yes, you are awake. What you are seeing is real. The U.S. is leading Portugal 3-1 at halftime!"

Some U.S. reserves are warming up right in front of us. A few of us sing, "Tony Meola, give us a wave. Tony Meola, give us a wave." After a few bars, he obliges, as did Wolff a few moments later. When they leave, some cameraman asks us to give some cheer, but we do not understand it, so we do not do it. However, the Brazilians behind us run down and start it right in front of us, so we join in, chanting in, what else, Portuguese!

Having enough, the cameraman says in English, "You'll be all over Brazilian TV in the morning!"

Halftime is about over, and it is time to put the game face back on. I turn to a few Yanks behind me and say, "Get ready, it's all going to happen right here." Everyone agrees that the goal that Friedel will be defending, just a few yards from us, will be under siege and that many tense scenes will unfold on the green grass right in front of us. There is little question that Portugal will come at us hard.

Just before play begins, the player that U.S. soccer fans love to hate, Cobi Jones, checks in for Stewart.

The first few minutes, the Portuguese do come, but are turned away by the now captain, Friedel. Hejduk and Pope thwart other challenges. The whole time, we sing encouragement. We chant "Super Power. Super Power. U!S!A!"

Suddenly Donovan wins a yellow card, and McBride draws a foul just outside the box. I yell, "Come on Goose," as he and Donovan stand over the ball. I have seen Agoos put this shot into the net before and hope he will do it now. I can sense he wants it badly, perhaps too badly, as he powers it well over the bar. However, in that series, we serve notice that we will continue pushing forward.

After a few U.S. counter attacks, Portugal wins a corner when Sanneh inadvertently touches the ball while trying to shepherd it beyond the end line while under heavy pressure from Pauleta. Figo drives the ball in and Joao Pinto gets off a week shot. However, Jorge Costa has taken a dangerous position right in front of Friedel. Costa brings the ball down and attempts to turn as I hold my breath. He is screening the ball from Friedel with his body, but Friedel reaches his arms around him, perhaps knocking Costa slightly off balance, so that when he turns, it is not all the way around, and his shot is wide.

We have dodged a bullet. An attacker had the ball inside our goal box but was unable to finish. I am thankful not only that the shot has gone wide, but also that the referee has not given a penalty, as some of the Portos had appealed. But before I can think the sequence through, Donovan suddenly finds himself behind the defense. We all gasp in anticipation, but alas, his left-footed shot from an angle rolls just wide.

The game is wide open and exciting. The noise in the stadium is increasing as if everyone knows the game is far from over. Cameras flash as constantly as we sing.

We serenade our hosts with "Ole, Ole, Ole Ole Ole Ole, Ole, Ole." Then we decide to give the world's best player some noise and we all chant, "Figo is a *puta*! Figo is a *puta*!" After a few lines of this, the Brazilian cameraman who had filmed us at halftime, turns with a dumbfounded look and shakes his head as if to say, "No. He is not." He is almost scolding us for our disrespect. "Why are you saying that about this great player?"

I guess he does not realize that I have yelled insults at such greats as Emmit Smith, Roger Clemens, and even Michael Jordan. With this in my past, Figo is not going to get off lightly. The other Yanks concur, and we continue our mockery.

As the clock ticks down, our anticipation grows. The clock has hit the 70th minute when Pauleta swings in a cross from my right side. I quickly glance to the front of the goal and see an attacker streaking in, unmarked. The ball is heading right for him, but then I see Agoos there. He desperately reaches out his foot to clear the ball. Only rather than putting it out for a corner, it shoots into the goal.

I maintain my composure, as I thought that there was nothing else he could have done; either stab at the ball the way he did or watch as the runner puts the ball in the net. I watch Goose and amazingly, his first move is to look at Friedel. I then see him smile. I am not sure if it is a smile of disbelief or if he is signaling to Friedel that it will be all right. Whatever the reason for it, it does not last long. To his credit, he gets up rather quickly and then turns away from me.

I think that if this was going to happen, better it is to Goose than anyone else. The left-footer is a seasoned pro, and I am sure he will put this behind him; that it will not affect his play. Where others may fall apart, I am confident that Agoos will continue playing his game.

I watch the replay, and I realized it did not happen the way I thought. Agoos had been under control; there was nothing desperate about his touch of the ball. He had been positioned brilliantly and should have made the clearance.

Now it is 3-2 with some twenty minutes to go. We are as loud as ever as we will our team to hang on. The Portuguese fans, backed by the Koreans, are making a ton of noise as well. I am certain the Portuguese will come forward with everything they have. The tension in the stadium is thick.

Where I would have gladly taken a tie before the game, now all I care about is victory. Maybe in a few days, the one point would be nice, but should it come to that now, I think we will all be devastated.

Joe-Max Moore comes in for Donovan, and I am somewhat surprised that Arena brings in another forward. I anticipated a more defensive player. However, Moore is not the typical forward. The Everton bench warmer has an incredible work rate. He is always running and seemingly never tires. He helps on defense as much as any forward I have ever seen. These skills certainly have their place in this situation as he can contribute on defense while still being able to go forward to keep the Portuguese defenders honest.

Immigrant Song plays on drums behind me as we sing "USA AYYY!" I am exhausted. My throat is sore. I am hot and thirsty. My feet hurt. I do not want to sing any more. Right in front of me, my boys, my countrymen, are up against some of the most expensive and talented athletes in the world, and they are giving it everything they possess. There is no way I am going to stop my singing, chanting, screaming, and encouraging. It is as if I am part of this great thing. To be quiet now is to surrender. The players are not giving up and they have to be at least as spent as I. No. This is crunch time. The time when winners step up and losers fold. Nobody in our section is folding.

On the field, the heat and running have got the best of Eddie Pope, and he cramps up. Despite Mastroeni's best efforts to stretch them out, Pope must be substituted. In comes his former D.C. United mate, Carlos Llamosa. Llamosa is a player and a person for whom I have the utmost respect. He has a great story and is a fantastic positional defender. However, these are not the things going through my head. All I can think about is that he is slow. Now with he and Agoos in central defense, I cringe. There is no way these two can keep up with the speedy forwards from Portugal. I fear that someone will go right by them to equalize.

Ten minutes left and I am sure they will be ten hard, nail-biting minutes. I notice my legs beginning to shake. Our boys do provide some relief as they hold the ball and even have possession deep in the Porto's end. Now it is Sanneh's turn to ease my suffering when he, deep in his own corner facing the end line and under pressure, rainbows Joao Pinto and clears the ball up field, to our applause.

Five minutes left, and I am wondering where the attack is. Friedel has not been called on in some time. The Portuguese seem exhausted as well; their passes are not crisp, and they often lose position with poor crosses.

Three minutes to go and a lot of play has mercifully been at the other end. "U!S!A! U!S!A!" We chant on and on. Our boys are able to waste a lot of time on throw ins and occasionally on fouls. Cobi Jones does well holding the ball in the corner.

Injury time! The long balls the Portuguese are sending are intercepted, and again we are in their corner. "Keep it down there," I hear Jimmy yelling. "I don't want to see anything!"

Two minutes is shown and our song changes again. "Nah-nah-nah-nah, Nah-nah-nah-nah, Ayy-Ayy-Ayy Goodbye!" I have sung this song at many events in my life but never with this much feeling and passion. It is as if I can give everything I have left to the singing of this song, everything will be just fine. I have never been prouder of any team for whom I have sung this victory song than I am of these boys. Our section is beside itself with anticipation. Surely, we will not have our hearts broken now. Our players will not let it happen, and our opponents do not seem capable of pulling off a miracle finish. Never did I think I would be singing this song at this game, however our song is loud, proud, and strong.

There is an incident with Beasley as he is taking a throw in. I see him put the ball in one of the Porto's face in a taunting-like gesture. The referee sees it too and books the young midfielder who has played an amazing game. Moments later, the whistle is blown and we erupt. I am not sure what to do. I am too tired to jump around like a fool. I guess I had done too much of that during the game, so I turn and look up at our section. What an amazing site. Red, white and blue everywhere. Flags, face paint, and red shirts. Everyone is hugging and high fiving. Drums are beating, and people are loudly voicing their approval.

***

We have done it! We have stunned Portugal. The world has witnessed the U.S. play it's best soccer, on the grandest stage. We quickly organized ourselves back into song. Then the players made their way over. First was Mastroeni who hurdled the signs along the end line, pulled off his jersey, ran all the way up to the wall, and flung it upwards. It was too high for me to reach, but the guy right behind me reached back and came away with as great a souvenir as I can imagine. The rest of the team arrived and applauded us. Some stayed and chanted along with us.

"This must be how it feels to win a big game in Europe," I thought to myself. I have heard stories of away fans singing in an empty stadium for hours after the game has ended. I was still going but was not sure if I could hold up much longer. Nearly all of the photojournalists came over and photographed us.

It was now at least a half hour since the match ended, and we were alone in the stadium. We were still singing and chanting. It was an amazing show of patriotism. I walked up the steps, but continued to go down various aisles whenever I recognized someone from Nashville last night. Finally, Jimmy and I made our way out into the concourse. Most were still singing in the stands, but people were beginning to move out.

Immediately upon reaching the concourse, I saw about six Yanks and I ran to them. Drums were blaring and the acoustics were amazing with the upper deck

59

serving as a roof. The six other supporters and I quickly formed into a circle, with our arms around each other's shoulders. We began jumping and spinning to the beat. As more supporters made their way from the stands to the concourse, they joined us. We were all in a big circle, jumping and spinning. The drums were unbelievably loud. Some people were whooping it up, but were barely heard over the drums. This was as exhausting as anything I have done, yet I did not want to stop.

After long minutes of frantic movement, I left the circle. I saw a food stand nearby and surprisingly there were still workers staffing it. I made my way over and bought two Cokes, 20 ounces of that glorious liquid in plastic bottles, just like at home. I gave one to Jimmy and he looked thankful.

Suddenly, we heard a loud bang from outside the stadium. We all ran towards it. Yet another big cheer went up when we realized it was a fireworks display! It was as if we had never seen them before. We cheered each colorful explosion. We were now out in the "World Cup Zone" where we had assembled before the match.

The night sky had replaced the hot sun, but there were still people everywhere. Many, if not most, were American. We were still overjoyed from the game and many U.S.A. cheers went up. A conga line formed, and I joined in as we ran around like lunatics, singing all the time. Then I saw somebody holding up a blowup of the World Cup. It was much larger than the original. I made my way over to it, and it was handed to me. I kissed it and held it aloft, something that most every kid in the world dreams of doing for real. I joined in with people chanting, "We want the Cup! We want the Cup!" At that moment, it did not seem like a far-fetched dream. In fact, it seemed downright possible!

Something caught my eye, and I looked toward a stage to see a band come out to play. They were Korean, and I wondered just what kind of ridiculous techno-pop they would play. I think they surprised us all by breaking into 4 Non Blondes' *What's Going On*. I thought this was perhaps the most appropriate song I had ever heard. With Senegal, and now us, pulling shockers, the world may have been asking this very question. I am sure the Portuguese were.

Then they got to the chorus and rather than singing, "I said Hey, Hey, Hey, Hey-Hey, Hey, Hey, Hey, I said Hey. What's going on?" it seemed every American there sang, "I said U, S, A, A-A, U, S, A. I said Hey. What's going on?" On a night full of improbabilities, this may have been the most surreal. The song lasted a long time, but we never lost track of that new chorus that will never allow me to hear this song the same way again. I will forever equate it with joy in Suwon.

After a few more songs, which were far less memorable, some guy with a microphone began inviting people up on the stage. About ten Americans accepted, and the emcee went to each of them asking their name and where they were from. I nearly fell on the ground when the first one, a white guy with blond hair, answered, "I'm Joe, and I'm from Korea!"

We were all showing our fatigue, and though there were still pockets of singing, most were simply talking in groups. I looked around for a familiar face and saw Tonya sitting on a ledge, talking to Doug and someone draped in a flag, and I went to her. As I approached, I heard the guy telling her to name the baby "Suwon."

"That's perfect! You have to do it," I said, and for a split second, saw a glimmer in Doug's eye. I think Tonya thought about it as well. "You could call her Sue and never forget this night."

Over my shoulder, I saw the camera crew approaching Scott and Neil. This was the first time the crew had seen them since before the game. I realized this as the producer asked them to recreate coming out of the stadium. She wanted them to jump around and act crazy, as if the game had just ended.

Scott took a deep breath. He and his tall brother did as instructed. Being someone who loves the camera, I could not resist and decided to help with the recreation. I ran over and acted like I was seeing them for the first time after the game. The three of us jumped around and yelled stuff about America and the players. The producer looked happy. I guess my policy of not cheering for a camera will be suspended for the trip.

Jimmy and Chuck approached, and we decided to head back home. It was tough to leave this place, as the whole time here had been magical. As exhausted, tired, and hungry as I was, I did not want to leave. I wanted to revel in this moment as long as possible. I think the feeling of victory, particularly and upset one, is better than any drug.

Leaving the area, we paused while some used the bathroom. As I sat on a wall with Jimmy and Doug, a short, round man with a greasy black mullet approached us. He looked at me and said, with only a hint of an accent, "Are you in Sam's Army?"

Since I was wearing a red shirt that said "Sam's Army," I thought it was a stupid question, so I just pointed to it. I guess he did not understand me, or maybe he could not read, because he asked Jimmy the same thing.

Jimmy, who was also wearing the shirt, said that we were. Mr. Mullet did not like this and said, "You guys are assholes." I was in too good a mood to hear this guy, so I basically ignored him, while keeping an eye on him, and I continued the conversation I was having with Doug. But Jimmy wondered aloud why we were assholes. "Were you at Nashville last night," the mullet asked.

"Yes. But I know we didn't see you," answered Jimmy.

Although this guy's English was unaccented, he did not have much of a vocabulary. He proved it by again saying, "You guys are assholes." He stood there for a few moments and then just walked off.

We were soon joined by Tonya and Chuck, and the five of us continued on our way to the shuttle buses that would take us back to the train station. Along the way, an older, white-haired gentleman approached and said he was from Fox Sports World and could he ask us some questions.

"Is this bigger than the Miracle on Ice?" he asked and held his microphone out to Doug.

Doug hesitated before answering, and I feared he was about to give the absolute wrong answer, so I jumped in front of him.

"Of course not. It is not even close. As great as this moment is for U.S. Soccer, it, in no way, measures up to that."

As we walked down the nearly deserted sidewalks outside the stadium, I felt the need to justify that answer to our group, who seemed in no mood to have the greatness of this night slighted.

"Here is how this could have measured up to the 1980 Olympic hockey team. We would have played Afghanistan and not Portugal. We are not directly at war with them, but stuff going on there is causing heartache for us, much the same as the Cold War did. Then Afghanistan would need to be, by far, the best soccer team in the world. Not, the heavy favorite in our group, but the overwhelming favorite to win the Cup.

Then, instead of our team, we had sent a team much like that of our 1990 World Cup team, which was made up of mostly unproven, untested college players. Of course, this would not have happened in the first round, but in the semi-finals, like the match where we beat the Soviets.

If this was the case, I could see it measuring up. Beyond that, let's not get too big headed about this thing. I don't mean to bring us down; this is the greatest night I have ever witnessed in sports in person. It is one of the top, I don't know, maybe four moments in U.S. Soccer history. It has already made this trip worthwhile, and I really wish that guy had not asked this question because perspective is not something we need right now. However, the Miracle on Ice is the greatest sports story ever and one of the greatest stories in the history of our country."

They all seemed to agree with me, but we did not dwell on it. We turned our attentions to food as we boarded the bus. We rode alone on the bus to the train station, but rather than heading back to Seoul, decided to hit Pizza Hut for a classic American dinner. Still enjoying the buzz of the game, we spotted the restaurant and hurried to it. We were only feet from the door when they locked it. They were closing for the night.

We pleaded with them to let us in. Maybe it was the starving looks on our faces or perhaps they wanted to share in our celebration, but in any case, they unlocked the door and welcomed us. This would have never happened back home and was just another example of the Koreans proving to be excellent hosts.

As we had the pick of the place, we chose a table that was close to a small television. I was disappointed to see Germany was leading Ireland 1-0. We ordered two pizzas and a pitcher of Coke. I was watching the game and really pulling for Ireland. It is the anglophile in me that causes me to put Germany last in rooting preferences, behind even Argentina and Mexico. Not only that, but as my sister is married to an Irishman and I have spent time there and I am familiar with their team, I almost always support Ireland. So I neglected the others who had immersed themselves in conversation as I concentrated on Ireland's efforts to equalize late in the match.

The waitress arrived with the pitcher of Coke as the clock was nearly out on the *Bhoys* in Green. I took the pitcher and poured for everyone. When finished, I set the empty pitcher down and looked up to the TV. I was not sure what was happening, but it seemed that the Irish were celebrating! At first I thought a fight had broken out, but was elated to realize that Robbie Keane had scored. With a fantastic finish, the game ended 1-1. It capped off what had been one of the happiest nights of my life.

The subway was crowded and I had to stand nearly the whole hour-long ride back to Seoul Station. I had been drained of energy hours ago, and the pizza had not done much to replenish my stores. With the euphoric match spurring me onward, I did not mind standing in a crowded subway car. It was a feeling I would be happy to relive many times over.

Chuck, Jimmy, and I caught a cab to the *Dong-Il*, and at 2:00 I fell asleep with a huge grin on my face. June 5th, Suwon, U.S.A. 3, Portugal 2.

Day 5
Thursday, June 6

PC Bang

I think I woke up at 10:00, though, again, I was not sure because there was no clock in my room. I knocked on Jimmy's door and woke him up and then did the same to Chuck, though he and his wife, Rebecca, were already up. I quickly realized that my voice was not normal. In fact, it was shot. I was hoarse, however it did not hurt. It did sound funny and both Jimmy and Chuck commented on it. I can only wonder why they did not sound the same way.

The four of us took the subway to Itaewon. Chuck and Rebecca wanted some western food that they said they could not get where they live in Gwangju. On the trip, I realized that Rebecca is an extremely patient woman, which is a good thing because her husband talks non-stop. She is a very nice young woman with dark, curly hair and brown eyes, which she often rolls at Chuck's observations.

We stopped at Seoul Station so they could check the train schedule. There, Rebecca showed me what kind of calling card to buy and how to use it. Calculating the time, I thought there was a good chance Ivy would be awake, so I went to a phone booth. Rebecca talked me through the codes and soon the phone rang. Ivy's voice was tired when she answered, but became very happy when I said "Hey, baby!"

She told me she woke up early to watch the game. Said she was screaming at the TV and the neighbors must have thought she was nuts. She commented on my voice and I told her that I had done some screaming myself. Then she told me that I was on TV! Not during the anthem, which I was hoping, but after one of the goals. She said a few of my friends called to tell to her they saw me as well, so it must have been a good shot.

The phone card was great, because as I was talking, the phone displayed how much credit was left on the card. Mine cost 10,000, so it counted down from 10,000. We talked for about 10 minutes before we were cut off. I have to say that it was great to hear her voice.

Felling wonderful, I led the others onto the subway and on to Itaewon. I felt at home there. I had spent an entire day there two days ago and thus felt that I knew where things were, and because of our victory last night, I felt almost untouchable. It was as if people saw the U.S. gear both Jimmy and I were sporting and looked at us with a certain envy. The spoils of victory are not held solely for the participants, but are shared by the fans. Though in soccer, unlike other sports, I feel the supporters in the stadium have some affect on the match, albeit a very small one. I do believe, that the crowd is able to lift the players and carry them when they are exhausted from running for over an hour.

Chuck asked us if there was anything we needed, anything we forgot to bring, because, he said, "We can get anything here."

I said I was fine, but Jimmy said that he needed deodorant. "I am almost out," he said.

Chuck and Rebecca exchanged foreboding glances. "You can get anything except deodorant. Koreans don't use it," Chuck said in his booming voice.

"What? You mean I'm going to have to smell Jimmy for three weeks? What do you mean they don't use it? I haven't noticed any terrible smelling people here."

Rebecca answered me, "They don't smell. It's strange, but they just don't need it." She then asked Chuck about a black market store. He agreed that we could find some there. So off we went, turning off the main street and heading down a hill for a few blocks until we came to an unmarked red door. Inside was a small room that was filled with familiar items. Filling the shelves were Campbell's Soups, Delmonte vegetables, Clorox, and Brillo pads. It was a far cry from what I had in mind upon hearing "black market." I was expecting a cloak and dagger mission. I thought we would whisper our needs to some young boy who would hurry off to tell his boss, a well-dressed man that strikes fear in those who know him. He would secure the deodorant, and through some back channel, would send it to us. No, this was simply a small shop run by two older Koreans.

Rebecca said U.S. Servicemen buy this stuff at the PX on base and then sell it to these types of stores. Chuck spoke a few words of Korean and the old shopkeeper produced the Mennen Speed Stick. There was no selection, but it would do. Jimmy paid and we were on our way without the need to check to see if we were being followed.

Our next stop was an underground shop where Rebecca bought me two colorful, wooded ducks. She explained they are traditional Korean wedding ducks. Instructions in English accompanied them and said that the bride's mother is to throw them to the bride. She is to catch them in her dress. If successful, she will have a boy. The penalty for dropping them is a baby girl.

I thanked her as she pointed me to the leather goods. Ivy had heard that Coach bags are inexpensive in Seoul, but all I could find said Coach Sport.

I talked to another suit maker and he quoted me the same price as before, $180.00, and I could see another pattern.

Rebecca then led us to a Mexican place. I should say a place that serves Mexican food. It was a large open restaurant on the second floor very near Nashville. The prices on the menu were as expensive as I had seen over here. I ordered the Two Beef Taco Platter for W12,000 or almost $10.00. I was given a large plate that had two soft-shelled tacos. They were basically the size of the same thing from Taco Bell, beef, lettuce, and cheese on a small flour tortilla. They tasted fine, there was just not much of them. I was pretty disappointed, but if you want good Mexican food, you have to go to San Francisco not Soeul. In any case, Chuck and Rebecca were happy with the food. They said again that there is no food like this where they live.

After lunch, they had to leave to catch a train home. I told Chuck I would see him in Daegu for the U.S.-Korea match. He and Jimmy made plans to meet up tomorrow in Jeonju for the Spain-Paraguay match for which both had tickets. I was staying behind for the most anticipated game of the tournament, England-Argentina.

Jimmy and I were pretty tired so we caught a cab to take us back to the *Dong-Il*. This proved to be a mistake. The streets were crowded. The harrowing ride took a long time. These cabs are terrifying. The roads are wide, most have at least four lanes, but people do not respect them. It is a free for all, with cars and trucks darting in and out. We eventually made it home, but it cost us W8,800.

Once home, we went to the PC Bang near the *Dong-Il*. I made friends with it's owner a Korean who calls himself Damien. He spoke good English, which helped Jimmy and I on our first visit when we had no idea what to do.

PC Bangs can be found on almost every block in Seoul. They contain many computers with high-speed Internet access. Prices are very affordable. Damien charges W500 the first half hour, then W1,000 every hour. That is less than $1.00 an hour. Damien says that is the standard rate. Jimmy and I, and other Americans, spend the time reading and writing e-mails and surfing the web, mostly for soccer articles. However, most patrons do not. Damien's typical customer is young, maybe 18. They chain smoke the hours away while playing video games. Damien tells me that they all have computers at home, but come to the PC Bang to play interactively with others on-line.

The PC Bang is generally a shade of yellowish-gray. Once clean, white computers are now colored, stained from the smoke, which hangs thick in the air. The room is a hazard for anyone with asthma or healthy lungs, for that matter. As one who grew up in a smoking household, a smoky bar or restaurant does not bother me, but in here, my eyes watered as I read an e-mail from Ivy.

She was worried that something would happen to me. Reading between the lines, I knew she was talking about terrorism. I had convinced her that hooliganism would not be a problem. I told her that hooligans are typically poor kids who could never afford to travel to the Orient. A white lie, to be sure, but certainly worth her piece of mind. I was not able to easily explain away the post-Sept 11th world.

I go back and forth on the World Cup as a target of terrorists. On the plus side (for not being a target) it would be extremely difficult with all the security. Also, they may not even care to hit this tournament because they follow it. I realize the fundamentalists of the Muslim faith denounce sports or at least the playing of it in short pants. On the other hand, soccer is such a world passion; Iran played in France 1998 and Saudi Arabia is here. An attack on this tournament would certainly cause these terrorists to lose support of many of their backers.

On the negative side, it is a worldwide event, and if they could hit it, they would show the world that no one is safe anywhere. These zealots could show their followers that regardless of how the rest of the world feels, their cause is right, and they will fight the infidels everywhere. In any event, our team and fans would almost certainly be the target.

These few days here, I had not feared for my safety at all. In general, I am not worried about being attacked on a small scale, but I did have some hesitation about a stadium being targeted. After the Portugal game, I no longer fear that. My worry now is the game against Korea.

We have been treated with nothing but kindness and warmth by the hosts, but we are hearing about the Red Dragons, their fanatical supporters. They are so very passionate. I do not believe they are looking for trouble, however, I do worry that if the game does not go their way, particularly if there is a costly, bad call that goes against them, things could easily get out of hand. I have not seen evidence of it, but there seems to be an active, anti-American sentiment here. Chuck talked about it often, but I also read about it in English newspapers. They say that security is being beefed up at the U.S. embassy.

Many Koreans resent our troops here, particularly the young who do not recognize the help we gave them during the Korean War. Many feel that we are preventing them from uniting with North Korea. Of course, that is not true; we are protecting their border, but a few incidents of our troops breaking laws, have soured them. There is a fear that some students will target us at the match. I cannot say that I feel entirely secure about it.

Of course, I mentioned nothing of this to Ivy when I replied to her. I only answered her terrorism concerns by telling her I have not seen anyone that even looks Middle Eastern. I told her that a few people have stared at Jimmy because of his dark hair and skin. Almost everyone is Korean and foreigners stick out like a sore thumb.

Once I had written enough to convince her I am safe, I pulled up my list of buddies and wrote my third letter of the trip to my friends. Today, I tried to put into words the emotions of the game. I was hoping to give them a sense of my trip. It is actually relaxing, writing my buddies, and I spent over an hour doing so.

Jimmy was busy updating his site. When he finished, he read my note to my friends and asked if he could post it. I agreed and within minutes, onthesidelines.org had two reports from Suwon.

Although, my lungs hated it, I enjoyed a relaxing afternoon in the PC Bang. It was the first chance I had to do nothing since we arrived. Damien has a small TV that shows the games. Denmark was playing Senegal, but I did not pay much attention. I was more concerned about our team.

I read that Claudio Reyna is still questionable for the Korea match and that Earnie Stewart is probably out. That was not good news; not only will we miss their talent, but they are our leaders, our captains. With as young a team as we have, there is a need for the calming experience of a veteran.

67

I was enjoying reading accounts of our historic victory, but Jimmy spoke up and said he was hungry. I realized I was as well, so we said goodbye to Damien. He said we owed him W3,500. When he gave me change for my W5,000 bill, I used the only Korean word in my vocabulary, *Com som nee da*, "thank you," I said.

He laughed and said, "You're welcome," in a way that let me know I had it right. And I should hope so; I had only practiced it for four days now.

We decided to go back to the place where we ate the first night. After a short walk, we were there. This time, I pointed to our selection on the wall. The waitress recognized us and soon served us that delicious meal of beef and other stuff, wrapped in lettuce.

Over this meal, Jimmy and I discussed the situation in which the U.S. now finds itself. "Poland looks to be the weak team, the one with no chance," Jimmy said.

"I think so. This next game is huge for us. We really need a point. Portugal will not lose again, which will give them six," I said while shoving the concoction into my mouth.

"If we tie Korea, we'll both have four, but then Korea will lose to Portugal, and we only need a tie with Poland to give us five and put us through in second place."

"Yeah, but if we lose, they will finish with six, and we will need to beat Poland to tie them with six. Then, it will be a three-way tie, and it will come down to goal differential. Right now, Korea is plus two; we are plus one. I don't want it to come to that," I said. This exercise was confusing, but we felt we must know how it will all come to pass.

"I don't either," said Jimmy. "I guess a tie is much better for us than for Korea."

"Right, because we would be tied on four, but they have to play Portugal, and we only play Poland. Man, that was huge last night!" I grinned as I recalled the game. The France-Uruguay match was on TV, but I was not paying much attention. I figured that France got their wake up call and would take the three points.

"Yep. I am glad I am here. I can't believe I almost didn't come. I would be upset if I watched that on TV."

"Wouldn't it be great if we won the group. Then we could play Mexico. That would be awesome," I said, knowing full well the understatement in that comment. "We should be able to beat Korea. I mean, who are they? But they looked good, and they are so fired up, it will be tough."

"Yeah, the crowd gives them so much energy. Whoa, look at that!" Jimmy exclaimed, pointing to the TV.

I turned in time to see the referee holding a red card, pointing to Theirry Henry. The score was 0-0 and the French striker was gone. "This could be trouble for France. They can't lose this." Then I hurriedly added, "If they lose, they are out! That would suck for me."

"Those France-Denmark tickets you have wouldn't be that great, the game would be meaningless. Now you won't get to see Henry play." Jimmy informed me.

"I'm not worried about that, I saw him play for Arsenal last year, but I want the game to mean something. If they are desperate, they'll have to play Zidane and that's who I really want to see," I said. Zinedine Zidane was injured just before the Cup started and sat out the first two games.

We finished up, paid our W10,000 and headed home to watch the second half of the game.

The game was very exciting because both teams tried to win. Ten man France went forward and were unlucky a few times. At the very end, Fabien Barthez had to make a huge save to keep the defending champions alive. The game did end 0-0, and due to the earlier game finishing in a 1-1 draw, I quickly figured that France will need to beat Denmark by two goals to advance. I smiled, believing that should make for an exciting, attacking French team. I was already looking forward to going to that game.

I watched the late game from my room and was happy that Cameroon beat Saudi Arabia. It basically meant that the Africans needed to beat Germany to advance. I like their chances. In fact, in the poll I filled out, I had Cameroon and Ireland going through, with Germany heading home early.

I also watched replays of the Portugal game. It had been on TV all day on a few different channels. Although I did not understand any of the commentary except for some funny English words the announcers had incorporated, I enjoyed every moment of it. Then I saw myself! Just after McBride's goal, they went to a shot of our section. We were chanting "U!S!A!" I clearly saw Jimmy and myself at the bottom of the screen. It was pretty exciting, but I looked somewhat reserved. I guess at that point, I was too stunned to go crazy.

The Korean announcers were really funny because they used words like, "shooting", "heading", "goalkeeper punching", and my favorite when describing a header on goal, "heading shoot!" It sounded hilarious because I could not understand anything, then suddenly there would be a high-pitched word I knew. For example, a call might go like this. "Blah, blah, blahblahblah, blah blah, blah Heading Shoot! Blah blahblah."

I fought off sleep as long as possible, and finally dozed off around 1:00.

Day 6
Friday, June 7

The Owner is a German!

The most anticipated day of the first round caught me sleeping until 10:00. Jimmy was still sleeping when I knocked on his door, but we were soon ready to head to our favorite place in Seoul, Damien's PC Bang.

In the smoke-chocked room, I found an urgent e-mail from Big Dog from the day before. Big Dog was panicking about his Home Stay. He said he was not eating well and asked about our hotel. He and Monty would be in Itaewon today to watch the games.

On the Yanks in Korea Yahoo Group, I read that the NY Crew was going to watch the big match at the 3 Alley Pub in Itaewon. Because they are so much fun to be around, I decided that I would watch the England-Argentina match there as well.

Jimmy did not spend too much time on-line and left quickly for the bus station. He had decided to take a bus to Jeonju for the Spain-Paraguay match that he was attending later that day. He had discovered it was cheaper than the train and almost as fast. Buses have their own lane on the interstate and they make great time.

I had a few hours to kill before heading to Itaewon. The first match, the other in the Group of Death, Sweden-Nigeria, was at 3:30, and I was looking forward to watching it. However, I needed to eat.

Since I was alone, I decided to play it safe and found a sub shop with the strange name of Tantalus. To make ordering easier, I opted for a combo of an Italian Hoagie, soup, and a Coke. It was W5,000 or $4.00 in my rough translation. I carried the bag back to the *Dong-Il* and ate while watching TV. They were really hyping the big match.

The ads began with footage of warships and it soon became clear that it was the British taking back the Falken Islands! The ad showed troops firing upon each other, and then cut to the two flags. Finally, they got around to showing soccer footage. Diego Maridona's "Hand of God" goal was shown followed by his fantastic goal later that same game in Mexico, 1986. Next, were the same two teams going at it in France. First, Michael Owen's amazing goal, then the moment that turned a young soccer player into the most hated man in England: David Beckham was lying flat on his stomach when he kicked out at the Argentine, Diego Simeone, and was promptly red carded. Finally, the Argies were shown rejoicing their penalty-kick victory. The music was dramatic and the message, even in another language, was clear: These two teams and countries do not like one another. They had fought a war and played some classic soccer matches. Today, they will meet again.

I easily made the two-change subway ride to Itaewon and emerged into the hot sun hoping to find Big Dog and Monty. It seemed Big Dog was not happy living as a Korean, and I thought it would be great to have two more Yanks staying at the *Dong-Il*.

I first went into Nashville, the scene of the big U.S. party the night before the Portugal game, but it was all but empty. I hoped I was not too early. It was about 2:45 and I wanted to find them and get a good seat to watch the Sweden match.

The next place I looked was Gecko's, another sports bar just around the corner from Nashville. There was a small crowd gathering there, but no one I recognized. Thus, I set out to find the 3 Alley Pub. I had not yet been there, and it was not on the main street but I had been told it was easy to find. "Go behind the Hamilton Hotel" which is a western-style hotel where a lot of Yanks were staying, "turn left and go down the alley and you'll see the 3 Alley Pub," I had been told. That certainly sounded easy enough.

I made my way, through the heat, between the Hamilton and a KFC and turned left down the alley. I saw a few restaurants and what may have been a pub, but no 3 Alley Pub. After about two blocks, the alley ended, and I retraced my steps, but again did not see that for which I was looking. "Maybe they meant to turn right," I thought to myself, and so I walked the other way, passing behind the Hamilton hotel, but not finding the 3 Alley Pub.

I was now frustrated, not to mention hot and thirsty. I was beginning to sweat and knowing I would be spending the next eight or so hours sitting and watching soccer and did not want to spend that time all smelly, I returned to Gecko's. It was gathering some atmosphere, and I hoped that Big Dog and Monty would show up.

Though there were a good number of people there, I was able to sit at a table with a good view of a television. Just before the match kicked off, two guys in England shirts joined me at the table. It was a father and son from Nottingham. The son was an English teacher in Seoul, and his father had decided to visit during the Cup.

They were impressed when I asked if they supported County or Forrest. "How does a Yank know about that?" they asked.

"It's just football," I answered and then upon learning they supported Nottingham Forrest, asked if they had liked Ben Olsen.

"Yes, very much. He was quality and fought hard, too," the father replied. He seemed to be the bigger soccer fan of the two.

I was drinking Cass on tap that was W2,500, but the father would not allow me to pay for any of the three I drank during the match.

Seated at the next table was a group of Nigerians. When they took an early lead, they really got into it. As the goal scorer, Julius Aghahowa, was doing a number of back-flips, they were dancing between our tables. It was a sort of tribal dance mixed with some hip-hop. Their joy was great to behold. Their faces beamed with pride. Their countrymen were winning a match in the World Cup, beating a strong European foe. Though Nigeria has had some wonderful international results and is considered the best team in Africa, it was apparent that these fans still thought of themselves as underdogs.

Their joy did not last, and when Henrik Larsson added a penalty giving the Swedes a 2-1 lead late in the game, they knew all hope was lost. At the whistle, the one sitting closest to me sighed and said simply, "We are out."

Sweden now had four points, which made the evening's match all the more important. Argentina had three and England only one. A loss by either would be devastating. Even a draw would leave both seeking a win in their last match and for England, even that may not be enough.

During the second half of the Sweden game, we were joined at the table by five guys from New Zealand. I asked if they knew Ryan Nelsen, the D.C. United defender who is from their country and whom I always seek out after a game for a good quote. They did know him and proceeded to tell me that he was on the radio on September 11th. He had lived near the Pentagon and had helped to bring the reality of that terrible day to his native land.

The English father and one of the Kiwis struck up a conversation about cricket, and it was apparent that they were both huge fans of the strange, baseball-like sport. I played a lot of baseball in my youth and have always loved the game, thus cricket had intrigued me. I asked a couple of questions, and they delighted in trying to explain the game to me. It was funny because I would understand it, then they would make a side comment to one another and laugh. I guess would be like me explaining baseball and then, under my breath, mentioning the Infield Fly Rule.

At about the time I was giving up hope, an American pulled up a chair. Ben was a lawyer from New York, and I mention him to warn everyone about proper planning. Ben was distraught because he had made plans to visit an old friend who was stationed here that night. Because he had not checked the schedule before making plans with his buddy, Ben was doomed to miss tonight's epic. On the other hand, there was me. If you are wondering why I did not go to the Spain game with Jimmy, it is because I checked the schedule, and when I saw it was the same day as England-Argentina, I told Jimmy to have fun without me. To recap, Andy=Good planning, Ben=Bad planning.

What I had not planned on was that everyone I knew was going to a bar that I could not find. I mentioned my plight, and the son from Nottingham said he would take me there. These two Englishmen were great; not only did they buy all my beer, but they served as a tour guide as well. When they dropped me off at the 3 Alley Pub, a place I had walked by twice and was right where the directions said it was, I wished them the very best of luck in life, and more importantly in the game against Argentina.

The first thing I saw upon entering the Pub made me smile. The New York Crew was there. I knew that with Leo, Joe, and Brent in a room, there would be good times. I asked if they had seen Big Dog or Monty and they said they had been here and would be back. With that news, I knew that this was the place I would be for the rest of the day, and night. I immediately sat in a comfy chair that was directly in front of the big screen TV. Most of the others were lounging on couches and other living room style furniture while the rest were sitting on regular wooded chairs.

When the game kicked off, Brent made it clear that he was rooting for Paraguay in the only way he knows, high volume. He complained that Spain subjugated his Filipino ancestors. He told the whole room all sorts of nasty things they had done while ruling the Philippines, and then asked if everyone else was still rooting for the Spanish. We all still were.

At halftime, some of us ordered food to go along with the happy hour OB drafts; W2,000. Most ordered burgers, steaks, or other western food. I ordered *Bulgogi*, beef and rice. Of course, it was served with *kim'chi*. It was not only delicious, but at W6,500, it was about half the price of the American food.

As I was eating, Big Dog and Monty returned. They had been shopping, and Monty was showing off the Cuban cigars he had bought and was visibly very proud of. I told Big Dog about the *Dong-Il* and that I was sure there were rooms available. He disappointed me a bit, saying that he had written the e-Mail in haste. He said their host family was great, but that he was having a hard time with the food. For a big guy, he is a surprisingly picky eater and was not at all adventurous in trying new foods. I had to laugh when he said he wrote the e-Mail while he was hungry, but after some rice, he was fine. He was eating a lot of rice. Plain rice. On the other hand, Monty was enjoying the home cooking. I was glad they were OK, but, selfishly, would have liked them to stay at my hotel, giving Jimmy and I someone else to hang with and talk to.

In the game, Spain, who trailed 1-0 at the half, answered with three in the last 45 as everyone's favorite goalkeeper, Jose Luis Chilavert, had a nightmare of a half.

The Pub was filling with both people and anticipation. There was a buzz, unlike that before any other match. It was as if everyone was keenly aware of the ramifications, not only for the two teams, but also for the entire Cup. It was very possible that one of these two giants would be sent home early. For us neutrals, it is why we love the game, two great teams facing off with so much history and so much at stake. For the good number of English who had joined us in the pub, it was as tense as sport can be. Their countrymen were about to face off with their bitter enemies. An enemy that had eliminated them from two of their last three World Cups. An enemy against whom they were desperate for revenge.

Maybe there was too much tension and the soccer gods did their best to relieve it. After the Spain game everyone was mingling around, some securing seats in the now crowded room. No one was paying attention the TV. That was about to change. Someone commented that it was showing an old Korean woman or more accurately, her feet. I had been vaguely aware of some scene from a sort of doctor's office, but now the sight of this old lady receiving a foot massage sickened me, along with everyone else in the room! The lady was so old she could hardly walk, and they had to help her onto the table. It was horrible; she had corns or bunions or maybe both. They were rubbing them like they could rub them right off her old wrinkled feet. I have never seen such gross looking feet, and there they were with hands all over them.

Of course, everyone was making sophomoric comments but after literally three minutes of this stuff, we started chanting, "Change the channel" clap, clap, clap-clap-clap "Change the channel" clap, clap, clap-clap-clap!

Finally, to our relief, the feet disappeared as the channel was changed. At first we could not tell what the new station was showing, but then we realized it was the only thing on earth more disgusting that an old Korean lady having her bunions rubbed off. You guessed it. We were treated to the sight of a dog giving birth! In less than two seconds we went from nasty old feet to an extreme close up of a juicy, misshapen, little puppy clawing it's way out of it's mother! Our collective gasp sucked the air so much that Monty's Cohiba was extinguished.

The puppy was rolling in its bloody placenta, and we were too terrified to make any sarcastic comments. Other than the gagging, the room was quiet. The silence would not last long as the scene became much worse. The veterinarian overseeing the birth picked up the puppy and while snot-like strings hung from it's body, began the circumcision. It was more than any male could take, "Put the feet back on! Put the feet back on!" we all seemed to beg at once. Our cries were heard and the channel was changed. We breathed a collective sigh of relief now that the ordeal was over, but we were still to traumatized to speak. That is until Joe broke the silence.

"What are you all worried about, they are just showing the menu." Most groaned at the unbelievably bad joke, but not me. I fell out of the comfy chair and rolled on the floor I was laughing so hard. I even think I spilled my beer. Truly, I laughed as hard at that as I ever have at anything else.

After about five minutes, we were recovered and ready for the match. Right in front of me was a Scotsman who was every bit as loud as Brent of the NY Crew, and every bit as vocal in his hatred for England and his support of Argentina as Brent had been in the earlier match. As for us Americans, we were probably 60-40 in favor of England. I was nervous at kickoff because of my love of the English team. I was hoping they would avenge their losses to the South American power, and I was hoping that it would be their captain, David Beckham, who would lead them.

For some reason I was surprised that as the teams were shaking hands, Beckham shook, his nemesis, Diego Simeone's hand without incident. I am not sure what I thought would happen. Certainly I did not think they would begin fighting right there, perhaps I thought Becks would snub the Argentine. But there was nothing out of the ordinary, and the game was on!

The game went back in forth with each team having a good chance. The English in the Pub were singing, but the Scott was heard as well. About 30 minutes in, I realized I had over extended myself in taking advantage of the still happy hour

74

prices of OB. I always make it a practice to never go to the bathroom during play, particularly in a game of this importance, but to my dismay and pain, I had to make a run.

I pushed through a sea of people and realized for the first time that the Pub was much larger than I had thought; there was a second larger room. I guess I should have made this trip during the first three hours I had spent in the Pub. The bathroom was empty, but I was surprised when a guy in an England jersey entered, having apparently made the same mistake I had.

"I hope you score while I'm in here," I said. But he did not seem to be in a good mood.

"Some of you Yanks are supporting the Argies," he told me in a manner that suggested I do something about them.

I was caught a bit off guard at his tone and did not know how to respond, so I said, rather lamely, "Hopefully the game will shut them up." I then hurried out and returned to my seat.

People had been cursing the referee for allowing some rough play from Argentina, particularly Batistuta, go unpunished. Just before halftime, though, the referee showed he had no rooting interest as he awarded England a deserved, but not obvious, penalty.

The room exploded, and I felt I could hear shouts from around the world. Cheers from Thailand, India, South Africa, Brazil, America, and of course England. Curses from Germany, Ireland, and Argentina. If there was one moment this year where the world was making a lot of noise, it was now.

Beckham quickly grabbed the ball, and it was apparent he would take the kick. He was going to shoulder the enormous pressure, the weight of his nation. After his sending off in 1998, he had been vilified like no other athlete. I do not believe we, in America, can draw an analogy to his plight. Perhaps if Bill Buckner had been playing for the United States against the Soviet Union when the ball went through his legs, but I doubt even this example does Beckham's ordeal justice.

However, Beckham responded to the curses of his countrymen, not by leaving his beloved Manchester United for a foreign team, as some of his advisors recommended, but rather he gave them everything he had. He was protected by their fans and responded by giving them one of the greatest years in the history of the fabled club. With Beckham playing wonderful football, United won the Premier League and the FA Cup. Then, on a glorious night in Barcelona, off two of his corner kicks in injury time, they defeated Bayern Munich to win the European Champions League, having already eliminated Diego Simeone's Inter Milan. He had risen in the face of adversity like few, if any athletes had ever done, to become the toast of European football.

Now he saw fit to start over. Miss this kick and endure the wrath all over again. Make it, become a hero to millions. Before the kick, he had one more hurdle. The wily Simeone, in an attempt at gamesmanship, approached the English captain, offering his hand in an obvious effort to distract the young Beckham. This time, the hand was not returned as Becks stared right through him, unnerved.

The referee blew his whistle and Beckham began his approach. I could now sense the world holding it's breath. This was possibly the quietest moment in recent history. The goalkeeper moved slightly and with the force of the British Empire at it's height, Beckham struck the ball. It never rose more than eight inches off the ground as it passed tantalizingly close to the moving keeper and struck the exact center of the net.

There was chaos in the 3 Alley Pub, and I pumped my fist and tried to watch the hero in his victory run. Moments later it was halftime. Just as the game went to commercials the TV went off. A few of us commented that this was good because they could be showing more feet or dogs or some other disgusting thing that should never been seen, much less televised. I spent the break talking with Monty and some English, who were much happier, but not yet counting the three points.

After about ten minutes, we began hearing rumors that a fuse had blown. "Good," I thought, "That is easy to fix." However, a bit later, another rumor circulated that they had flipped the fuses and nothing had happened. Then a big guy, with a shaven head and dressed in all black came in the room and started working on the set. Word spread that he was the owner. That was followed by the fact that he was German. I had faith that he would fix the problem, but when he left and the screen was still off, everyone got uneasy. Some English, fearing a plot by their other enemies, began a chant that we all joined in, "The owner is a German! The owner is a German!"

Everyone was laughing at this, but then a sense of dread overtook the room. From out the large windows, we were able to look across the alley and into another pub with a large screen. On it we could see players returning to the field. A lot of people fled the pub, but the other was just as crowded and most just stood in the alley and watched through the window. I was feeling very good from a mixture of the 1-0 lead and the numerous OB's I drank, which were no longer sold at the happy hour prices of W2,000 but had gone up some 40 cents to W2,500, so I did not seem to care that I did not have a great seat. I was very content to revel in the atmosphere and circumstances that led me here. Besides, it was a lot harder to get an OB in the alley.

As I watched the second half kickoff through a window, across an alley filled with people, through another window, and across a room filled with people, I noticed most of the Americans had stayed indoors with me. We had the room to ourselves except for one Englishman who was doing his best to turn the room into a pub in London. He would loudly sing some English song, stop half way through it, and appeal for us to join him. I did so a few times, but he was doing songs I had never heard, and I was also trying to talk with some others about our train ride to Daegu. After a while, he became annoying and was on all of our nerves. Then he started yelling at us, not in the angry manner of the guy in the bathroom, but somewhat good-naturedly about getting on his side.

We had had enough so we all broke into, "You'll never beat the U.S! You'll never beat the U.S!"

After seven or eight bars of this, he yelled at us "Come on! We're ranked 5th in the world, you're 37th!"

We did not miss a beat and quickly responded in unison with, "That's what Portugal said!" Clap, clap, clap-clap-clap "That's what Portugal said!" Clap, clap, clap-clap-clap! He did the only thing he could and that was to laugh and nod his head in agreement.

However, he was not deterred. "Come on, we all speak the same language!" he pleaded us to join him, as if together we could will England to hold on against the ever-mounting Argentine pressure. Despite his best efforts, we were rapidly turning on him. Then he demanded, "How many are with me?"

I had to answer, so I yelled, "One less than before the match!" This drew a lot of laughs, and everyone joined me as I started singing, "Oh I'd rather have Clint Mathis than Beckham!" It was a take off of the now famous Figo chant and although it did not fit as nicely, it served its purpose.

He was nearly defeated, but tried one last time. "Come on lads, stand with me!"

I was caught up in the moment and answered, "I can't believe it, but now I'm rooting for Argentina!" With that some others started chanting, "Argentina! Argentina!" and despite myself, I joined them. The Englishman was done, and he watched the final few minutes without any singing or coaxing.

It did not take long for me to regain my senses and I cheered England as they dodged bullet after bullet. Eventually the referee blew the whistle and I could feel England erupt! They had done it. They had beaten Argentina 1-0. Revenge for a nation, redemption for Number Seven. I was as happy for Beckham as I was for England.

After the cheering died down, our English friend began asking for a cell phone. He said he had "to call me mates," because, "they'll never believe I was out shouted by a bunch of Yanks."

Big Dog and Monty decided they would go back to the *Dong-Il* for the night rather than the hour long trek back to Suwon. We decided to have a few more beers and then head back. I spent most of the time congratulating and chatting up the English. The look on their faces was priceless. They were absolutely beaming. I made my way into the larger room, which had filled back up, and had a conversation with a few English. Finally I decided it was about time to get on home.

I pushed my way through the crowd. I was in a great mood from the game and the many OB's, but as I approached Monty, I suddenly sensed he was not sharing my joy.

"Did you pick up my bags?" he asked quickly.

"What bags?" I asked, slow on the uptake.

"My backpack and shopping bag, they were right here," he frantically answered.

"Oh shit! How long ago did you see them?" I was suddenly very sober and trying to calmly think things through.

Big Dog answered "Just a couple minutes ago. I moved them from by the wall over to right here." He motioned to a table where he and Monty had been standing.

"What was in them?" I asked.

The answers came too rapidly for me to properly digest. "Passport, game tickets, cash, clothes," they were both talking at once.

"Oh my God." I was stunned. I could not imagine anything worse than losing these things.

We asked around the room, which had mostly emptied out, but nobody had seen anything. I went to the bar, hoping they had them, but they did not. We did another quick search which turned up nothing before Monty said he wanted to get out of there.

Out in the alley I poured over everything with my eyes, looking for someone with a backpack, but we saw almost no one by the time we reached the main street and hailed a cab. The ride back was quite, until the cab driver appeared lost. He looked to me, as if I could offer some assistance. I was thinking there was no way in hell I knew how to get us back, when I suddenly recognized a restaurant. It was called China Fusion, a name I had commented to Jimmy about on our first night. From there I was able to direct him to the *Dong-Il*.

The neighborhood was more alive than I had ever seen it. There were hundreds of Korean men in business suits, stumbling drunk, some being carried by a friend. It was like night of the living dead. These businessmen were all hammered. Their eyes were glazed and even I could recognize their speech was incoherent.

I was happy that Monty got a laugh from them, but we had an idea. The three of us went to the PC Bang, and my two friends posted a few messages on the Yanks in Korea group, hoping someone had mistakenly grabbed the bags, but also appealing for tickets for Big Dog. They had determined that Monty lost his passport, and the gifts he had bought including the expensive Cubans. Big Dog had, for some reason, put his tickets for both the Korea and Poland matches and some two thousand dollars in Monty's backpack. He was understandably very upset.

Monty had a different view of things; of course he had not lost nearly as much as his friend. "If I can't get a new passport in a week, I'll have to stay here for the second round!" They had both planned on returning after the Poland game. Now he had the excuse that his boss could not help but accept.

We returned to the *Dong-Il*, where I saw Jimmy's key still at the desk. It was after midnight and I was surprised he was not back yet. I slyly grabbed it and gave it to Big Dog. Jimmy would find company in his room when he returned. Monty and I went across the small street to the Cowboy Bar, where we each enjoyed two large

OB's and a plate of "Popcorn Chicken" which turned out to be some good chicken nuggets. It was 2:30 when I gave Monty my blanket and cleared just enough room for him on my small floor.

Day 7
Saturday, June 8

Where is Jimmy?

I woke up and looked down to the floor to see Monty fast asleep. I stepped over him to get to the bathroom. When I returned, he was awake. After shaking away the cobwebs, we went up to Jimmy's room and knocked on the door. A dreary-eyed Big Dog opened it. I looked in, but did not see Jimmy.

"He never came in," Big Dog said, anticipating my question.

"Hurry up and get ready," Monty advised. He was anxious to get to the PC Bang to see if anyone answered the e-mails he and Big Dog sent last night.

It did not take long and we were soon on our way. It was 9:00 when we entered the PC Bang. Monty quickly pulled up the Yanks in Korea list. I was reading over his shoulder, hoping for some good news. There were a few replies to his message, but alas, none had any news on the bag. A few people offered their extra tickets.

I tried to cheer them up, telling them that at least they could get in the game. I had been worried about this, as tickets for the Korea game seemed to be scarce.

Finding no real news at the PC Bang, we decided not to waste much time there, and so we left after just a few minutes. Our destination was the American Embassy.

The guidebooks indicated that it was very near the *Dong-Il* so we decided to walk. We had not gone far when we passed a Dunkin Donuts and could not resist. I had a chocolate donut and a coffee. It cost W2,200 or only a bit more than it would back home.

After walking about three blocks, we came to a huge intersection. There was a statue of some old military guy on the corner. To the right, the apparent direction of the embassy, about a quarter mile down was a huge gate, the kind of gate you picture when thinking about the Orient. I suspected that there was some famous park or palace beyond the heavy wooden doors and brick walls. We were obviously in the very center of the city.

We made our way along the sidewalk; the road to our left was ten lanes wide. We joked about the traffic, which was weaving in and out, as we walked. We were glad to be on foot rather than in an amusement park-like taxi.

About halfway to the gate, we saw our flag atop a non-descript building. When we were a block away we noticed the security guards who had the embassy surrounded. They were Korean, dressed in black, held a long club, and were stationed about every ten feet.

When we reached the block that held the embassy, we had no idea where to go, so we kept walking, hoping to see something that would direct us. As we passed the guards, each one kept a very close eye on Monty. Big Dog and I thought this was funny and even Monty had to laugh. He looked suspicious enough with his olive complexion, but he also was carrying a large bag. The guards attempted to glance into the bag as he passed.

At the middle of the block, there was a gate and a guard quickly snapped to attention when we approached it. He waved us off and it was clear we were not going to get in. However, there was a list posted that gave phone number to call for a lost passport. Monty took it down, and we made our way back, past the same guards who were still keenly aware of Monty's every move.

A block down was a newsstand and I showed Monty how to buy and use a calling card. I bought one myself, but when we tried to use them, they did not work. It was extremely frustrating as I would have liked to talk to Ivy, and Monty still had no idea how to get his passport. He was scheduled to leave one week from today, the day after the Poland game.

The three of us decided to meet at Seoul Station tomorrow morning for the trip to Daegu where I had made hotel reservations for us all before leaving the States. We would be spending two nights there. Then Monty and Big Dog ducked down into the subway to head back to Suwon and their host family.

I slowly made my way back to the *Dong-Il* to see if Jimmy was back from Jeonju, but he was not in his room. I headed to our second home, the PC Bang, and again, no Jimmy. Damien confirmed that he had not been there. Of course, I realize we are all adults and he is under no obligation to "check in" with me, but as we are in a very strange land, and he had planned on returning the night before. I could not help but wonder where he was.

Outside the PC Bang I saw a street vendor selling small alarm clocks. They were cheap and plastic, but were exactly what I needed. I paid the W1,500 with three 500 *won* coins and made sure it was set for the correct time before walking away.

It was just after noon and despite the earlier donut, I was getting hungry. There is a place just around the corner from the *Dong-Il* that we pass on the way to the PC Bang. In the window, they display a few of their dishes. A lot of restaurants do this here and though some of the dishes are quite strange, others look fantastic. I had wanted to try this place out since the first time I had seen its samplings in the window. On this day, I was hungry for some sushi and I had seen some on display.

I took a moment to work up the nerve to go into the place; it is always a bit difficult to go into a strange place over here. You just never know what to expect. Will they speak English? Are the menus in English? If the answer to both these questions is no, it can be extremely awkward. But, as they say, nothing ventured, nothing gained. In I went. A young lady pointed me to a table and handed me a menu.

I breathed a sigh of relief to see that not only did the menu have English alongside the Korean, but is also had pictures. In the section for sushi, it had only two options: large and small. The picture showed pieces of salmon, tako (octopus), something I think was squid, and some sort of fish. It looked good, but I was worried that they would not give me soy sauce. I love sushi, but I have to have the soy. My fear got the better of me and I decided not to risk it. What I found to order was described as "spicy soup." When the waitress came, I pointed at the picture.

She returned with *kim'chi*, the staple of Korean dining. The guidebooks say Koreans eat this dish of cabbage marinated for days in a spicy red pepper sauce at every meal. From what I have seen it is true. In fact, Big Dog and Monty reported that their host family eats it at breakfast! It has taken me a few tries, but I have the taste for it.

A few moments later, the soup was served. Brown broth containing Raman noodles and seafood. There were a few mussels, clams, and tentacles of either squid or octopus. It was very good, but very spicy! I enjoy the hotter foods and it is a good thing, because this was hot. As I ate it with a combination of chopsticks and a spoon, I began to sweat. Then my nose began to run. The small cup of water I was given was empty and I could not get the waitress' attention. I was actually eating *kim'chi*, spicy in its own right, to cool my mouth. I was going through napkins like I was home with the flu because my nose was running like Joe Max-Moore, non-stop and all over the place.

Eventually I noticed a sign that read, "On second time, bring water for yourself." I took that to mean, "Get your own water" which I did from the ever-present water cooler. A few times. At one point, I had a momentary lapse with the chopsticks and dropped a mussel into the broth, which splashed up right into my eye! I was blinded! It felt like the time I stored my soft contacts overnight in solution for hard contacts. But through all the pain, I continued eating the stuff. It was the best thing I had had since arriving. Flavor and pain, all for W4,500. I will be back.

After eating, I returned to the *Dong-Il*, but still no Jimmy. I left him a note saying I would be at the PC Bang and then would go to Itaewon for the games later in the evening. I spent the next few hours at the PC Bang. I talked to Damien about a game that I see played on TV. It is a board game that is so popular it has it's own channel! The board is a grid and the player's alternate putting their stones (black or white) on the board. Every now and then they remove one of their opponents stones. I have seen people playing in on the streets, much like people in the park in New York City play chess. I had been curious about this game and asked Damien about it. He told me it is called Paduk and that he was a master. He said he gives lessons, and I can buy a set most anywhere, some not expensive at all and that he would teach me to play.

Just when I was about to leave, Jimmy showed up. The first thing he said was, "Chuck drove me crazy!" I showed great concern by laughing my ass off. He said they met up and sat together for the game. When it ended they got lost leaving the stadium, though Jimmy said he knew right where to go. Chuck kept leading them in the wrong direction. It took them so long to get away from the stadium that they just got a room for the night. Upon arriving back in Seoul, Jimmy forgot which subway stop was ours and spent nearly five hours wandering around.

This was scary as it was funny. He said every stop he got out at looked the same. He was a bit frazzled, and we decided just to go back to the *Dong-Il* to watch the games.

The first one was over, and South Africa had beaten Slovenia. That eliminated the Green Dragons who I heard had some of the best supporters at the Cup. Next was Italy and Croatia. I was excited about this game and was hoping that Croatia would pull the upset. That would leave Mexico sitting pretty to win the group and setting a possible match with us! I did not want to play Italy in the Round of 16 because I did not want to be sent home then. I know we can beat Mexico!

However, the game was very boring. Almost nothing happened in the first half, and when Christian Vieri scored ten minutes into the second half, I was sure Italy would apply their notorious bolt and the game would degenerate further. So confidant was I that the game would end 1-0, I told Jimmy we could go eat. He did not argue, but said he wanted a burger.

I led the way to a Burger King I had passed earlier that day and had a Whopper Value meal. We ate on the second floor, next to a window that looked down on a large, outdoor bookstore. The sun was setting, and we ate quickly, hoping to go through the books, but they put them away for the night before we finished.

I told Jimmy about our trip to the embassy, and we walked that way. I mentioned to Jimmy that I had read that they were going to close it at noon the day of the Korea match over fears that a Korean mob could cause trouble. We walked past the embassy and continued on to the large gates. I was interested to see what was behind them, but when we arrived, they were locked! We tried to walk around, but all we saw after a ten-minute walk was another gate. There was no way in at this hour. As we walked back toward the embassy, we noticed people congregating and looking toward the gate.

Just then, a light show was projected onto the large gates. At first it was entertaining but quickly became dull, and we left after just a few minutes.

Back in the *Dong-Il*, I was stunned to see that Croatia had come back to stun the *Azzuri*. In the next game, Brazil piled it onto China in a game that featured Roberto Carlos scoring on one of his trademark free kicks. He is amazing the way he hits the ball.

After the Brazil game, I found a channel showing the Italy game and watched as Croatia scored two goals, but was concerned as Italy had two seemingly good goals called back. One of them was not even close. I felt a bit bad for them, but seeing as we will play one of the teams that advance from their group, it would be great if they did not make it through.

I noticed Survivor on Armed Forces Network and laughed to myself because it was the final episode, the one where Ethan won the million dollars. I had suspected they were a little behind the times and my suspicions were confirmed as they showed a commercial previewing the upcoming opening of *Star Wars Episode II*. I thoroughly enjoyed that movie about a month ago.

After Survivor, my clock showed 1:00 and I turned out the light, looking forward to a long train ride to Daegu tomorrow.

Day 8
Sunday, June 9

Beer and Soccer, Dangerous

My new alarm clock went off later than I had hoped on this, our first big travel day. I went to explain to the two women who run the *Dong-Il* that we would be in Daegu for the next two nights and that I would pay in advance for our rooms because we did not want to carry our luggage with us. However, I guess she had anticipated this and actually carried our bags to a storage room! This was a great coup as we had planned on just paying for the rooms to keep things simple. Now, we apparently had about $50.00 extra! We will keep our fingers crossed that we will still have rooms upon our return.

Despite the late start, things worked out, and Jimmy and I were only two minutes late getting to Seoul Station. Big Dog did not seem to notice it was just after 9:00 when we met him in front of the noodle stand in the subway area of the sprawling station. He told us Monty was with some other Americans inside the train station. As we walked there, we saw a sight that was becoming a normal scene in Seoul, a stand selling t-shirts supporting the Korean team. I think everyone in the country owns one. They are red and say, in English, "Be the Reds" in white letters. I hate these shirts as each time I see someone wearing one, which is at all times on the streets, it reminds me of just what we will be up against tomorrow. Our boys will not be playing a soccer team; they will be playing a whole nation. A nation that has come together to support its team in a way that is surprising even the European media.

In addition to the "Be the Reds" t-shirts, Koreans are waving scarves, signs, and banners that say "Korean Team Fighting!" Upon our arrival, we snickered at the slogan and though we still think it is amusing, we do understand what it means. Adopted as the official slogan of the team, "Korea Team Fighting!" has come to represent the side's heart, determination, and spirit. They may not be the most technically gifted team, but they make up for that in hustle, guts, and relentlessness. They have an undying belief in their coach, their system, and each other. This is what their slogan means to them.

Their apparent ability to run forever frightens me as well. The heat has been stifling here in Seoul and from everything we read, it will be worse in Daegu. I worry that we will run out of gas trying to keep up with them. I hope Arena has devised a plan to slow the game down. The schedule is also working against us. Our players will be on four days rest, while the Koreans have had one extra day to recover from the first match.

On paper, at a neutral sight, with weather not a factor, I do not think we would have much trouble with them. However, with these fanatical fans in the stadium and the whole country urging them on; in the hot, humid summer weather of

85

Daegu, and on one less day of rest, I am not sure we will get it done. I draw seems like a great result.

We saw Monty inside the station. He was hard to miss in his Sam's Army shirt and a large flag tied around his neck. Jimmy handed out the tickets that we had bought just before leaving for the Portugal match. The roundtrip ticket had cost 25,000 won or about $20.00 for the four-hour train ride.

I was hungry, so Monty and I each grabbed a Whopper combo meal from a Burger King in the station. There were a few Americans in the line, and we passed the time talking about our experiences here. One of them mentioned the World Cup souvenir stand outside and Monty wanted to check it out. We still had about thirty minutes before the train boarded, so he and I went to see it. On the way, we encountered some extreme anti-American sentiment. We were outside, negotiating our way slowly through the crowded plaza that led to the store, when Monty was attacked. He was startled as he was punched from the front and then from behind. He looked at me for help, but I was not getting involved in this one. It was not that I was afraid; I just was not sure how to handle the situation. I have never had a friend attacked by an elderly, woman who stood only four feet eight!

I am not entirely sure if she was anti-American, anti-Indian, or just anti-Monty. Whatever the case, she was not happy and threw two punches that Monty may not have noticed had he not seen them. In between blows, she cursed him. I do not know what she said, but the tone indicated it was R-Rated. After she had her say, she continued on her way as Monty and I broke into laughter.

Undeterred, my Indian-American friend defied the abuse by hanging his American flag proudly on the window as we took our seats on the train. The train was nice and clean, the seats large and comfortable. We settled in and decided that this was not a bad way to travel.

After about 30 minutes we pulled into Suwon, Monty and Big Dog's home base, for a quick stop. Big Dog and Monty cursed that had they thought ahead, they would just now be boarding. Instead, they had caught an early subway to Seoul. They were worried their tickets that were for a Seoul-Deagu trip might not be accepted, boarding in Suwon. Monty said it cost him about three hours sleep. I told him that it really sucks, but better safe than sorry.

A few minutes later the suburban sprawl finally gave way to the countryside. Big Dog was reading The Game of Their Lives, a book about the 1950 World Cup in which the U.S. famously upset England. Jimmy was reading one of the many papers he purchased here. Monty and I were without material, so we decided to see if the train had a bar car.

We were in luck and found it only two cars behind us. It was about 10:45 in the morning when we took our seats, which faced the windows, giving us a great view of the mountainous countryside. Monty and had I come to know each other quite well the last few days and over an enjoyable stout and then an OB, we continued forming a tight bond.

Monty was born in India, but came to the U.S. at an early age. He is Boston through and through. Though his accent is not as pronounced, he would have fit right into a scene from *Good Will Hunting*. He is an active member of Sam's Army and is thus recognized and greeted wherever we go by other Americans. He has many friends here. He is also a huge sports fan, not just a soccer lover. He said the greatest day of his life was this past January, when he traveled to Atlanta, scalped a ticked outside the dome, and cheered his beloved Patriots to their first Super Bowl victory.

I told him that I have heard a theory that New Englanders all secretly hope that the Red Sox never win the World Series, as it would give them nothing to look forward to. He strongly denied that, saying he is actually worried that he might injure himself in that celebration, but that he prays for it everyday.

After a few more OB's and a few hours, we decided we were neglecting the others. We were in a good mood as we returned to our seats, singing something about the bar car and all of its wonders. As we sat down, a train worker pushed a cart of food by. This happened about every 20 minutes or so. This time, I heard him say, "Ice cream." I could not resist and asked for one. I was given a cup of Dots! Chocolate and vanilla. Jimmy had never seen them before, and I was surprised to see them here. It just showed that they pretty much have anything here that one could want.

It was just before 2:00 when the train pulled into Daegu Station, and we disembarked. I had reserved a room at the Union Tourist Hotel for the four of us. When I called, I was aware that the person making the reservation did not speak great English, and I had made it clear to the others that while I thought we were all set, I was not 100 percent confident that a room would be waiting for us.

Outside the station, in the brutal heat, was an information booth. At first nobody there seemed to have heard of the Union Tourist Hotel, but then they remembered it and advised us to take the subway. We really did not want to get on another train and asked if we could take a cab. The girl in the booth was extremely nice and wrote the name of the hotel on a piece of paper and pointed us to the taxi stand.

As I have mentioned, Korea is a very modern country. There is very little one cannot find here, however, there is a glaring omission of something we take for granted . . . addresses. In short, they do not have them. I have no idea why and do not think it would be difficult to start numbering buildings and creating a system, but they have not done so. This makes getting into cabs tricky. If the driver knows where you are going, no problem. If not, well I have not had that happen yet. Only once, in Seoul, a driver waved us off after we told him the *Dong-Il*. I assumed he had not heard of it and did not want to waste his time trying to find it.

Luckily, the driver took a quick look at the note and nodded as we all piled into his cab. About ten minutes later we arrived and upon checking in, the desk clerk said we had two rooms. At W30,000 apiece, or $24.00 a night, split two ways, we gladly accepted them both. We decided that Monty and I would room together; as it was likely we would be out late, drinking. Jimmy, who does not drink, and Big Dog, who does not drink beer but enjoys a few mixed drinks now and again, were in the other room.

We met an American family, led by Jim, a retired New York City police officer, and his wife and two young children. They had just arrived and had a room on our floor. We told him that we had learned, through the Yanks in Korea Yahoo list, that there would be a gathering of Americans at a club called Old Blue.

After dropping our bags, we decided to find a PC Bang. I was dying to know what happened in the Mike Tyson-Lennox Lewis fight, which I calculated would have ended just a few hours earlier. At the front desk, they advised we would find one downtown, which they pointed was a few blocks straight out the front door.

We decided that despite the heat, we would walk because we had no idea what to tell a cab driver. We drew a lot of stares as we walked through the city. Chuck had warned that outside of Seoul, they see very few westerners and not only would people stare, but children would poke at us. I was not sure whether to believe this or not. I am pretty sure that there is an American Army base here. In fact, Jimmy has been looking forward to seeing Amanda, the girl he met the first night at Nashville, again. She is stationed here. But we were attracting a lot of attention. I felt like I was in one of those movies where some young Americans are in the wrong place in Mexico and all the natives are staring at them. It was that hot and we were getting those stares, though there were not many people on the streets.

We considered turning around a few times, but finally we saw the famous PC Bang symbol and went quickly up the steps and into the welcome smoke-filled, but cool room. I went immediately to Yahoo and read that Lewis had knocked Tyson out. We also read that Reyna is still questionable but that Mathis might play. I sent my usual e-mail to Ivy and other friends, but we all wanted to get back to the hotel because the first game of the day would start shortly.

We all wanted to see Mexico and Ecuador. Though Mexico is our bitter rival, many Americans want them to do well. A good showing from our region could possibly lead to more bids and thus easier qualifying. It also helps to gain respect and that is something that we U.S. fans are more than preoccupied with.

We stopped on the way home and buy Gator-Aid and sodas. Our plan was to watch the game at the hotel until halftime. Then we would leave for Old Blue and spend the rest of the night there with our countrymen.

We groaned as Mexico's keeper, Oscar Perez, failed to stop a header and Ecuador took an early lead, but felt better when Jarred Borgetti equalized.

At halftime, we headed down the elevator, and a Korean gentleman struck up a conversation with us. We continued talking outside, where we planned to catch a cab, and he revealed that he is an umpire in the Korean Major Leagues. I had seen a baseball stadium from the hotel window and he said he was on the way for that night's game. For some reason, I broke into an umpire routine and started belting

88

out, "Steee-Riiiiike One!" while really putting my arms into it. The umpire just stared at me as I yelled, "Steee-Riiike Two!" At this point, I nearly punched someone who walked up behind me.

It was Ellen and she was holding her baby. Tom was there also and they said they were also going to Old Blue. Three cabs pulled up and the umpire hurriedly climbed into the first, obviously thankful to be away from me. I ended up in the third with Big Dog, Ellen, and the baby. Ellen commented that Erin had been so well behaved all day on the train. Of course the moment the taxi pulled out, Erin decided she had kept it in long enough and began crying at the top of her very strong lungs. This went on for a while, as traffic was heavy. At one point we did not move for five minutes. It was hot and frustrating, but at least Erin stopped crying. We were stuck in the middle of what had to be Bridal Row. There was nothing but wedding dresses in the windows, and Ellen joked with me that I should jump out and pick one up for Ivy. All the dresses were white except for one that was red with gold trim, and I said that I would take that one. Ellen scolded me for this and then advised that none of them were very attractive.

The traffic did clear and we were dropped off at the *Dong Inn*, from where we had directions to Old Blue. With only a little trouble, we found the bar. It was on the second floor and was made up of one large room that had the feel of a TGI Fridays but was dominated by a large, square bar in the middle of the room. I was disappointed that there were only a few small television sets behind the bar. However, the hostess led us to a back room. It was much smaller, rectangular in shape, with a bar against the long wall, but had a large screen TV at the far end. There were about ten or so Yanks there, and I recognized a few, including Mark from D.C.

I sat with him, and we all drank OB Beer from large pitchers. Most everyone cheered when Mexico took the lead and although they missed a number of good chances, they earned a deserved 2-1 victory. Mexico was sitting pretty with six points, but were not through yet as they will face Italy who will be desperate for a win as they only have three. Croatia figures to beat Ecuador, which would give them six as well. For Mexico, a point and they are through as first place winners. A loss and it will probably come down to goal differential. The good news is that Italy are in trouble of advancing, meaning that should we go through, we would play either Croatia or, in a dream match up, Mexico.

After the match, the bar was still relatively empty so Monty and I decided to head out in search of food. A few doors down, at an intersection, there was a large, outdoor stand. I noticed some tempura among the other Korean treats. However, it was outdoors, in the heat, and Monty and I walked on. We passed a number of eateries, but were a bit shy about going in. None seemed to have any English menus at all.

The narrow streets were crowded with people. At one point, a shop had some speakers that were playing John Denver's classic, *Country Roads*. I stopped and sang along with it. "Take me home, to the place, I belong, West Virginia, Mountain Momma, take me home, county roads," I belted out the words, showing Monty how Southerners sing, but he was apparently familiar and sang with me!

Finding no luck with food, we were circling back to Old Blue when we came upon a life-sized Elvis statue outside a pub. We took turns posing for pictures with the King, before deciding we had to go in for a beer. The inside of the bar's theme was a cave. The walls replicated the inside of a cave. There were stalagmites as well as stalactites. Monty and I argued which hung up and which hung down while waiting for the waiter to bring us large mugs of OB. This bar was empty, save the staff and posters of the Flintstones on the wall.

We were given some sort of chips. They were tube-like, round and hollow, and very good, though I have nothing to compare them to. After the beer, we were going to leave, but the waiter brought us a bowl, which was boiling. I thought I heard him say, "Egg soup." But it was steaming so much I could not see into it. After the stem subsided and it went from boil to simmer, I took a spoonful that burned my tongue. Monty did not like it, but I did, as it resembled egg drop soup. The waiter also brought us a plate of peanuts, pretzels, and dried things, perhaps squid, but I left that alone. Of course, we had another round of OB, so that when we left the Elvis bar, we were feeling fine.

So good was our mood that when came to the outside food stand near Old Blue, we had no problems with the health concerns that had earlier frightened us. We were having a hard time deciding what to get, but the guys behind the wooden counter began giving us food. First was a bowl that looked to be pasta in red sauce, but turned out to be potato cakes and were very good. Then I ordered some tempura. It was octopus. Long tentacles dipped in the light tempura batter. I dipped it in the large bowl of soy sauce that had certainly been in the sun all day. I am sure most everyone who used it also double dipped into it, but I figured as long as all these people can do it, I could as well.

As we were eating, we were joined by a father and his two sons who were about my age. They were from Minnesota. The older of the sons, Steve, had been an English teacher here and helped us ask a few questions about the food. The workers continued to give us samples, and I continued to enjoy it.

After the tempura, I ordered *kimbop*. This is a traditional Korean snack that I see everywhere. It looks like a California roll, without the avocado and crab. It is rice wrapped around vegetables and sometimes meat. I picked up the first roll with the chopsticks and as I do with all California rolls, I dipped it in the soy sauce. This turned out to be some cardinal sin. Everybody around, workers, other patrons, and passer bys groaned and waved for me to stop. They all stared in disbelief as I ate it. I was confused, because it was good, and I had no idea why everything can go into the soy, but not this.

I smiled sheepishly at the guy who gave us all the food and ate the next one without the soy. It was not nearly as good. "Why don't they dip this in the soy? Isn't it just like sushi?" I asked Monty, but he had no answers.

Then the guy behind the counter pushed the soy closer to me and motioned me to dip away! I gladly did so and enjoyed the rest of the *kimbop*, to the dismay of the onlookers.

We returned to Old Blue with our bellies full to find it had filled up significantly. Inside we saw the New York Crew, or more aptly, we heard them singing before we saw them; the brothers, Scott and Neil, were there sans their film crew, then I saw Jimmy sitting at a table for two with none other than Amanda!

The Costa Rica-Turkey match was on and everybody was cheering for the Ticos. Everybody except for one, that is. There was an American there in thick, horn-rimmed glasses and a bright shirt, loudly cheering for Turkey. No one knew who he was, but we quickly learned he was a person with whom we were all familiar. His name was Sven, and he was a prolific poster on the Yanks in Korea board. He was a lawyer who was living and working in Japan. He had offered a lot of advice leading up to the trip.

When asked, he was unable to properly explain why he was for Turkey. Joe of NY brought up that CONCACAF had won all of its games so far, an amazing achievement from a small, lightly regarded region. We all agreed that trend needed to continue. Turkey went up one-nil, but Costa Rica mounted a furious comeback to score a late goal and split the points. We all cheered the goal, and when the final whistle blew, the NY Crew led a cheer against the thick glasses wearing Sven, a soccer favorite, it is sung to *Guantonamero* "One Drew Carey, there's only one Drew Carey, one Drew Ca-ary, there's only one drew Carey!" we all sang while pointing at a smiling Sven.

Kaela showed up, and I realized that she and Monty were friends from back home. The atmosphere in the bar was fantastic as the NY Crew led us in many songs. We also spent a lot of time teasing Jimmy and Amanda. We were very childish and accused them of being "in love." We suggested to Big Dog that he should find somewhere else to sleep that night. It was all in fun, and to Amanda and Jimmy's credit they took this ribbing in stride and were able to laugh off even our crudest suggestions.

Another topic of conversation that we dealt with was our safety tomorrow. For years there has been resentment over our military having bases here, and though I agree with our presence here, I can understand their point of view. Then something happened at the Winter Olympics last year that has galvanized the anti-American sentiment.

It happened in short-track skating, a wild race on ice. In a final, an American, Apollo Anton Ono, was blocked as he tried to pass a Korean. The Korean finished first, but was later disqualified, giving the gold to Ono. Evidently short-track skating is a huge sport here because the country erupted in anger. They saw it as America using its clout to award the gold to their athlete. It probably did not help that Ono is of Japanese descent. They even created a phrase, "Hollywood acting," which means to draw a foul when none has been committed, like they have accused Ono. The term is used when soccer players take dives.

I had heard of this controversy before leaving America and had thought about having a red shirt with a large printing of Ono's face on the front. I am glad I did not as it would have been a waste of money. I would not have dared wearing it. The Koreans are really fired up about it.

If we lose, there will be no problem. If we draw, there will probably be no problem. If we win, there may be a problem, but I am confident in the security here. I am not afraid, even though we will be outnumbered something like 60,000 to 2,000, which breaks down to 300 to 1. There are rumors that the Red Dragons, the loud, organized supporters club, run predominantly by students, have some leaders who have strong anti-American feelings. The rumors say that here in Daegu, the third largest city in South Korea, these feelings are stronger, due to the military base.

I have no idea if these rumors are true or not and I would be lying if I said I had no trepidation at all about the game, which will be held in the largest stadium in Korea. However, nothing I have seen has foreshadowed any violence. I have felt welcome everywhere. The Koreans have shown themselves to be gracious hosts. Even while being stared at, I have sensed no danger. I have enjoyed this trip immensely and the warmth of the Korean people has been a large factor in that.

That said, I really hope the referee does not make a bad call to give us the game. Should that happen, I could see where normal, peaceful people could lose control and attack us. In my life, have been good at avoiding trouble, however should a mob become caught up in this at the stadium, it would be hard to avoid. I have faith in the Koreans, but not a mob.

We have discussed for days what to wear to the game or more specifically, what color to wear. Usually, Americans wear red. However, 60,000 Koreans will be wearing red so many have suggested we wear blue so that we may be seen. Others say to wear white, while others say we should not give up our colors. This argument has raged on the Yanks in Korea list for weeks and is still raging. For a while it seemed we had settled on blue. However, as it stands, there is no agreement and I am planning on wearing the same thing I wore to the Portugal match, a red Sam's Army shirt with a flag tied around my neck.

Late in the night, Big Dog and Jimmy decided to head back to the hotel. The bar was thinning out, but Monty, Kaela, a few others, and I decided to stick around. We had drunk a lot and were having a great time. Big Dog left us in charge of the soccer ball he carried everywhere he went. We told them good night and then sarcastically asked Amanda if she knew the way to our hotel. She really is a great girl for taking all our crude jokes.

At some point, Monty mentioned the Elvis bar, and the others demanded we take them there, so off we went. We found it easily and went in. Our waiter smiled and waved to us. We drank pitchers of OB and ate the tube-like chips. I convinced some cute Korean girls to sit with us, but they stayed only long enough for pictures. When we finally left, I was feeling that I had reached my limit and was concerned about a hangover.

Outside, Monty, Kaela, and I began to kick the ball around. Kaela has some skills, and we decided we would walk back, even though all we really knew was the direction that we should head. Finding the hotel was something we, in our drunkenness, did not consider. We went through the streets, kicking that ball all over. It was well after midnight, but the streets were crowded with what we took for college students. Many times, we passed the ball to a random Korean and each time they took great delight in kicking it back.

It was such fun. Crowds were cheering us as we passed by. Monty and I tried to aim our passes to the females. A few of these young women shied away from the ball, but others aggressively booted it back. We were ruling the road and some Koreans followed us a block or two, joining the game, before turning back to where they had been.

We were really into our game, and I soon lost track of which way we should be heading. However, that did not stop us. At one point, I was met by three very cute girls walking the other way. "Where are you going?" I asked.

"Dancing!" they said, their eyes inviting us along.

"Wow! That would be fun," I thought and from the look on his face, Monty agreed.

"Where do you dance?" Monty asked.

They pointed and said, "Not far." They were really interested and we were in the process of getting their names when Kaela arrived and pulled us away, much to our dismay.

Monty took it very hard and as the three cuties walked away, waving, Monty decided that Kaela had just earned a Red Card.

I agreed, and we both mimed pulling out the card and sending her off. Being she could not be sent away, we simply avoided in giving her the ball.

It was just Monty and I and the Koreans kicking it around and Kaela making sexist remarks to us. Then, Monty sent the ball to me. His pass was a little in front of me, he had led me too much. I stretched to reach the ball, but when my foot came down, it landed half on and half off a short curb. My ankle rolled and to try to lessen the impact, I, too, rolled over.

I was on the ground and knew it was bad. Monty laughed at first, but he quickly saw from the look on my face that I was hurt. Kaela really gave it to me, making joke after joke.

"Is that one of the dance moves you were going to show those girls?" I heard her say.

"I need a cab," was all I said to Monty. My knee was bleeding, and though the beer was keeping me from feeling it, I could tell that my ankle was in bad shape.

We all got in a cab and Kaela was dropped off at her hotel and then we at ours. Rather than going in, we decided to play some more. During the cab ride, I had forgotten about my ankle and Monty and I began kicking the ball around. We had left the crowds behind and the street was deserted. There was a 15 feet high wall in front of the hotel and it made for a great third teammate. I would play the ball off the wall to Monty and he returned it the same way.

I was limping on my ankle, but it was the left one, so I was able to kick with no problem. For some reason, the experiences of the day, the excitement of tomorrow, the beer; this was the most fun I ever had kicking a soccer ball. I treated each trap and pass as if I was playing in the Cup. I was very serious about placing the ball right on Monty's foot.

Our fun was interrupted by the hotel manager. He stormed out, scolding us and motioning us inside. We had not considered that we were making a racket outside a hotel. As we tucked our tails and walked up the steps to the front door, he said, "Beer and soccer, dangerous!"

"Don't I know it," I thought as I limped onto the elevator. I was asleep within minutes of entering the room. It was 2:15.

Hollywood Acting

It was 9:30 when I woke up. Monty was also stirring. I pulled down the covers to look at my ankle and was horrified at the sight. It had swelled to more than twice its normal size and had turned an ugly shade of purple. I opened the small refrigerator and took out the can of Coke I had bought the day before. It was cold, and I used it as an ice pack, pressing it on my injured ankle. I wished I had thought of this the night before.

"Oh my God!" exclaimed Monty when he saw my ankle. "You did that last night?"

"Yeah, I'm dreading the game today, standing for two hours and all," I said, wondering if I would be able to stand in support of the team. I would really hate it if I were forced to sit.

"You'll be alright," Monty lied.

When I stood up, the ankle seemed OK. It held up to pressure, and I walked with only a slight limp. I was glad of that, but not so happy with my condition. I did not have a full-blown hangover, but was not at the top of my game. I drank a bottle of cold water in attempt to hydrate myself. This day was sure to be long and hot.

Monty was moving slowly as well. "I feel like shit," he said as we began to get ready to go.

Last night, all the Americans had decided to meet at TGI Fridays for lunch and a pre game rally. Some folks had assured us there was one near the train station and that all cabbies knew where it was.

When we were ready, we went over to the other two's room, certain they would be anxious to go. They were not, and it was not until a half an hour later that we headed out of the Union Tourist Hotel to catch a cab for Fridays.

When a cab pulled up, the four of us got in and told the driver, "TGI Fridays, near the train station." He nodded and drove off. After about five minutes, we saw that we were near the train station, but the driver did not seem to have any particular destination. He was making turns here and there. He obviously did not know where Fridays was. I was about to tell the others to look out for the red and white stripes of the restaurant, when I saw them myself. "Over there!" I instructed and he let us off right in front.

There were a number of Yanks milling about outside. They told us it does not open until 11:00. We had about 15 minutes to kill. Big Dog came to the rescue and pulled out the ball, the one that had led to my injury the night before. My ankle was not bothering me too much, and I could not resist having a kick. Big Dog displayed surprisingly good touch for someone of his size. A few other Yanks joined in and soon the staff was unlocking the front door.

Inside, Jimmy, Monty, and I grabbed a table, but Big Dog sat with someone else. I told Jimmy and Monty to order as soon as possible. There were well over one hundred Americans and the staff looked to be overwhelmed. They agreed, and we quickly grabbed a waitress and placed our orders. I had a hamburger with fries and ordered both a Coke and water. Monty shocked me by ordering a Long Island Ice Tea along with a steak.

"How can you drink that?" I asked.

"Got to get ready for the game," Monty answered with a big grin.

More and more Americans arrived and soon there was a line just to get in. Some had been sitting for 15 to 20 minutes before ordering. Our food was the first out of the kitchen, and we ate while those seated around us looked on with hungry, envious eyes.

As we were finishing our meal, I saw Chuck coming through the doors. He looked around a few times and his eyes lit up as he waved to us. He approached our table and did not hesitate to sit in the empty seat. As quickly as he had joined us, he began complaining. He loudly told us how a taxi driver had tried to rip him off. He continued to complain about Koreans everywhere. Again, I wondered, "Is Chuck treated that differently than us, or just crazy?"

I told him that he might not want to eat here because we will probably leave before his food would be served. He did not mind, and in his booming voice called a waitress over and ordered a burger and fries. He then told us how the waitress would not have come over if he had not called on her.

Monty had had enough and got up to mingle. Jimmy is a slow eater, and as soon as I had finished, I was off as well, leaving Jimmy with Chuck.

Most folks were either still waiting on their food or were just beginning to eat. Monty found Kaela, and we sat with her for a while. For as many Yanks as were there, it was pretty mellow. I guessed that most were in the same quasi-hungover condition as I. However, after folks finished up, songs began to ring out.

The NY Crew was sitting at the bar drinking beer, and they were starting to sing. Monty and I made or way up to join them. After leading the whole place in America the Beautiful, we took a break from the songs and discussed the game. We were having a good discussion, but not really saying anything new; "a win would be great, but we will take a tie. We will be outnumbered like never before today, so we all need to be as loud as possible." Again, nothing new, just rehashing what had been said many times before. Then, we noticed someone coming in the door. It was the commissioner of MLS, Don Garber. At once the NY Crew began chanting, "Don't let the league fold!" Clap, clap, clap-clap-clap! "Don't let the league fold!" Clap, clap, clap-clap-clap.

After a few rounds of this plea, the commish looked our way and smiled. He pushed by a few people and quickly approached us. "The league's not going anywhere, fellas," he exclaimed as he shook our hands.

Monty had his camera and told me to pose for a picture. After he snapped the shot, Garber was leaving and I yelled out, "Don't take less than 15 million for Beasley!"

He left the restaurant without eating. I guess he just wanted to see what the fans were up to. Monty and I were talking about going to the stadium. But Big Dog got upset and said we should all leave together. He wanted all 200 or so Americans to travel en mass. While that would be great, it would also be nearly impossible to organize. Some were already beginning to trickle out. Some were talking about cabbing to the stadium while others were planning to walk to the shuttle bus stop for the free ride.

I went back to the table to see what Jimmy wanted to do. Chuck was complaining that they still had not brought his food. Predictably, Jimmy was ready to go. We collected Monty, and Big Dog gave up his fight, and we were soon in a cab, on the way to the stadium.

It was a fairly long ride of about 20 minutes. The stadium was well outside the city, at the foot of a mountain. The moment we stepped out of the cab, a Korean family asked us to pose with their children for a photo. We agreed, and someone said that we would be doing a lot of this today. After the photo, we chatted for a bit with the father. As we turned to leave and were shaking hands, Big Dog told them, "I hope we tie."

Monty and I jumped all over him for that, "I hope we tie!" exclaimed Monty, "What the hell is that? Who are you for?"

Big Dog had no answer and muttered something like, "I was just trying to be friendly."

"You don't have to hope we tie to be friendly," I said. "Wow. You hope we tie."

We continued ribbing him as we searched for a fountain where we were all supposed to meet. Outside the stadium, the color was red. Thousands of Koreans were streaming about, most wearing a "Be the Reds" t-shirt. Many wore traditional masks that looked like they were out of *Shogun*; of course I would never say to them that they looked Japanese. As we walked, we were stopped for pictures. After each one, we all shook hands. The Korean's English was generally limited and they would say something like, "I am happy to meet you." Big Dog did not tell anyone else that he was hoping for a tie.

On our walk we found Kaela and a few others who were also looking for the fountain. We were enjoying the experience of walking through the colorful crowd when I saw a familiar face approaching from the right side. My heart started beating rapidly and I felt my temperature rising. My mood changed, and I felt angry. It was Steve Sampson, the previous coach of the National Team; the coach who many, including myself, blame for our terrible showing at the 1998 World Cup.

A few others recognized him and began shaking his hand. They were all happy, excited to meet a "celebrity." As he was shaking hands, I just walked away from the group. I did not want anything to do with him. It was strange. I know I do not like him at all, but I was really feeling angry. The mere sight of him had ruined my mood. I was a bit shocked at my reaction to him.

Someone said, "Can we take a picture?" Sampson was happy to oblige.

After a few photos, Sampson said, "Now I want one with you guys." He handed his camera to a Korean who had been drafted as the photographer. "You guys are what all this is about," he continued and then pointed at me and said, "You too, come on over here."

At first I was going to decline, but then I quickly thought of the idea of him having a picture of me, and I liked that idea. The original outline of this book discussed the 1998 team at length, and I spared no harsh words in my criticism of him. I hoped that one day he would read those words while looking at this picture of us in Daegu. I gladly posed and was happy when he left.

We found the fountain, which was conveniently located near a beer stand. The brothers, Scott and Neil, were there. They told us they had hailed a cab and told the driver to take them to TGI Fridays. After driving for about 20 minutes, he pulled up to the stadium and let them out! They had been here for a few hours and were happy to see some Americans.

It was very crowded, as if all of Korea was there. However, despite the mass of red, I did not sense any danger. I pulled out my camera to take some pictures, but my camera's battery light was flashing and it would not take any pictures. This was upsetting, as this was the one game I was hoping to have pictures of. I anticipated the scene in the stadium and wanted to show it to my friends, but I realized I would have to obtain pictures of this day from others.

Some more Americans arrived; and many were drinking beer, Budweiser to be exact, which was the only choice at the stand. I had a Power-Aid. I was happy that the heat did not seem so bad. The sky was thankfully overcast. We were all happy about this and knew the team was.

A lot of Americans were around and we were singing which drew stares from the passing Koreans, but they paid us no real attention, other that the occasional request for a photograph. There were many Americans wearing costumes, a few ladies were dressed as Lady Liberty. There were three Elvis. Many wore face paint. In this patriotic crowd, with my modest outfit, I was not as popular with the Korean photographers as were others. At one point, I started a cheer that went, "600 to one, I like our odds! 600 to one, I like our odds!"

I saw Ethan Zohn, the Survivor, and spoke with him for a while. He said he was having the time of his life, and I agreed.

Jimmy and I decided to get in early. I had a fear of missing the start of a game due to lines getting in the stadium, so at 1:30, two hours before game time, we began heading to the gate. We walked with Tonya and Doug. We realized we had to get to the other side of the stadium, the side at the foot of the mountain. About halfway there, I noticed a stage with a band playing. There were Koreans packed in front of it. Then I recognized the song. It was, *Oh this is Korea!* A song the TV had played a lot in support of the Korean team.

I could not believe that band was here. I also could not believe the frenzy that the Koreans were being whipped into. As we walked by, I had goose bumps. This was unlike anything I have ever conceived. I would not have believed it had I not seen it, but these fans would put any fans of any American sports team to shame. NY Yankees fans, where is the joy? Green Bay Packer fans, where is the noise? Duke basketball fans, where is the passion?

I said to Doug, "I hope we can shut them up."

We waited in a long line for about 20 minutes before entering the stadium. Jimmy and I quickly found our seats. Fortunately, we were under cover. The sun was going in and out, but we were in the 3rd row from the top of the lower deck, covered by the upper deck. Unfortunately, this stadium was not nearly as cozy as was Suwon. We were in a corner, a goal to our left. I have never seen such a large stadium. I guessed were 100 yards from the nearest part of the field. I thought that as loud as it would be, the field was so far from the stands that the players should be able to communicate. As bad as it is to watch a game in a stadium like this, it was a blessing for our team.

Before the game, they announced the lineups. I was relieved to see Friedel still in there. I was worried that even though he beat Portugal, he had given up two goals and had a few other shaky moments and that would have given Arena a reason to bring in Kasey Keller. As I said well before the Cup began, "I'll take Friedel."

The defense was the same four from the Portugal match and that made me wonder, "Just what did David Regis do to end up in this dog house?" The left back was so far down that Hejduk, a right back, had replaced him for two games.

In the midfield, our Captain was back. I was very happy to see him, apparently recovered from the injury. I never thought we could beat a marginal team without him, and though I was proven wrong, I was glad Claudio Reyna would be playing. Also, Landon Donovan had moved to right wing from his forward position. I hoped this kid could handle the position change. Absent from the midfield were Pablo Mastroeni and the injured Earnie Stewart who started against Portugal.

At forward were Brian McBride and Clint Mathis. I guessed whatever caused Arena to sit Mathis against Portugal had been resolved. I was very excited to see what he could do on this stage. I was hoping he lived up to his considerable hype. "Can he become the goal-scoring predator for whom we U.S. fans have waited for so long?" I wondered.

Despite some efforts to familiarize myself with the Korean players, I did not recognize any name. I made it a point to remember the goalkeeper is named Lee.

The stadium was full and it was red. I saw a European Championship match from Holland two years ago on TV. The entire Amsterdam Arena was in the orange of the home team. I thought it to be the most incredible display of support I had ever seen. This was very similar. I tried to imagine what was going through our player's minds, but I did not have a clue.

***

A lady sings our anthem and the place goes quite. We all sing as loudly as we can and I know that this may be the only time all afternoon that we are heard. I appreciate the Korean fans for their show of respect during our anthem.

As soon as it ends, the fans in the opposite end zone unfurl an unbelievably large Korean flag. It covers the entire lower deck. I have chills as some 60,000 sing their countries anthem. The second the song ends, the flag just drops out of sight beneath the stands. Incredible organization.

Now the chant starts, "Tey-Han-Ming-Go!" Clap, clap, clap-clap-clap-clap. "Tey-Han-Ming-Go!" Clap, clap, clap-clap-clap-clap! The entire stadium not only dresses the same, but they all chant in perfect unison. We try some chants, but are drowned out as soon as we start.

After their chant, they sing that song, "Oh, this is Ko-Rea! Oh this is Ko-Rea! Oh this is Ko-Rea! Oh-oh-oh-oh-oh, Hey-Hey-Hey!" On and on it goes, without stopping. We are trying to chant the old standby, "U!S!A! U!S!A! U!S!A!" But we can barely hear each other.

The game kicks off amidst 50,000 flashbulbs. We are attacking the goal away from us. It is probably 200 yards from where I am standing, on an ankle that I can now feel. I am happy that we go on the attack right away. With some sustained pressure, the volume drops, but only a little. Then there is the sound of a drum, which cues them to start the "Tey-Han-Ming-Go!" chant. Nobody has any idea what it means. All we know is that every Korean in this stadium is yelling it with everything they have.

Now they attack for the first time, down the right wing and the noise becomes shrill, high-pitched until Friedel collects the ball. They are cheering every little thing. They react to a stolen ball as if they have scored a goal.

Jimmy and I look at one another as the red crowd begins singing Beethoven's *Ode to Joy!* I am not sure I have every heard that sung before, but I do hear it now. About five minutes in, Korea has a close range volley, but the player puts is high, and we breathe a sigh of relief. An early goal would set this crowd on fire, and I am not sure I could imagine that.

We have tried a few other chants, but we cannot be heard at the other end of the two sections that we Americans occupy. Then we discover a weakness! While they are doing the clapping after chanting, "Tey-Han-Ming-Go!" We all chant "U!S!A!" It fits perfectly and goes like this: "Tey-Han-Ming-Go!" "U!S!A!" "Tey-Han-Ming-Go!" "U!S!A!" A few Koreans in the section next to us hear it and look our way with a look that is both perplexed and annoyed.

100

The Koreans are able to set up their offense and create a few half chances. Other times our defenders make big stops. Friedel is not really tested and handles everything with no trouble. We do not have much possession, and on our forays into their zone, our attackers fail to connect on the last pass and the Koreans are quick to counter.

They are fast and are running everywhere. The crowd is really lifting them, willing them to push themselves. Friedel is forced to make a save with his feet on a close range shot. We are being outplayed.

Then Donovan is released and crosses to McBride, but he is a step late and the defense puts it out for a throw. O'Brien centers, and again, it just misses McBride, however it does find Donovan and he shoots just wide! This sudden burst of offense has given us a boost, and I look to the clock to make a mental note of our first real chance when I realize that I cannot see a clock. I look all around the stadium, but no clock. I scream at Jimmy, asking him if he sees one, but he just shrugs and shakes his head.

We can see a replay scoreboard, and what we see is a Korean with blood all over his face. He is down in our penalty area. The Korean crowd sees it as well and from their horrified shrieks, one would think that his head had fallen off. I see a Korean girl near us and she is crying! And, I sense she is not the only one doing so. The replay shows he knocked heads with Hejduk. The cut is nasty, but get serious. They wildly cheer as he gets up and walks off the field.

I am trying to find someone who may know the time when I see Mathis bring down the ball. He seems to be in on the keeper. He shoots and he scores! We erupt! I am jumping up and down and my ankle is killing me now, but I do not care. I can sense that the rest of the stadium is very quiet, but our two sections are rocking. I think to myself, "This is the way it should be. They are not real soccer players. We are better than them! Mathis is the man"

We break into the chant of "U!S!A! U!S!A! U!S!A!" But the Korean fans are not down for long. They wave the injured player back onto the field. The trainers evidently just wrapped a huge bandage around his entire head. He looks like a wounded soldier and his re-entry fires up the crowd. However, their team is rattled, and we are able to possess the ball. We create a few half chances, and I am feeling much better. It is not often that we Americans feel that we are the better team. Against most teams in qualifying we are, but on this stage, it is a strange feeling. I sense victory.

They do their chant, and we answer. "Tey-Han-Ming-Go!" "U!S!A!" The whole stadium is standing, and I may be the only one on a really bad ankle. It is bothering me, but there is no way I will sit down now. It is hot and humid, but I have felt much worse. The relatively mild weather and the cavernous stadium are playing into our hands. I am giddy. Is it possible for us to have six points after two games? I feel like singing Ode to Joy along with them.

The game has broken down some, and the Koreans make a substitution! I did not notice an injured player; Hiddink must not like what he sees. As a fan, I think it is a great sign when your opponent substitutes in the first half.

Off a free kick, I see bodies fall in the box and immediately see the referee pointing to the spot. We fall silent, but a few moments later the Korean fans realize the call and go berserk. I look at the replay, but from well over 200 yards, cannot see anything. Agoos, their player, and Pope all fall down. I cannot see enough to argue. I cannot believe we will be tied.

"Come on Friedel!" I urge. And the big man comes through! He dives far to his right and pushes the shot away. But there is chance for a rebound. Pope is racing one of their players, the ball loose in front of the goal. I hold my breath, but Pope gets there first and clears the ball. We go nuts! We chant "Free-dul! Free-dul! Free-dul!" Pope is injured and is stretched off but comes right back on.

The penalty save has taken a lot out of the crowd. They try to get their voice back and are still extremely loud, but not as loud. They have suffered two major blows and have not recovered.

I have no idea how much time is left, but there cannot be much. Soon I see the fourth official signaling but cannot read his sign, thus I remain in the dark about the time. "How can they build a stadium with no clock?" I wonder, and moments later, the whistle blows.

Halftime! We lead 1-0, thanks to Mathis and Friedel. I slap high-fives with the fans around me and sit down for the first time at the stadium. Most of the stadium does. We all need the break. The Korean fans have mercifully stopped their singing. It is even quiet enough for us to hear others in our section. A few guys in front of us sing, "How much for the doggie in the window?" But have to stop after that first verse because no one knows the next verse. Then I hear the NY Crew singing that old Bob Marley favorite, "No *kim'chi*, No cry!" The whole section joins in, "No *kim'chi*, no cry. No *kim'chi*, no cry!" Everybody is laughing as they sing. You may need to have been there to understand it, but it has all the trademarks of the NY Crew, creative and hilarious and loud enough to be heard.

The second half kicks off with the U.S. now attacking the goal nearest us. Jimmy starts his stopwatch and we see others in our section doing the same. Korea goes on the attack right away and just a minute in forces Friedel to get down quickly to save a goal. It was a great save. It is now apparent that without Friedel, we would be playing catch-up.

The crowd is rejuvenated and as loud as they were at the start of the match. "Tey-Han-Ming-Go!" "U!S!A!" We go back and forth, though I am sure only the sections of Korean supporters bordering our sections hear us at all.

Korea forces some corners and all the action is at the far end of the stadium, a long way from us. The players are slightly bigger than ants they are so far away.

Finally we have some possession in their end, and it seems that we have an opportunity to shoot, but both Reyna and Donovan elect to pass and Korea is quickly on the attack again. Our boys are not packing it in, thankfully. Sanneh makes a few runs forward. However the Koreans are all very fast and cover so much ground, it seems that we are out numbered.

Hiddink decides to make another change, subbing one forward for another. The incoming player seems to be very popular among the Korean supporters as they all scream for him when he is announced.

In the stands, we have virtually given up singing and chanting, except for the "U!S!A!" that we answer their chant with each time they do it. Perhaps some Yanks are singing, but we cannot hear them.

Though we do have some penetration into their end, nothing comes of anything, not even a weak shot. I have to remind myself that we are winning. Their players impress me with their skill and I wonder why the European clubs have not found more of them.

There is a scary moment as Reyna is stretchered off, but he comes right back on. Soon after, we do get a shot off. Beasley crosses to McBride. I do not think he got much of it but does force Lee to make a save. As usual, Korea pins us right back into our zone. Friedel is kept busy.

Suddenly, Reyna sends Donovan in alone, but he whiffs on his first time attempt and a great chance is wasted. A second goal would be very nice. I am not as confident as I was earlier. Hiddink makes his final substitution and Jimmy tells me there are 20 minutes left. Immediately, Friedel is forced into another big save. "Free-dul! Free-dul! Free-dul!" Becomes the one chant of ours than can be heard. He has been huge, and I hope he can keep it up. He is our best player on the day.

Korea's pressure is relentless. They are not tiring, at least not to my eyes. The crowd is willing them onward. We try to urge on our players, but know they cannot hear us. I hope they know that we are here for them.

In the distance, we see more shaky moments in the U.S. defense. We no longer work the ball out, choosing to boot is up field when possible, out of play when necessary. We are bending but not breaking.

Now Arena makes his first sub and it is not a popular one. Beasley gives way to Eddie Lewis. There are a lot of angry American fans questioning this move. Even I, who normally has the opinion of whatever Bruce does is fine with me, am perplexed. From my vantage point, Beasley has done well, starting a few breaks. He has tried to use his blazing speed, but has been unable to outrun the equally fast Koreans. I fear Lewis, who has nowhere near the wheels of Beasley, will be left behind. On the other hand, it is a defensive move. Lewis has much more experience and is a better defender. Again I have to remind myself that we are winning.

Jimmy says 15 minutes. Korea has a free kick, and I see a dangerous ball played into the box. A red shirt goes up and the ball is in the net. For a second, there is no reaction, and I hope my eyes have deceived me. My ears soon alert that they have not. The stadium is making more noise than I thought possible. I am disgusted that we have given up the goal, but I see other Yanks, looking over to the

103

Korean section, just to our left. I do the same and have to smile, though do so grudgingly. They are jumping and hugging and screaming. Some are crying. As over the top as I thought our celebration after O'Brien's goal against Portugal was, I think they are surpassing it. I am not sure they are merely celebrating a goal. I see other Americans looking on with amazement. I turn my eyes to the far end of the stadium. It is awash with movement. Before, it was a solid red block; now it reminds me of a game we used to play in first grade. Our gym teacher would line us around a parachute. Each of us would grab the edge and shake it with everything we had. She would throw a few plastic balls on the parachute and they would be tossed by they movement of the parachute. That is what the far end looks like, a red parachute being pulled in every direction by school kids. It is an amazing sight.

Enough of that, the game is back on. I hope we hold on. To lose this game would be devastating. The stadium is no longer organized; it is just loud. I am surprised these people have enough energy for this. We see on the reply that the goal scorer beats Agoos in the air.

Lewis has a free kick saved easily by Lee and the crown erupts again. They have pulled it back together and are chanting in unison once again. The game is going back and forth, but they are faster. Arena now substitutes Josh Wolfe for Mathis. I like this move. Other than the goal, Mathis has not done much. Wolfe is very fast.

Lewis makes a bad play losing the ball in the corner nearest us and our two sections groan. Though I am praying we hold on, I am holding out hope that we can get another. I think that maybe the speed of Wolfe will catch them off guard. However, they are still running all over. They are like a swarm of gnats; they are annoying, and they are everywhere.

I ask Jimmy for the time again and he says five minutes. Then I think I see it raining. I say so and Jimmy says he noticed it a little earlier. Then a Korean misses what looks like a point blank shot. I have changed my mind and only want the point now. I ask Jimmy again and he says "Almost 90."

"Just blow the whistle!" I yell to the referee. But he plays a few minutes of injury time. Korea attacks and I hold my breath. We get it out and the whistle blows. Another sigh of relief. The crowd salutes both teams. A few Yanks, most notably Hejduk, come our way to applaud us.

I sit to give my ankle a break, wondering what further damage I have done to it. I think about our group now. Both Korea and we have four points. I feel certain Portugal will beat Poland today, giving them three and eliminating Poland. Because Korea play Portugal they will either both get one or one of them will win three points. Doing some quick work in my head, I determine that, provided Portugal does beat Poland, a draw against what would be a winless Poland would put us through. This thought makes me very happy.

Coming into the tournament, I was hoping that if we won the last match, we would go through. The way it will stand, we only need a draw. I decide I must share this news, so Jimmy and I head down to the NY Crew. They look as exhausted as I.

"If Portugal wins today, we only need a draw to go through!" I announce.

"What, no. Are you sure?" Brent asks. We go through the scenarios and agree. Then, Leo points about five rows down to an American with a long mullet. This guy's hair goes half way down his back. In unison the NY Crew serenades him with, "One Michael Bolton! There's only one Michael Bolton! One Michael Bolton, there's only one Michael Bolton." Jimmy and I join in and we have to sing it through a few times before the guy realizes we are singing to him. He good-naturedly gives us a wave and runs his fingers through his hair as we break up in laughter.

As Jimmy and I turn to go, Joe, the New Yorker that I had played darts with that first night at Nashville, grabs me and says, "Keep up the noise. I'm outta here."

"You're leaving! No way, you gotta stay!" I tell him.

He sadly shakes his head and says, "I have to leave."

I tell him it was great to meet him and I'll do my best to keep the boys going.

***

With that, Jimmy and I headed out of the stadium. On the concourse, we ran into Monty and Kaela. The four of us left the stadium and headed for the buses that would take us back to the train station. From there we would make our way to Old Blue, where everyone had decided to meet for a post-game party. As we were outside the stadium, walking around, we saw some of the Korean fans carrying their huge flag. It was rolled up, but still an impressive sight. There were at least 40 people carrying it. We continued walking, but noticed we had lost Jimmy. Monty speculated that he must have seen Amanda and was with her.

The line for the buses snaked for a quarter of a mile so we decided to try our luck catching a cab. We continued past the buses and approached the wide road. This was the first time all day that we were away from a crowd. We virtually had this stretch of the sidewalk to ourselves. A few cabs came by, but despite our waving, did not stop.

We were exhausted. I only wanted to sit down and eat something. Kaela seemed worse off than I. She was funny as she cursed each cab that passed us. I was thinking that we would not get one, but she and Monty overruled me.

I heard someone call my name and turned to see three Yanks approaching. It was Doug, Tonya, and Amanda. "Where is Jimmy?" I asked Amanda. She had no idea. They were also seeking a cab. "None of them are stopping," I informed them when out of nowhere a cab pulled up! Before we could believe our luck, the other three jumped in and the cab sped away.

Kaela was pissed! "That was our cab! We were waiting here!" she vented. Though she was right, Monty and I would not have felt right, leaving a pregnant woman standing on the side of the road. Not long afterward, our chivalry was rewarded and we happily climbed into the cab, me in the front, Monty and Kaela in the back. The driver, however, was not satisfied and cruised around looking for one more fare. He was hailed and a pulled up to two Koreans, a mother and daughter. We could understand that he was saying that he could only take one. They were torn, but in the end, the daughter reluctantly climbed in. He somehow communicated to us that she was going to the bus station, but we had no idea who was going to be dropped off first.

The answer became clear as he sped through downtown, very near to Old Blue, we were sure, but kept going. Kaela was upset with him. I was growing hungrier by the moment, but was entertained by a small wide screen television that he had mounted on his dashboard. It was showing highlights of the game. For the first time I had a good look at the penalty call. In my biased opinion, it was a bad call, but I can certainly understand it; it looked bad. I saw that the goal was scored by Ahn, who had out jumped Agoos. Then I saw something that I had not seen during the game. After Ahn scored, he ran to the corner and broke into a speed skating routine! A few others imitated him, however, it was another who drove their point home. Number 14, Lee Chun-Soo, rather than skating, jumped back and threw up his hands. He was playing Apollo Ohno, mocking what they perceived as his "Hollywood Acting," in essence drawing a foul.

Eventually we found the bus station and the girl was let out. We headed back into town. The driver, who was very talkative throughout the ride, grew even chattier. He spoke almost no English and was driving an already angry Kaela out of her mind. She did not hold back her opinion of him, and I was glad he could not understand her.

He was paying much more attention to us than with driving. "Baseball?" he asked.

"Yes, I like baseball," I answered.

"Oh baseball!" he said. "Park Chan-Ho." I had no idea what he was saying. "Park Chan-Ho!" he was excited. "Park Chan-Ho!"

Then I got it, "Oh, Chan Ho Park, the pitcher, yes I know him," I said, then corrected myself and pronounced his name as they do in Korea, "Park Chan-Ho."

He turned around, "You love her?" he asked Monty.

"No!" Kaela almost shouted as Monty giggled.

The driver pulled out a Mariah Carey DVD. I saw Kaela's face turn red. "Mariah Carey?" he asked.

We three quickly answered, "No!" he looked dumbfounded, but put the DVD in anyway.

"I love Mariah Carey," he told us and then to our horror, he sang along with her. I thought Kaela was going to strangle him, but he was saved by a humorous moment. We came around a corner and saw that a deliveryman had had an accident. There were about ten cases of bottled beer broken on the side of the road. "Oh sheet!" Our driver cried. "Oh sheet!" He was pointing at the spilt beer and even Kaela had to laugh.

He rolled up his sleeve and stroked his arm hair, looking at me for approval the whole time. I think he was proud of this hair. He then reached over and sort of rubbed my arm. Again, I think he was saying that we both had arm hair. Then he pulled up his shirt and grinned widely as he rubbed the hair on his stomach. I had no idea how to react, but Monty was laughing in the back.

"I think he loves you, Andy." Monty and Kaela would have a good time with this for a long time, I was sure. The driver continued singing with Mariah and showing me his body hair. I had to put up with this until we reached Old Blue. The second he pulled to a stop, I bolted, leaving the others to pay the fare. It may be a cliché, but this was a "ride from hell."

Inside, Old Blue was nearly empty, but in a booth I saw Tonya, Doug, and Amanda. They were exhausted, but eating. I left them to their food and ordered a pitcher of OB for Monty and Kaela who were just then coming in. By the time they sat down, I had a mug ready for them. The beer changed our mood and though tired, we were ready for a party.

The waitress came by and I ordered the seafood spaghetti, it was W8,800. Kaela asked for the fruit and cheese platter. My dish was good, though a bit sweet for my taste. The tomato sauce contained clams and mussels. Kaela's platter had some cheese that tasted like Brie on bread. I laughed at the fruit, sliced tomatoes and sweet pickles!

As we ate, people trickled in and by the time we finished, they bar was jumping. On TV, we saw Tunisia and Belgium play a lackluster one-one draw.

I saw Big Dog and asked if he was happy. "Why?" he asked.

"You got the tie you were hoping for," I said.

Monty jumped in, "Yeah, you should have seen him celebrating when Korea tied it."

"I did not," he said, and then changed the subject. "Have you seen my ball?" We shook our heads, and he said, "It's gone."

We were drinking OB, when Monty tapped me on the shoulder and pointed to the entrance. Chuck was coming in. Chuck saw us and came right over. He was upset at how long the bus had taken. We told him we took a cab, but wished we had waited in line for a bus. Then, he complained that his ticket for the game had not been with Americans. He had sat in the middle of all the Koreans and was upset that they had cheered the whole game. To his credit, he bought the next pitcher of OB.

Despite Chuck's negative attitude, we were feeling good. The OB was taking effect and I was no longer tired. I got up and began to mingle. I noticed Jimmy sitting at the table with Amanda. Doug and the expecting Tanya had thrown in the towel and returned to their hotel.

Big Dog introduced me to Mark Spacone, who was the founder of Sam's Army. We had a good time discussing the Cup. I had once read that he said his goal was to watch the U.S. play in a sold out stadium where everyone was wearing red. I asked him if today he reached that goal. He laughed and said it was not exactly what he had in mind.

The night was interesting because there were a good number of Koreans celebrating along with us Yanks. They were on one side of the bar, in a section that was raised a step over the main area. When our singing began in earnest, they were content to watch. However as the night dragged on, they began singing back. This went on for a few songs.

Monty suggested we go introduce ourselves. He bought a pitcher of OB, and I followed him up the step, into "enemy territory." There were two large tables of Koreans, one with all guys and the other with mostly young ladies. Monty briefly hesitated and then offered the beer to, can you believe, the ladies table! Then he and I applauded them and they returned the favor.

The next thing I knew, we were in a singing contest. First the Koreans sang, I don't think it was a soccer song. Then Monty and I, along with a few others who joined us for the occasion sang, *I'd Rather Have Clint Mathis than Figo!* in appreciation for his goal. Then they sang and we went back and forth for a few songs. It was great fun. I love to sing, but have a terrible voice, so situations like this, drunken soccer songs in a pub, are made for me.

One of the songs we sang was the *Old MacDonald* song, *Bruce Arena Has a Team*, only the words changed slightly. The first verse was for Josh Wolfe and said, "With a goal, goal here and a goal, goal there. . ." The next verse was for Jeff Agoos and originally said, "With a stop, stop here . . ." However, this time, although it was not premeditated at all, we all sang, "With an own goal here and an own goal there . . ." We could not finish the verse we were all laughing so hard.

The Koreans then did their chant, "Tey-Han-Ming-Go!" To which we instinctively shouted, "U!S!A!" When we finished that round, I asked what it meant. They said it means "Republic of Korea", they were basically chanting their countries name. Then, in a diplomatic move that would make Jimmy Carter happy, we Americans began chanting, "Tey-Han-Ming-Go!"

We were rewarded for our gesture as they enthusiastically responded, "U!S!A!" It was truly a heartwarming moment, as we continued chanting for each other's country. I think we were saying just how nicely we had been treated, that the Koreans were perfect hosts, and that we appreciated their hospitality. I am not sure what they were thinking. However, if all the rumors are to be believed, that the youth of Korea is strongly anti-American, I was touched that because of this match a simple act of song had caused them to cheer my country. I hoped that they would remember this moment and think that Americans are not so bad, that we are all just people and that maybe all the rhetoric they heard about us just might not be all true.

When the chanting ended, I started us in singing their other song, "Ohhh, this is Ko-Rea, Ohhh, this is Ko-Rea, Ohhh, this is Ko-Rea, Oh-Oh-Oh-Oh-Oh, Hey!Hey!Hey!" Suddenly a conga line formed, and we danced all around the bar, hands on shoulders, Americans to Koreans. It was a unifying experience, and I knew that I was at the World Cup. It was strange, but this song that had annoyed me all day had transformed itself and was now no longer the song of the Korean Team, but was now, at least for me, the song of the World Cup.

Once we had circled the bar and were back in the Korean section of seats, we stopped to catch our breath. We Americans applauded them, clapping our hands over our heads. They responded with bows and waves and we retreated to our seats and more OB.

The Poland-Portugal match had been on, and the rain was pouring down. It was torrential and we were all thankful that we were not in it and that the weather was clear where we were. Portugal responded as I thought they would and hammered Poland 4-0 behind a hat trick from Pauleta. For the second straight game, Poland's goalkeeper, Jerzy Dudek, was terrible. I had been concerned that the Liverpool keeper could carry his team, now I was only hoping that he would not find his form against us.

It was now official, a draw against the Poles and we will advance to the second round. For Korea, it was not that easy. They would need to draw with the Portos. For the group favorites, a victory was needed to assure advancement, only a loss by us would put them through with a draw. I was confident that Portugal had received their wake-up call after suffering the embarrassment of losing to the U.S. I felt they would beat the Koreans and join us in the second round. Everyone was of the opinion that we needed to take care of business in our game, because if we lost, we would need Korea to win and nobody thought that likely.

In the crowd, I bumped into Mark Spacone of Sam's Army, again. I told him of my brief encounter with Steve Sampson, expecting him to echo my feelings, but to my surprise, he had the opposite reaction. "Why don't you like him?" he asked.

I told him I did not have the time to go down the whole list. He said he thought him a good coach who had just had a bad Cup after the players turned on him. Mark pointed out that not only had he qualified us for the Cup in 1998, but that he had guided us to a fourth place finish in the 1995 *Copa America*.

These were good points, but I responded that it was talent that qualified us and for the Copa, it was not really his team, just the leftovers from Bora Milutinovic. I said that he made good moves by adding Kasey Keller and by allowing them to play more offensively, but he really had no business being coach. I said it was unfortunate that we had that early success because it forced US Soccer to keep him on as coach.

Mark argued that he was as qualified as anyone, having been assistant to Bora.

I said that I doubted that, and although I have no proof, he was probably nothing more than a translator for the Spanish-speaking, Serbian-born coach.

Mark looked at me like I was crazy. At that point, a taller guy said he had been listening to our conversation and that he agreed with me. He said that he had been a minor-league player who had been called up to the Metro Stars while Bora had been their coach. He went on to say that Bora ran everything and assistant coaches had no freedom to interject anything. He continued to say that he thought Sampson had been a decent college coach but was in way over his head with the National Team.

I was pleased that my ideas now had some backbone. Mark looked as if his world had caved in. "Cheer up, Mark," I told him, "we're going to the second round."

It was getting late and the bar was thinning out. I was sitting at the bar, making a new friend. Mike was traveling alone, on a graduation gift, having just earned his degree from his hometown University of San Francisco. He said he was having a great time, but did not appreciate a culture where they eat dogs. I did not mention I was looking for some myself.

Mike had spent the few days between U.S. games traveling to China. He had eaten at a famous restaurant, but said it was pretty ordinary. He had walked on the Great Wall, and I could see that he was amazed and proud of this, and he said, "I mean, I was standing on the wall, thinking, 'I am standing on the Great Wall of China!'"

He was staying in Korea through the first game of the second round and was then going to Japan for the rest of the Cup. I was quite jealous of his itinerary, but reminded myself that I was staying through the quarterfinals, while most Yanks were leaving after the Poland match.

He and I sat at the bar for a long time and drank a lot of beer, when I realized I had hit my limit. I found Monty and he was good to go as well. We caught a cab home, and when I lay down, the clock read 3:00. It had been another fantastic day in Korea.

Day 10
Tuesday, June 11

If Frogs Had Wings, Would They Score a Goal?

The second I closed my eyes, or so it seemed, the phone was ringing. It was our wake-up call. "5:45." the voice alerted me. I felt sick. "How can I possibly be up this early?" I thought.

Monty was not helpful when he said, "Think about it this way, it's 6:45 in the evening back home."

It did take my mind off the pain because I thought of my softball team that was on the field. There was no time to dwell on that. We had to get moving. The train left at 7:00, returning to Seoul around noon. From there I had to catch the subway to Incheon for the hour-long ride in order to make it to the France-Denmark match, which began at 3:30. I had been concerned about making it there in time, but since the early train was available, there should not be a problem; only a hurried day.

The promise the day held motivated me, and I was shaking out the cobwebs minutes later. Monty and I quickly packed and amazingly Jimmy and Big Dog were ready to go when we knocked on their door.

After a quick cab ride, we were at the train station and aboard with no problems. We settled into our seats and prepared for the long ride. I was hoping to sleep, but despite my lack of sleep the previous two nights, I could not. I thought about going to the bar car for some food, but as I remembered the menu from the trip down, it contained nothing I wanted this early. I was also holding out hope that I might fall asleep. I spent the entire five-hour ride, waiting for the sleep, which never came.

Every time I was about to fall asleep, my mind would remind me that I was going to see what promised to be an exciting, drama-filled match. Unbelievably, France had only one point and had not yet scored a goal. My pick to win the whole tournament was on the brink of a humiliating exit and the only thing that could save them was a victory by two goals or more. Their opponents, the solid and professional team from Denmark, only needed a draw to advance to the second round.

I was sure that Denmark would pack it in and allow France to attack and was looking forward to seeing all of France's great players fighting the odds to score the goals that they desperately needed. Things were not all bad for the French as one of the very best players in the world, Zinedine Zidane, would be making his first appearance at this Cup, having sat out the first two games because of injury. I was certain his presence would inspire his mates and that they would regain the form that saw them lifting the Cup in 1998.

When I ordered the tickets for this match, I did so because I wanted to see France play a strong team. Then I worried that by the time the group stage reached this match, both France and Denmark would have qualified and would be resting top players. The reality of the situation could not have been further from the truth. Senegal had shocked France, and even their opponent on the day, Uruguay, still had a chance to advance. The game for which I held tickets was of unbelievable importance. France was fighting for their lives.

When the train pulled into Suwon Station, we bid Monty and Big Dog farewell until we would meet them for the train to Daejeon for the Poland match. I was sorry to see them go, not only because I had a good time with them, but I was also losing what would have been my travel partners for the day. Big Dog and Monty had tickets for the France game, but they had been stolen. Though U.S. Soccer had been able to provide Big Dog with replacements for the U.S. games, they could not help with this one. So our two friends headed back to their host families and I continued to Incheon alone.

Back in Seoul, Jimmy and I caught a subway back to the *Dong-Il* where the two women greeted us by holding up both index fingers, indicating the 1-1 draw our two countries played. Just after moving our bags back to our rooms (I kept my same one, but Jimmy was given a new room) we headed to the PC Bang. It had been nearly two days since we had last checked our e-mail. Like drug addicts, we craved the Internet and although I was hungry, I did what any addict would do and skipped lunch to satisfy my habit.

I felt at home, entering Damien's smoky PC Bang. He greeted us just as the two ladies had at the *Dong-Il*, by holding up the score. Unlike them, he spoke English.

"One to one! Good game!" he said.

"Great game, very loud," I told him, but did not elaborate; I was worried that if I did not get to a computer soon, I would start shaking.

It felt great to have the world at my fingertips once again. I sent a number of e-mails, detailing the trip to Daegu, the amazing atmosphere inside the stadium, and my still swollen ankle.

Then I proceeded to read every account of the match I could. Understandably, Brad Friedel was given the credit. On Big Soccer, most posts had elevated Clint Mathis to god-like status. In short, everyone was elated with our position, beat or draw with Poland and go through. Lose and pray for Korea to beat Portugal. I kept that last notion in my head although I felt neither was likely. Our team is too confident to lose to Poland, it just will not happen. On the other hand, as hard as the Koreans play and as much as the country is behind them, I do not think they will beat Portugal. The Koreans here are certain they will win and advance, but I think they are a bit delusional. We need to take care of our own business.

I stayed in the PC Bang too long and had to bolt for the subway without eating. I guess I could have stopped for a quick bite, but despite my hunger, I was more concerned with getting to Incheon in time for the game. I had read that it was an hour on the subway, from Seoul Station, so I hurried out of the PC Bang at 1:30, and hoped that in that hour before the match, I would find some food.

I easily found the subway for Incheon at Seoul Station and upon entering the car and taking a seat, realized I was sitting next to an American. He was about my age, perhaps a bit younger, and was with his father. They were of Turkish descent and had been following the Turkish team. I was shocked that they had not planned on attending even one U.S. match. I thought to myself, "How can we gain the respect of the world when we don't even have the respect of our own soccer fans?"

They were from Boston and were pleased with the play of the Turks. I told them that I thought Costa Rica was going to tie Brazil, which would eliminate Turkey, but they scoffed at me. The son told me he had been to Turkey a few times and had seen the team he supports, Fenerbache. He said the atmosphere there is incredible and intimidating. I enjoyed the conversation we had, but could never understand why they cared so little about our own team.

On September 15th, 1950 General Douglas McArthur landed at Incheon and thus the U.S. entered the Korean War. Today, France came hoping not to exit the World Cup. When I arrived, via the subway, the Turks and I split up. They had told me we were at the stadium; there was no need for a shuttle bus, so I decided I needed food. Badly.

The subway stop was in a mall, but I was pointed toward the exit when I asked where I could eat. Just before taking the elevators out, I saw a small stand. It was selling the usual Korean snacks, dried octipus, squid jerky, and chips none of which appealed to me. Then I saw something that looked like sausage, wrapped up like a Slim Jim. I have never eaten sausage from a wrapper before, but my stomach was paining me and I decided to give it a shot. Just before I reached for one, two Germans stepped in front of me and picked one up. They spoke in German, but I could understand that they were trying to figure out what it was. When they shrugged and put it back, I decided that if Germans did not know if it was sausage or not, then I should leave it alone as well.

I rode the escalators out of the station, certain that I would find food, if not outside the stadium, than inside. Back above ground, I was met by a team of Christian missionaries. They have been very visible here, mainly outside stadiums. Most saw them as a nuisance. I understand the work they are doing and took their offerings and tried to offer a quick word of encouragement. Today, however, they were extremely aggressive. They swarmed as fans exited the subway station. I saw that they were handing out the same booklet that I received at the first two matches, so I quickly walked by them.

It was another beautiful, sunny day. The air was much clearer here than in Seoul and the sun brought out all the colors of the various jerseys fans were wearing. I had on my D.C. United shirt and was hoping to trade it for that of some other club. There was a lot of bleu and white of France and dark red of Denmark. I searched out a drink stand and waited behind a group of blond haired guys wearing Finland jerseys. Once they had bought their beer I ordered a Gator Aid. I had not eaten anything all day and this was the first drink I had. I gulped it down quickly and decided that inside the stadium was the best option for food.

The complex was well set up. Just outside the subway exit was a baseball stadium and beyond that was the soccer park. There was a wide walkway leading to the soccer stadium. I passed by a large group of Danish fans . . . or should I say band. Each of them had an instrument and were blowing, strumming, and banging them. It was not random noise, but actual music. Other Danes joined in and clapped and sang along. The impromptu rally drew many onlookers and after a short time, I moved along. I then passed by the box office where there was a line of Koreans just beginning to form. I realized they were hoping tickets for Korea's match with Portugal would go on sale. That important match would be played here in Incheon. I wondered how long they would need to wait for tickets. I was pleased that my tickets for the next U.S. match were already in my possession. I would not have to wait in any lines or do any scrambling to secure them.

Finally I entered the stadium, through almost no security which was very unlike the U.S. matches. Before stealing a look at the pitch, I went on a search for food. The gates had recently opened and there were very few fans inside. The walkways were nearly empty which led me to think that soon I would be eating. The first stand had a large menu, but none of it available. Other than drinks all they had was a package of five hotdogs. They were not cooking them or putting them on buns, just selling the package to be eaten raw. I walked around a bit, but found nothing better. I was hungry but did not want raw hot dogs so I found my seat.

I was in the first row of the middle section of seats, to the left of the goal. Behind the goal there was only one deck so I was low, only fifteen rows above the field. This stadium was similar to that in Daegu in that it had a lot of room between the field and stands. In Suwon, on the other hand, we were right on top of the field. I was about fifty feet from the pitch, not nearly as far as in Daegu. It could have been better, but it was not bad.

At the far end of the field, the France team walked onto he field and I stood to applaud Fabien Barthez, who keeps net for my beloved Manchester United. He was the only Man United player I expected to see in person. After Denmark had come out to warm-up, I went in search of food, again.

This trip turned up similar results to the earlier brushes with food. I was now so far beyond hungry that I did not have anymore pains in my stomach. I did notice in walking through the concourse area that there were no doors on the men's bathrooms. The sight lines provided the passer-by with a view of the urinals, and men making use of them.

A few minutes before game time, a 20 something young man wearing a Newcastle United jersey sat down next to me. He reached into his backpack and pulled out an England flag and began tying it to the railing in front of us. I helped him do so, not only because I am a big fan of England, but also I thought it would give me a target to look at to see myself on television.

The anthems were played, and for the first time, I was not shaking with pride and anticipation. It was good to be there just to watch. After the French anthem ended, I said to the guy from Newcastle, "That is a great song."

"It is, I hate to admit," he said in his Geordie accent. The game kicked off to flashbulbs even though the sun was bright, but he and I were only half paying attention. We were discussing everything else soccer related.

I told him I had seen Newcastle play. They had toured America in 2000 and had played a friendly with D.C. United, in which I was happy to point out, the home team won 3-1. He was interested to hear that at the press conference following the match I had stood next to their coach, the legendary Sir Bobby Robson.

He asked me if it was true that women's soccer is bigger than men's in the U.S. I could only laugh at that inane statement, but saw that he was serious. I answered him by saying, "When the women won the World Cup in 1999, the nation got caught up in it, it was a huge event. They sold out 80 and 90 thousand seat stadiums and were even named Sports People of the Year, but in general, they are not bigger then the men. When their league began," I continued, "they drew crowds of less than 10,000 on average. The MLS averages about 15,000. Mia Hamm is a major celebrity, bigger than any men's player, but not the game. Nobody really cares about their league or, to be honest, the National Team. The World Cup just got people excited, and it was a great story," I finished and wondered how he could have come up with that idea.

He seemed to understand what I was saying, but I was not sure he believed me. He changed the subject, "You are playing very well."

I agreed and related the Portugal game to him. I am still on a high from that night in Suwon. I told him that even if we crash out against Poland, we have done a lot of good. We have showed the world that 1998 was a fluke and that we can play this game.

He agreed with me, saying we played great against Portugal and that he thought we are one of the better teams here. After that, we were quiet for a while and settled into watching the important match before us. About 20 minutes in, Denmark scored at the far end. As the crowd erupted, my new friend from the north of England and I stared unbelievably at one another. The game had not begun as I had predicted. Denmark did not pack it in and France was not attacking in waves.

France kicked off, but looked like a beaten team. They now needed three goals, which was three more than they had scored all tournament. As I was wondering just what had gone wrong with the defending champions, my new friend said to me, "You know, I can see you in the finals."

He said it so matter-a-factly that I believed him. Before answering him, I took a moment to reflect on this. A guy from England just said he could see the U.S.

in the final game of the World Cup! Had we really come that far in eight days? Had 1998 been forgotten, or at least forgiven?

As I pondered his statement, he explained, "If you avoid Italy in the second round, then you will play probably Ireland or Germany, neither is at the top of their game. Then maybe the other bumps off Spain and you get them in the semis, I see you through."

I did not tell him I had thought that same scenario through a hundred times, rather I said, "It is too bad you have such a difficult road to the finals. You'll probably get them," I pointed to the field, obviously meaning Denmark. "And then probably Brazil. It looks like the tougher teams will all be in Japan."

"Yes, that is true, but we cannot beat Brazil."

"Sure you can. I think you are as good as anyone in the world. Look, France are out. You have already taken care of Argentina. Don't be scared of Brazil, you are every bit as good as them."

He seemed cheered to hear that, as if he had not considered that himself. It is funny that I have found some English that have an overly optimistic view of themselves while others are at the exact opposite end of the spectrum and with that, there seem to be none in the middle.

Halftime came and I told him I needed to find food. He said to stay away from the hotdogs, that they were horrible. Because those were the only things for sale, I simply ran out and bought another drink.

The second half kicked off and I took a moment to take in the great French players I was seeing. There was Barthez, four years ago, the finest goalkeeper in the world. Now with Manchester United, he had gone through a difficult year, but was still immensely talented. I saw Lillian Thuram and Marcel Desailly, two tall, strong center-backs who had shut down the world four years ago. To their left was Bixente Lizarazu of Bayern Munich whom some say is better than Roberto Carlos. In midfield was the toast of Highbury, Patrick Vieira, his Arsenal mate, Sylvain Wiltord, and the player of the year, Zidane. Up front was the Juventus striker, David Trezeguet whose wonderful golden-goal had won the European Championship for France. Was I witnessing the end of a dynasty?

Newcastle and I renewed our conversation. He had come to Korea because Japan had been too expensive, but he had wanted to get as close to the action as possible. That is another thing I find curious about the English. They will travel great distances, to the sight of a match, knowing full well they cannot get into the stadium. They say the atmosphere outside the stadium and then inside a nearby pub makes it all worthwhile. As for me, I could not stand to be left outside while my team was playing. I would much rather be far away than that tantalizingly close.

A question popped into my head, "Have you ever played Championship Manager?" I asked.

He stared back at me, dumbfounded, and said, "I lost two years of my life to that game. How do you know it?"

116

"I play it. A lot of us do in the states." That may have been a bit of an exaggeration, but I do know people who do play the addictive game of soccer management. I had recently read an article in an English magazine that compared this video game to heroin! It said that it has the same addictive qualities and pointed to a number of actual marriages it has destroyed.

"Who do you play?"

I answered him, "I have been playing the same game for almost a year now. My team is Plymouth."

"Plymouth!" he yelled out, "That is where I am originally from!"

"Well, I started out with Port Vale, but they fired me after I had taken them to the Premiership but then went right back down. That's when Plymouth hired me."

"Can you name any Plymouth players?" he asked.

"Wow, ummm, I can tell you that they now have Rui Costa, Carl Cort, and Brad Friedel."

"No, I mean real players. Come on, name me one Plymouth player."

I tried, but could not come up with any. I thought I had one, a young goalkeeper, but he did not know him.

As we were discussing this great video game, Denmark scored again! At the end of the day, France did hit the post twice and had a few other near misses. Barthez made one fantastic save, but they did not score. 2-0 and the Champions were out without scoring a goal. I shook my new friend's hand and wished him luck. "See you in the finals!" I said and somehow it did not sound ridiculous.

I left the stadium quickly, beating most of the crowd. Outside, the line for Korea tickets had grown very long during the match, but I broke through it and was soon on the crowded subway and heading back to Seoul where I knew I could find food.

I was sitting next to an old man who repeatedly folded and unfolded his game ticket. He folded it many times over until it was the size of a dime and when he could fold no longer, he carefully undid the folding before starting again. From the forlorn expression on his face, as well as the odd pairing of clothes, I guessed he was French.

He and I remained silent until about halfway back. Eventually he spoke, "Mozart." His accent combined with the fact that I was not expecting him to talk, caused me to miss the word.

"I'm sorry, what did you say?"

"Mozart." He was now strangely smiling and he pointed to a speaker that was playing some classical music. "If you want to be happy, listed to Mozart." These words struck me so that I made a mental note to buy some Mozart when I get home. I was sure that if my team had just been eliminated, there would be no music on earth that could make me smile, but his whole face had lit up and had joy written all over it.

"You cannot hear this and be unhappy," he continued, but I had to ask.

"You are French?"

"Yes."

"And you can smile after that game?"

"Those players were terrible, just no good. I cannot waste anymore time worrying about them. But Mozart . . ." his voice trailed off.

"I thought they would win again," I said, trying to steer the conversation back to soccer. I always try to pick the brains of foreigners. They know so much more about the game than we Americans. I can do all the reading and watching I want, but I can never replace those formative years. While I was hearing stories about Babe Ruth, Ted Williams, and Jim Brown, they were learning of the great soccer players of the past.

"They could have, but the coach. He does not want to win. Only to show he is the boss. He is stupid and lost for us. He does not pick the best players."

"Any of your players should be able to win, they are all so talented," I said.

"Yes, but some have no heart and they all want to be fancy. Just play simple. Like the midfielder from England, what is his name, he is the best."

"David Beckham," I told him.

He crunched is face as if he had eaten a lemon, "No, he is fluff. What is his name?"

I was taken aback with the Beckham comment and could not think at all. "Who does he play for?"

"Manchester, Scholes."

"Paul Scholes?" I asked, not believing what he was trying to say.

"Yes, Paul Scholes. He is so good. He keeps everything simple. If somebody is in front, he passes to the side. If somebody is here, he passes there. He never tries to do something he cannot do. Very simple. Beautiful. That is the way to play."

He asked me what stop I was getting off. I did not know how to pronounce it, so I told him it was two stops after the stop for Seoul Station. He said that was his stop as well. He was staying at the YMCA. I knew that to be nearby, but was not exactly sure where it was.

We continued talking about soccer, but, sooner than I wanted, our stop was upon us. I was enjoying talking to this gentleman. As we exited the car he said, "Come, I buy you a drink."

As hungry as I was, I took him up on it. Alcohol was the last thing I wanted, but even more I wanted to continue our conversation. We exited the station at a different exit than Jimmy and I used. He made a quick turn and we were off the main street and in one of those small, yet alive alleys, much like the one the *Dong-Il* is on.

"Where do you want to go?" he asked.

I saw a number of pubs, but had not been here before and was about to defer to him, when I noticed one was called the Mafia Bar. I had read earlier in the day that John Gotti had died. In a gesture to the former mob boss, I said, "Let's go in here, the Mafia Bar."

The Mafia Bar was a little darker than I would have liked, but it was empty and quite. From the menu, I ordered a Mafia beer; my French friend had a scotch.

My beer arrived with a lemon in it. It was light and refreshing and did not sicken my empty stomach. The waiter also brought the round, hollow chips and I dug into them as if I had not eaten all day.

Taking a sip of his scotch, he told me that he loved soccer, but it was music that was his true passion. He loved the opera, and I was surprised to hear that he never goes to soccer games in France, only the opera.

He told of a black American singer, I missed him say her name but think he was talking about Denyse Graves. He said he had heard her sing the French National Anthem on the day of their 200th birthday in 1989. He said he had never heard anything more beautiful, and he had fallen over crying.

I guess we Americans are not passionate about anything like that. Certainly any self-respecting male would never admit to crying, particularly over a song. However, hearing him tell this story, I had not the slightest thought of laughing. Rather, I felt sad, somewhat empty. Though we make fun of the French, I think that if we had that kind of passion about anything, our lives would be so much fuller.

For the next fifteen minutes or so, I sipped my beer and listened to him tell stories of old French television shows and musical acts. I really had no idea who or what he was talking about, but he constantly paused and asked if I had heard of them. I never was able to answer in the affirmative, yet he held my attention. His face was so alive as he recalled his memories. His passion warmed my heart.

As I finished my beer and he his scotch, I asked if I could buy another round, but he declined. He told me he had recently retired from Air France and as a going away gift, he had been given an around-the-world ticket. He was leaving in the morning for New Caledonia where he was going to spend a few weeks before returning to Paris to get on with his life.

He gave me his card and said if I was ever in Paris to give him a call. I saw his name was Bernard and it was with sadness that I shook his hand and bid him *au revoir*.

Upon leaving the bar, it took me a few minutes to figure out which way was home, but after a few wrong turns, I found my way and was shortly knocking on Jimmy's door.

The late games were beginning and we decided to watch them from the room. Ireland needed to win by two against a terrible Saudi Arabia team to advance. I was not only hoping that would happen, but that Cameroon would beat Germany and send them home.

Both games started off very well as Robbie Keane scored early for Ireland and Carsten Ramelow was sent off for Germany.

Ireland added two more after the break, but so did the ten man Germany, and it was those two who advanced, the latter as group winners.

119

At halftime, I heard that Senegal and Uruguay had tied 3-3, which had sent the African team through as group runners up to Denmark. This game had apparently been thrilling. Senegal opened a three-goal lead before Uruguay desperately came back, but were unable to get that extra goal that would have put them through.

With the day's matches over, I impressed upon Jimmy how important it was that I eat. He, gracious as always, told me to pick the place. I choose the closest restaurant to us. A chicken shack that has them rotisserie style in the window. They have a poster on the window advertising Ginseng Chicken Soup. I had actually read an article in the newspaper on this dish saying it was both healthy and delicious.

At 10:30, a bowl of this soup was placed in front of me. The bowl contained chicken on the bone, chestnuts, rice, and ginseng. They also gave us a bowl of salt. The first bite had no flavor so I added some salt, but it did not help and I added more. I ate nearly all of the still tasteless soup, and it did satisfy my hunger. It may have been healthy, though I doubt it with all the salt I added, but it was certainly not delicious.

I ended this very long day watching an episode of the first season of Survivor, the only one I had not watched all the way through, and fell asleep afterwards at 1:00.

Day 11
Wednesday, June 12

Argentina Crashes Out, Taxis Just Crash

For the first time in what seemed like forever, I got to sleep in. I rolled out of the small bed at 10:00 feeling refreshed. I was looking forward to a relatively lazy day, as we had no real plans. I showered and turned on the television. All of the morning show hosts and hostesses were wearing either the Korean jersey or the "Be the Reds" t-shirts. They had been doing this since we arrived. It was just a reminder of how World Cup crazy Korea is.

As I flipped the channel, I saw other shows that I would liken to *Today* or *Good Morning America*. Everyone was wearing the jersey. Other channels were showing repeats of the U.S.-Korea match. I think I have seen it in its entirety at least five times. A couple of the games from yesterday were also being repeated. I paused to watch the last few minutes of the Uruguay-Senegal match. Wow, was that a heart stopper! What a fantastic game that must have been great to see live. With so many channels showing games, this really is the place to be for a soccer fan. If you miss a game, you will have many chances to catch it later.

I continued channel surfing after the match and paused on a station that was hyping the Korea-Portugal match. It showed a lot of Portugal highlights, including many from the U.S. match. Though I could not understand the words, the message was clear: Korea will advance to the second round. This whole country is so confident. I fear they are showing their soccer naivety, thinking they will get a result against Portugal when Portugal need a win. I cannot imagine the letdown that is going to befall this land when Figo and company end their dream.

Two individuals were toasted above all others. The first is Ahn Jung-Hwan, who scored against us. He plays professionally in Italy, one of only two Koreans in Europe, and is a heartthrob to screaming Korean girls. The other is Guus Hiddink, the Dutch coach, who has transformed this team from a perennial whipping boy to that of a very dangerous squad.

Hiddink scrapped the tradition of seniority-based lineups and instilled a belief into the players that they can be world-beaters. Hiddink is one of the most popular men in Korea and his management methods detailed in a book, *The Hiddink Way,* are predicted to revolutionize the way business is done in this already economically strong nation.

The coach is so loved here that the *Korean Herald* did a piece yesterday detailing his movements during the game. It read, in part, "He gestured his discontent in the 21st minute when Landon Donovan made a threatening shot," and "Hiddink got carried away a little bit in the final minutes but resumed his calm when referee Urs Meier blew the final whistle." I also read that the one song they sing a lot

121

is not *Oh This is Korea* as I had thought, but rather *Pilseung Korea* which means "Victory Korea!"

The television show went to a segment that I found absolutely fascinating. The show sent cameras to homes, parks, and bars to record the reaction of the Koreans watching the U.S. match. I was enjoying watching their facial expressions when I was struck with the thought that I was not only watching them, but I was watching me. Not literally, but emotionally. When the game began, they had the same look of nervous anticipation that I had felt. When Mathis scored, they looked as if they had been shot, they could not believe what they had just seen. Of course, I had the exact opposite reaction, one of pure joy, but moments later, we were again going through the same trauma. A penalty had been called on Agoos. As the Korean advanced to take the kick, I realized that they held the same fears that I had. To their utter dismay, their fear was realized. Later, we again were at the far end of the spectrum as Ahn headed in the equalizer. It was now their time to celebrate. It was so eye opening watching them and realizing that although we had separate hopes for the match, at the end of the day we are only people supporting our team.

I went out and bought a calling card and tried to call Ivy. The phone would not accept it. There were four phones on the busy sidewalk, but none took the card. It was extremely frustrating. I had not spoken with Ivy for a few days and really wanted to talk to her. I went back to the convenience store where I had bought it. I pointed to the bank of phones. They did not speak English, but indicated to me that the card should work there. I returned to them, but again had no luck.

I felt terrible and started for home, but passed other phones. I put the card in every which way, including the way diagramed on it, nothing worked. I tried it in every phone, none worked. Finally, at wits end, I willed it to go through. I said aloud to the phone, "Accept this fucking card now!" Apparently, intimidation works on Korean phones, because moments later I was talking to my fiancée. She said she had been worried because she heard about riots in Japan and people had died. I had to tell her that the riots were in Moscow, because Russia had lost. Everything is safe here, I assured her.

Here is a reason I am so fortunate to be marrying Ivy. Should we ever be blessed with a son, she has agreed to my request to name him after a soccer player. We have debated a few names; I prefer Hristo Ryan or simply Ryan Giggs Gustafson. She is pushing to have Beckham in there somewhere as in Beckham Giggs or Ryan Beckham. When I mentioned the Korea game, she interrupted me shouting, "We are going to name our son Ryan Friedel Beckham Gustafson!" I am a lucky man.

Feeling much better after the call, I knocked on Jimmy's door and we headed out for the short walk to the PC Bang. We were there only minutes when Monty came in. He had a meeting at the U.S. Embassy. He asked us to wait for him before going to Itaewon, to watch the games later in the day.

While writing an e-mail, a funny thing happened that showed just how obsessed this place has become. I had just finished writing to my friends about the

Korean songs and cheers, *Tay-Han-Ming-Go*, *Korea Team Fighting*, and *Pilseung Korea*. I had told them how we hear them on the streets, in the stadiums, on television, in bars, and even on the subway. I had just moved onto a new subject when someone's cell phone rang. The tune it rang to was "Oh, *Pil-seung* Ko-Re-A! Oh, *Pil-seung* Ko-Re-A!" His damn cell phone was singing for the Korean team!

I was still writing e-mails when Monty returned. He was delighted that his passport would not be ready for another week. He had been scheduled to fly home the day after the Poland match. Now he had no choice but to stay through the second round game. "I am not sure my boss would have bought any other excuse! But there is no way I can get back on time," he was beaming, but then added, "Now that I am staying, we'll probably lose."

"Not a chance, man! We are going to party in the second round!" I encouraged him.

The three of us then went to a sub shop only a few doors down from the *Dong-Il*. Monty ordered Iced Coffee. I selected an Italian hoagie that had entirely too much mayonnaise on it. While eating, we decided to take a cab rather than the subway to Itaewon. It had started to rain, the first we had seen all trip, except for the light shower during the Korea match.

We hailed a cab and Monty got in the front, leaving Jimmy and I in the back. The driver tore out and made a right, taking us past the U.S. embassy, then a U-Turn and we headed back down the wide street, aiming to go past City Hall on the way to Itaewon where we would meet up with Big Dog.

We were flying down the busy road, when I saw a van up ahead that looked as if he was going to make a left turn. The problem was that he was to our right. The moment the van slowly crossed into our path, I knew we would hit it. The driver locked the brakes, but on the wet road, had no chance to stop in time. I put out my arm to brace myself. I realized that Jimmy had not been paying attention to the road when he suddenly emerged from his daydream and recognized our fate only moments before we slammed into the van.

"Oh Shit!" came his piercing, high-pitched scream. My ears were ringing from his cry when they heard the awful sound of metal on metal as we tagged the front left side of the van, just in front of the driver's door. It felt like we hit very hard.

When we stopped, I asked, "Are you guys alright?" They were, and I noticed Monty was not wearing a seatbelt. Maybe we did not hit as hard as I thought, he had braced himself with his arms, just as I had done.

Our driver shot out of his seat and began yelling at the driver of the van. Unsure of what to do, we stayed seated in the cab for about a minute. Our driver motioned us to get out as police were quick to arrive on the scene. He then hailed us another cab! I thanked him and gave him a few thousand *won* and said, "I'm sorry," before jumping into our new cab.

In Itaewon, we went into Gecko's. It was crowded and the only seats we could find were far from a television. However, the mostly English atmosphere was great and in any case, the view, bad as it was, was better than looking through a window, across an alley, and through another window, as I had done during the second half of England-Argentina.

England needed a draw against Nigeria who looked more than happy to earn a point before returning home. In the other game, Sweden only needed a draw whereas the Argies had to win.

The England game was pretty dull as both teams seemed to agree that 0-0 would do nicely. We could not see the other game and thought that with all the English here, they may not even be showing it. Therefore, at halftime, we went a few doors down to the Seoul Pub. There we found two large sets with no seats in front of them. I had no problem situating myself to get a great view of the Sweden match while still being able to keep and eye on England, just in case.

Standing next to me was a middle-aged man wearing a Turkey shirt. We began talking and he said that he and much of his family had immigrated to Australia. He even had a hint of that accent. I told him that I thought Costa Rica would get a point against Brazil the next day, which would eliminate his homeland. He said he was a little worried, but confident Brazil would come through for him. He also told me that he had a 14-year-old son who played for the top youth team in Sydney.

"So when the time comes to choose a country, will he play for Turkey or Australia?" I asked him.

"That will be his choice," he answered, somewhat surprisingly, I thought.

"Who would you have him play for, if he asked you?"

"I would love for him to play for Turkey, but I feel he will play for Australia," he answered.

As we were discussing the future Soccer-Roo, Sweden curled in a beautiful free kick. A number of others cheered along with me. Argentina could not get anything going and looked to be headed home, but then the match became exciting. The Argies pushed forward, needing two goals. Sweden countered, and Argentina attacked again. Just as it looked as if Sweden would hold them, the referee called a penalty. Replays showed Ariel Ortega had dived, as if that was news. Sweden's keeper, Magnus Hedman saved, but Hernan Crespo, who was so far in the box that he nearly passed the ball before it was shot, stuck in the rebound.

The South American's had life and threw everything into the attack. My ancestor's homeland held on for dear life and the final few minutes were as intense as sport can be. Then the whistle blew, ending the group of death. England, who finished 0-0, and Sweden had survived. England will play Denmark and the group winners will face Senegal. In the group of death, two powers had fallen, but it looked good for both advancing teams in the second round. However, it could have been a different story. Had France done what they should have and won their group, we would be looking at an England-France match in a few days.

After spending some two hours drinking beer in the smoky pubs, Monty and I headed out into the street for some fresh air, if that is what you call the stuff in Seoul, but not before I bought a Seoul Pub t-shirt for W10,000.

Monty and I walked the busy street, dodging other pedestrians and raindrops. Most Koreans were carrying umbrellas and seemed to have a different etiquette for this than we Americans do. This caused a lot of confusion and I was nearly poked in the eye many times. We passed the one end of the street where all the food vendors were and decided to grab something to eat. I wanted to hit the Afghan place for a kabob, but first Monty stopped at the Indian stand and ordered two orders of Curry Bread. It was cut into triangles and appeared to be bread dipped unto curry and then deep-fried. It smelled delicious. As we walked away, Monty offered me a bite. I dipped it into some green sauce that was supposed to be spicy.

While walking quickly away, I put the bread into my mouth. Within seconds I made a U-turn and bought myself some of this fabulous bread. The green sauce was indeed spicy, very spicy. I am sure this was not the healthiest meal I have eaten over here, but it may have been the tastiest.

After scarfing down the bread, we went into the large shopping center where I had bought Ivy the jade necklace the day before the Portugal match. It is not really a mall that we are familiar with. It is more like a large flea market. Not that the shops are temporary, but all the shops are in stalls, not their own stores.

I bought the chess set that I had looked at that first day. Again, they told me the price was W100,000, but I got it for W65,000. It is a beautiful set. The pieces are marble, one side painted blue, and the other brown. Rather than the traditional pieces, they are historical Korean figures. It will make a nice addition to my living room and is sure to be a conversation piece.

I also picked up a set of steel chopsticks, like those used in restaurants here. I got five sets not for the W10,000 price asked, but for W7,000. Ivy and I eat a lot of rice dishes as well as carryout sushi and these will be fun to use.

At 7:30, we met Jimmy and Big Dog at the Hamilton Hotel, where a lot of Irish fans were checking in. There were hundreds of green shirts around and those wearing them looked like they were up for a party. The promise of a night out with them made me sorry that we were catching the subway home.

Big Dog and Monty continued onto Suwon, as Jimmy and I changed trains at Seoul Station and were soon home, at the *Dong-Il*.

The two late games did not mean that much to me, and I wrote and channel surfed while they were on. At the end Spain beat South Africa 3-2, sending them home as Paraguay beat Slovenia 3-1. Thus Group B ended with Spain as winners going to Suwon to face Ireland in a game that made me regret not getting tickets for it. I had considered ordering tickets for this match, but was scared that if I spent $100 for them, I would be stuck seeing a game like Cameroon and Paraguay. Instead, the opposite happened and the match up was a dream match for me. Oh well, nothing I could do about it now. Paraguay ended up second and will face

Germany. That day, Paraguay will become one of my favorite teams. I guess it is the English fan in me that causes me to dislike the Germans so much.

I was about to turn off the television to go to sleep, but in my final tour of the channels, saw that Armed Forces Network was about to start one of the all-time greatest movies, *Patton*. I stayed up and watched most of it before falling asleep around 1:00, dreaming of the beautiful game that I would attend tomorrow, Brazil-Costa Rica.

Day 12
Thursday, June 13

There's Only One Pierce Brosnan

I woke up around 9:30 and watched more of the Korean team on television. The networks have climbed aboard this bandwagon and are riding it as far as it will take them, which I am sure, will be to a crushing defeat at the hands of Portugal tomorrow night.

Jimmy and I went to the PC bang to get some news before heading to Suwon for the Brazil-Costa Rica match. Along the way, we noticed many more vendors lining the sidewalks selling those "Be The Reds" t-shirts. I had thought that every Korean already owned one, but apparently not. I hope they are able to get rid of their inventory before the game tomorrow night.

At the PC Bang, I was disappointed to read that Roberto Carlos has a minor injury that will keep him from playing today. I am a big fan of his and was looking forward to seeing him. He scored the greatest goal I have ever seen. It was one of his legendary free kicks and happened at the *Tornoi du France*, which led up to the Cup in France in 1998. The ball had to have been placed some 30 yards from the goal. He took his usual long run up to the ball before hitting it with the outside of his left foot. The ball shot well to the right of the wall before making a sharp curve into the goal. The break was so dramatic that the French goalkeeper did not move as the ball soared within feet of him and photographers behind the goal ducked for safety. I was able to console myself in the knowledge that I would see Ronaldo and Rivaldo, among other great Brazilians.

After taking in all the news and sending e-mails back home, Jimmy and I went for some lunch. I took Jimmy to the place a few doors down where I had previously had the spicy soup. I had been craving it since first eating it days earlier. Just after we ordered it, an Irishman sat down behind us. It was apparent he was having trouble with the menu. I invited him to sit with us and he did so. Being that I was an expert in this restaurant because I had eaten here once before, I tried to help him.

I recommended the same spicy noodle soup that Jimmy and I were awaiting, but he said he just wanted something small for breakfast. He ordered a beef dish with rice. He told us a bunch of his friends had gone to Starbucks for breakfast, but as this was his first morning in Korea he wanted some authentic food.

He had been in Japan for the first round and was ecstatic Ireland had advanced, though he said he did not "fancy our chances against Spain." His dish was served at the same time as our soup and it was massive. The plate was larger that a normal plate and was overflowing with rice, beef, and vegetables. He was stunned, "I only wanted a light breakfast." Then he said, "Me mates have probably already finished." With that he began shoveling the food into his mouth, pausing only to say how good it was.

Jimmy said the same thing about his soup, though he was sweating and drinking a lot of water due to the spice. I enjoyed it this time, more than the first, perhaps because I did not splash the firewater in my eye. I was also much more comfortable using chopsticks in unison with the large spoon. What I did was first, grab some of the angel hair-like noodles with my chopsticks and suck them into my mouth. Then I would scoop up some broth with the spoon and slurp it in before going back to the chopsticks to grab a piece of shrimp or squid. The combination was delicious.

The Irishman quickly finished about a quarter of his plate before he said goodbye and ran out, hoping to catch his friends. Jimmy and I helped ourselves to his food and it was very good, but together, we hardly put a dent in it. We did finish off our soup, as well as the side of kim'chi, before we decided it was about time to leave for the train station in order to get to Suwon. There we were to meet up with Big Dog and Monty at the Sante Fe, the sight of the earlier debacle with the American fans.

The subway to Suwon was crowded, and we were forced to stand. I hoped that it would clear out and we could get a seat sometime before the hour-long ride was over. As usual, we were the only non-Koreans on the train and were greeted with the usual stares. Small children, in particular, seemed to be fascinated with us. They would often point at us while talking to their parents who answered them in hushed tones as if we could understand their mild scolding. Jimmy seemed to draw more stares than I. I hypothesized that it was because with his olive skin and dark hair, he is mistaken for a Middle Eastern terrorist. Perhaps the Koreans are on guard, making sure he does not try anything. In these dangerous times, the World Cup makes an inviting target and Jimmy is pretty much the closet thing I have seen to fitting a terrorist profile. Jimmy agreed with that, saying he has been mistaken for an Arab many times before.

As we neared Suwon, two women, one middle age, the other, probably in her late teens, were forced to stand next to us. They looked us over and give Jimmy an extra stare before the older one spoke.

"Are you going to the game?" she asked in accented, but clear English.

"Yes, we are," answered Jimmy.

"Where are you from?" the same lady asked.

"America," Jimmy answered. This is how most conversations with Koreans go.

They replied with the usual, "Oh, America!" And they nodded to one another. Generally the conversation ended shortly thereafter with them saying, "Nice to meet you." It is a routine that we have been through countless times on the streets and in restaurants, but this time it did not end as expected.

The older women introduced herself and her very cute young friend. She pronounced their name very quickly and I did not catch them. Then she told us that the young lady was a cheerleader in the ceremonies before the first match. At this point, the young one spoke for the first time, and although her English was not as good as the older one's, she said, "I danced and cheered."

When I told her she was famous, she got a puzzled look on her face, but the older one (was it her mother?) spoke to her in Korean and she giggled and blushed. She said, "No, no." And then something in Korean that made the older one laugh and nod in agreement.

"She wants to know if you are a model?" she asked Jimmy! I was stunned. A model? Jimmy? Ha!

I was in disbelief when the cute, young one said, "You look like Pierce Brosnan."

Jimmy looked at me, but all I could do was to blurt out, "Pierce Brosnan!" as Jimmy began to laugh. My mind raced as it seemed that this girl was flirting with Jimmy. Before things could go any farther, the train pulled into Suwon Station and as we exited, I heard the girl say, "Goodbye Pierce Brosnan!"

"You have to be kidding me, Pierce Brosnan?" I said, but Jimmy only shrugged.

It was hot outside and we worked up a sweat in the short walk from the station to the Santa Fe where the sign on the door still announced they served "Spainish Food." As we went up the stairs, I said to Jimmy "I hope it doesn't take 15 minutes to get a beer like the last time."

Big Dog and Monty were already there. In front of Big Dog was something that made me forget all about the beer. It was a milkshake! Served in a tall glass and topped with whipped cream and a cherry, it looked like something out of the 1950's.

"Is that good?" I asked the dumbest question of the day.

"Awesome," was The Dog's reply.

Unlike before the Portugal match, the Sante Fe was not crowded and the service was good. I ordered a vanilla shake and soon enough found out that it was indeed, "awesome."

As I enjoyed the shake, I told them about Pierce Brosnan. Monty and Big Dog delighted in teasing Jimmy about it.

"Did you get the digits?" Monty asked, referring to her phone number. Monty had taken some heat from us earlier because he bragged that he would get a girl's digits and go on a date while over here. Up until now, he had been unsuccessful.

We left the Sante Fe rather quickly because our two friends did not have tickets for the game and wanted to get to the stadium early to try to scalp them. The line for the shuttle bus was near and as we headed to it, I saw Andy Mead and Wade ahead of us, also walking toward the back of the line. Andy Mead publishes a soccer magazine, The Emerald City Gazette. He and Wade were averaging attending a match a day for nearly four weeks, leaving me with nothing to do but applaud their efforts.

As we were walking past everyone in line we saw Andy and Wade duck into the line, nowhere near the end of it! When we approached them, I yelled out "Line cutters!" And pointed to them, certain nobody else in line knew what I was talking about. We shook their hands before noticing who they had cut in behind. It was Lamar Hunt, the owner of the Kansas City Chiefs and Wizards (the MLS team that both Andy and Wade support). This man has done so much for soccer in America that the U.S. Open Cup bears his name. He was dressed in a dark gray suit and seemed to be alone.

I thought it odd that one of the richest men in America was waiting in line for a shuttle bus to a soccer game, but there he was. We all shook his hand and I managed to snap a picture of him posing with my three friends. I thanked him and we continued to the back of the line.

At the stadium, tickets were much harder to come by and after awhile, Jimmy and I went on our way, leaving Monty and Big Dog to search for the elusive ticket. As we neared our gate, I saw the first bit of violence at a stadium. A group of Turks had a handful of tickets for sale and there was a crush to get to them. Jimmy and I watched as people, nearly all foreigners as in non-Korean, pushed and shoved in attempt to buy these tickets. In a matter of minutes they had all been sold. A happy few ran off, clutching the precious paper while others dejectedly sulked off. Violence is a harsh word for the incident and no one was hurt. The fact that I used that word is a testament to the peaceful nature of the matches here.

The magical Brazilians had attracted a huge crowd and were proving to be the team everyone wanted to see. I was glad I had a ticket but feared that my friends may not get one. It was nearing game time so Jimmy and I headed into the stadium where ten days earlier we had shocked the world by beating Portugal. Our seats were similar to the ones we had that great night. We were in the same end zone, but were to the left of the goal. We were also, about ten rows higher than our 2nd row seats for the Portugal match.

The sun was out in force as were the legendary Brazilian women. Nearly as famous as their team, these lovely supporters wear nothing more than a green and yellow bikini. The more modest of them attach a mini-skirt. Jimmy and I were happy to see two of them only two rows above us. The Costa Ricans were occupying the same sections we had against Portugal. In our section, there was a wide variety of people, but more than a few Brazilians.

This was true Latin soccer, and the stadium was filled with the sound of drums. When the game began, I could almost sense what I had heard but never really believed, the Brazilians were playing to the beat of the drums!

The Ticos needed a tie to advance. They came out running, in their red shirts and blue shorts, with the knowledge that their region, CONCACAF, had yet to lose in this Cup. The U.S., Mexico, and Costa Rica sported an outstanding record of 4-0-2. Surely they believed, as did I, that they could hold the Brazilians to a draw. Perhaps had they played an ugly game of defensive soccer, had they clogged their defensive zone with players, they could have done so.

Unfortunately for them, ugly soccer is not their style and they tried to run with the masters. It was fun, and it was exciting, and it was over after the 13th minute. By that time, Ronaldo had scored twice. Costa Rica had a number of good chances, but missed them and in the 38th minute, Brazilian defender Edmilson scored what could possibly be the goal of the tournament. It happened at the far end, away from us. There had been some fancy play between the Brazilians and was finished with a spectacular overhead, scissors kick that brought an already appreciative crowd to it's feet.

While we were talking about the goal, the lanky one, Paulo Wanchope finally finished one for the Ticos to give them a glimmer of hope heading into the half.

The second half picked up where the first had left off. Both teams were out for goals. Costa Rica because they were desperate and needed two to advance. Brazil, because they are Brazil and that is how they play. This game reminded me of when teams tried to run with Magic Johnson's Lakers. The Lakers knew they would win, reveled in playing their style, and enjoyed every second of the up tempo play. Brazil may not have a Magic, but they do have Ronaldo and Rivaldo as well a cast of other entertaining players. Seeing Ronaldo in person was more of a treat than I had imagined. When the ball is at his feet, anything can happen. He looked like a running back, the way his hips swiveled, turning defenders this way and that. I told Jimmy that he looked like Walter Payton on crack.

About ten minutes into the second half, things got interesting as Ronald Gomez headed into the goal at the far end and the Ticos only needed one goal to tie. However, Brazil never panicked and six minutes later, Ronaldo fed Rivaldo who finished in front of us. Two minutes later Junior added to the total and the crowd was delirious. We had all hoped to see a show, but I do not think anyone envisioned seven goals. Even the Costa Rica fans seemed appreciative. The game ended that way, and as expected, we heard that Turkey had beaten China and will advance as group runner up to the Beautiful Brazilians.

Costa Rica went out on point differential, but showed well and I think gained some respect for our region. After Brazil had beaten Turkey on my first night in Korea, and Rivaldo had taken that ridiculous dive, I turned against them. Having seen them live, I am now with the rest of the world, in awe of their skill and in love with their play. I am once again a fan of Brazil. As for the two R's, Ronaldo and Rivaldo, they have each scored in all three games in the first round. I am very happy for Ronaldo who had played so little in the four years since his collapse in the finals in 1998. He is back, healthy, and having fun. It has been wonderful to see such a talent regain his form.

On the way out of the stadium, we bumped into Doug and Tonya and they wanted to get food with us so we decided to revisit the Pizza Hut that we had eaten in after the Portugal match.

We walked around the stadium and were across the eight-lane street from the shuttle buses, but when we tried to cross, the crossing guards waved us back and motioned for us to walk way down to the next block before crossing, which would force us to walk all the way back to get on the bus. As soon as they turned around, I looked at Tonya and Doug. They nodded and we took off, with Jimmy right behind us. This road was very wide, maybe 100 feet across and when we were about half way across, the guards turned back around and tried to tell us to stop. There was no way we were going to turn back, but I glanced over my shoulders and saw hundreds of others following our lead! When we reached the safety of the other side, we were all laughing, and Tonya said she felt like the Pied Piper.

The four of us did eat pizza and Jimmy and I returned to Seoul in time to catch the late games. I was really looking forward to Mexico-Italy and was hoping that Italy would lose. In the other match it was Ecuador-Croatia. Croatia was tied with Italy with three points and I was hoping they would get a better result than the Italians. Should the U.S. advance, we would play a team from this group. I was hoping it would be the Mexicans and was really hoping it would not be the Italians.

Italy figured Croatia would beat Ecuador and were thus desperate to win. However, Mexico was out to win the group and scored first on a fantastic header by their excellent forward Jared Borgetti. I cheered for Mexico, but only because they were from our region and I want more respect, which may translate to more births in future Cups. Amazingly, in the other match, Ecuador led Croatia 1-0.

If the results held that way, Italy would advance, but should Croatia have scored and tied, it would be bye-bye Azzuri. Knowing this, Italian coach Giovanni Trappatoni substituted in the once golden boy but now out of favor, Alessandro del Piero who got his head to a cross in the 85th minute and nudged the ball into the net. Italy went wild! This was a team that seemed to feel the pressure more than any other. Or at least they show that they feel it. They are so passionate about soccer that it is as if their nation will not survive if they do not advance. The coach always looks as if he is knocking on death's door and the players pout and cry every call that goes against them.

Shortly after the equalizer, the Croatia game was a final, 1-0. Should this game remain the same, both teams would advance. Both Mexico and Italy obviously had word of this as the final few minutes saw Italian defenders pass the ball back and forth while Mexico stood and watched. Finally even the referee tired of this and ended the game. Mexico are first and will play the 2nd place team from our group. Italy are 2nd and play our groups winner, which if we beat Poland as expected, will probably be us.

I ran out to the PC Bang and sent out an e-mail to my friends back home. Part of it read:

Well, should the US get through, we get Italy if we win the group and Mexico if we are 2nd! What kind of rotten luck is that? I think that if we played Mexico, not only would we have a good chance of advancing, but also the build up would be incredible. Tons of press for you back home. Our bitter rivals and us vying for a spot in the quarterfinals. That would be some event.

The rest of the night, I watched a repeat of the Brazil match and then caught *Survivor*, the original one, and fell asleep around 2:00 with visions of U.S.-Italy in my head.

Day 13
Friday, June 14

Street Party, Korean Style

This day started as most have here in the *Dong-Il*, with me slowly getting out of bed while watching Korean television. They were whipping themselves into a frenzy over tonight's game against Portugal and their dream of the second round.

For obvious reasons, I had not paid much attention to that match, other than being quite sure the Korean spirit would be shattered. No, I was completely focused on the U.S. game. Poland had not looked good at all in their first two matches. Coming into this Cup, all I had hoped for was to need a victory in this match to advance. The reality was much brighter; we needed only a draw.

Jimmy and I caught the 10:00 train to Daejeon, oblivious to the Koreans on the streets in their red shirts. Half an hour after leaving Seoul, we pulled into Suwon Station. This quick and easy trip had me wondering why I had not paid the extra 2,000 *won* for a train ride, as opposed to the hour-long subway ride, that I had taken twice.

In Suwon, Big Dog and Monty joined us and within minutes of pulling out, Monty and I made our way to the bar car. We both ordered the Curry Rice and a beer. We had wanted the curry on other trips, but had not been hungry. Now was our chance.

We ate the tasty, if unspectacular, curry while watching the countryside pass by and soon our conversation turned to the match. We were both confident, yet nervous. I tried not to look ahead to the second round, reminding myself that we were playing an established European team that had nothing to lose. Poland had certainly disappointed it's fans, but I did not think they would roll over, as some had suggested.

"No matter how humiliating the Cup has been for them, losing to the U.S. will at least double it," Monty said, agreeing with me that Poland still had a lot to play for. "Nobody wants to go home with no points. I'm sure they think they're better than us."

"Yeah, and in beating us they will avoid disaster. Plus, they would go home on a high note. But I do think we'll win. We are playing with such confidence right now," I said, before altering the subject. "Here is a bad omen, though. Consider this, in 1994, I thought we would go 1-1-1. Which we did. But, none of the games turned out the way I predicted. I thought we would beat Switzerland and we tied them. I thought we would lose to Columbia, we beat them. And I thought we'd draw with Romania, who beat us.

"In this Cup, I again thought we would end up 1-1-1. I thought Portugal would beat us, but we beat them, just like Columbia. I thought we'd beat Korea, but we tied, just like Switzerland. And I thought we tie Poland . . ." I stopped without saying where that train of thought led.

Monty was quiet for a while, contemplating the nightmare of a theory. Finally, he took a long pull on Hite beer, and said, "That's crazy. We're going to beat them."

"I hope so," I said, "Or even tie, that's all I care about." Perhaps my story scared me or maybe it was the early beer that did it, but as I stared out the window at the large, green mountains, I was not as confident as I had been minutes earlier. I sensed Monty was apprehensive as well.

I had somehow succeeded in bumming us out, so I changed the subject. "Have you seen Scott and Neil?" I asked. Back in the States, I had made reservations for the six of us to stay at a hotel called the Hole In One. It was strange, making reservations for four people I had never met, particularly considering that I only reserved two rooms. But things had worked out well, and I enjoyed being around all of them.

"They are on the next train, 15 minutes behind us. They want us to wait at the train station for them. Then we can all go to the hotel."

"That's cool. Their train is only 15 minutes behind us?" I asked. I wanted to make sure, because I did not want to spend hours at the train station, but 15 minutes would be no problem.

"Yeah. I don't know why they run them like that, but that's what's going on," Monty assured me.

We spent about an hour in the bar car before returning to our seats for the last half hour. Big Dog had finished the book The Game of Their Lives and Jimmy had started reading it. The Dog told me about meeting Scott and Neil in the train station, and soon enough, we were there.

The Daejeon train station had computers in it, though it was not a PC Bang. They were on long tables that were set up in the main building, where passengers were busy buying tickets and carrying luggage. In this environment, the computers were relatively smoke free, however, they were much more expensive than a PC Bang and required coins be dropped into them, like a video game.

We all sat down and deposited W1,000 for the ten minutes it was to buy us, only my computer did not work. It took my money, but the screen remained frozen, and I was reduced to reading USA Today and Big Soccer over Big Dog's large shoulder. I then walked around the station until I saw Leo and Brent of the NY Crew. We greeted each other and I mentioned that this was the first time I had ever seen them before I had heard them.

They laughed and said they were saving up for the game. "Do you have any songs for Poland?" I asked, sure that they had come up with a witty ditty for the important match.

They looked at one another, nodded, and began singing to the tune of the Village People's YMCA:

Poland! You're attacked from the east.

Poland! You're attacked from the west.
Poland! You are Europe's crossroads.
Eee-ven Mon-gols took you . . .Poland!

I was cracking up and had to ask them a few times to make sure I had all the words down pat. I thought it was a great song, but wondered where they had come up with Mongols taking Poland. Did they? I was a history major and know that they had reached the gates of Vienna before the Pope interceded and turned them back, but I did not think they were as far north as Poland. Well, in any case, it just makes the song funnier.

As I was contemplating the near fall of Western Civilization, I noticed a group of people coming down the stairs that led from the tracks. In the middle of the group, I easily noticed Neil, with his bleach blond hair and ever-present visor. As they neared me, I also saw his brother, Scott who preferred to cover his head with a star spangled bandana.

We collected Jimmy, Big Dog, and Monty and went out to find the Hole in One. The information booth advised us to get a cab and told us they would know where it was. Thus, we split into groups of three and caught two cabs that were waiting in the heat outside.

Big Dog and the two brothers got into the first one, leaving Jimmy, Monty, and I in the second. I told the driver to follow them and that we were going to the Hole in One Hotel. He nodded and I was confident that we would soon be checking in. However, moments later, the first driver got out and came back, speaking to our driver. We three Yanks looked at one another, trying to figure out what they were saying, but it became apparent that our driver told him to "follow us."

The first driver returned to his cab and once we were into the street, he pulled over and we sped past him. We drove about a mile or so and then made a decisive right. It was hot and stuffy in the cab, but I was sure we would not be in there much longer.

My hopes dimmed a bit as we made a U-turn, and then another. Each time we turned around, we passed by the other cab and saw that the other three were suffering in the heat as much as we were. We drove around for a few minutes. It was obvious from the look on our drivers face that he had no idea where we were going. His head was swiveling on his neck like Ronaldo's hips. Eventually, he pulled to the side of the road and made a call on his cell phone. The other cab pulled in behind us and the driver approached. They spoke and the other driver returned to his cab and pulled out ahead of us.

I was hoping that he had made a call and knew where we were going, but after he led us in a few circles, our driver passed him. The leather seats were flowing with sweat as I was drained of the nice, small buzz I had from the beer on the train. It was beyond miserable. However, as I was pulling my wet Sam's Army shirt to prevent it from sticking to me, we pulled up to a hotel and the driver announced, "Hole in One."

"About as elusive as a real one," Monty observed. We paid the driver W4,500, just over $3.50, and grabbed our bags from the trunk.

The three from the other cab fell out as they came to a stop and Neil remarked that "addresses rule and no addresses suck ass." This was as good an observation as I had heard regarding the pre-medieval address situation here. We all agreed and each expressed wonderment on how such a modern society did not have addresses.

At least the hotel had the reservation, and we were soon into the rooms. I had decided to go with a traditional Korean room, called an *ondol*, as this was for only one night, thus the room had no beds, just mats for sleeping. This ended up working well as we were three to a room, I being with Monty and Scott. We took a little while to refresh before heading out to find the other Americans.

Through the Yanks in Korea group we were informed that our gathering place would be the NASA bar. Some Americans had come in a few days early and scouted the area for an adequate place to prepare for the match and celebrate afterwards. Once again, we piled into two steamy cabs and told the driver, "NASA bar." He nodded confidently and we were off.

We drove for close to a half hour, driving for a long time aside a river and past an amusement park. How I would have loved to feel the air rushing by me as those on the roller coaster, but I had to make do with the nearly out of service air conditioner. We were hot and getting testy when the driver pulled to the side of the road and pointed to a sign on top of a six story building that read in big red letters, "NASA." I could almost taste the beer and was in such a hurry for one, that I did not mind paying what had been, by far, the largest cab fare of our trip of W12,500.

The six of us just about ran to the building. Upon entering, we saw that the bar was not on the first floor, which was nothing new. We made our way to the second floor, but there was nothing there but an abandoned office. We found the same thing on the third, fourth, and fifth floors.

"It's crazy to have this bar at the top of this deserted building," Big Dog panted out. The steps were particularly tough on the big guy.

"Don't worry, man. You won't have to move for at least five hours," Scott tried to comfort him. I was giddy as I took the last flight two steps at a time.

We were devastated, when we reached the top floor to find nothing there. Profanities were hurled out of all of our mouths, except for Jimmy who is just too nice a guy to ever curse, other then during car wrecks, but then again, he does not drink, so what would he have had to be upset about?

It was a sad group that made our way down those six flights of stairs. I suspected the cabbie may have been in some trouble had he still been there, but he was gone. It looked to us like we were on the outskirts of town and we wondered if we would find any more cabs. I thought I saw a restaurant across the street where we could at least get a drink, but, like the building, it was deserted.

We thought our luck had changed when a carload of Korean girls pulled up. A few jumped out and came up to us, obviously drawn to our red, white, and blue colors and flags and not to our humor of the moment. Monty took the lead in talking to them and one of them pulled out a cell phone saying she was going to call more friends to take us to the real NASA. Unfortunately, that idea fell through, for what reason I was never clear. As they drove off, four good-looking American girls along with two guys walked up. I thought that this was amazing because there were virtually no people at all in this area.

Our mood improved as we greeted them. "Are you looking for the NASA Bar, too?" Monty asked. We had assumed they were soccer fans.

"No," one of the lovely ladies answered. Monty then explained our situation and the girls were genuinely sad for us. They said that they lived in Daejeon and they would love for us to go with them. A few of us may have been tempted to follow these ladies to wherever they were going, but we did what millions of our gender were doing all over the globe this month, and put soccer over spending time with the fairer sex.

Our decision proved to be the correct one when we found out that we were talking to a group of missionaries who were on their way to church! Now, as I said before, I am a Christian and would never put soccer above God, however, this was not the time for church. It was time to find the NASA Bar. Monty tried to convince the ladies to come with us, but they were not about to be corrupted by any of us. Before they left, they preformed a good deed that should earn then gold stars in St. Peter's book. One of the guys called us two cabs and when they shortly arrived, told them where we were going, even giving him directions! We thanked them profusely and were off.

This time I was with Jimmy and Neil. We had not gone far when the two cabs became separated. I was not worried because both cabbies had been instructed on where to take us. After another long, hot ride, we were dropped off in a bustling part of the city. After paying him, again 12,500, I looked around, but did not see anything about NASA. Nor did I see the other cab. The three of us decided to wait for the others. We had driven on a busy highway and were sure the other cab would be taking the same route.

After some five minutes, Neil started to worry about finding his brother. I walked around the block, but did not see anyone from the other cab. I did, however, encounter two other Americans who, to my relief, told me that the NASA was only a block away. Secure in the knowledge that we were very near our destination, I returned to the corner where Jimmy and Neil were still waiting. As we stood there, in the heat, but mercifully in the shade, I saw two people approaching. The first was a pretty young blond. She was holding hands with a tall, well built young man with a tight crew cut wearing a Poland jersey. When they passed us, I tried to make eye contact, to give the guy a nod, but he stared straight ahead with a look of hate on his face. I had heard stories that Poland has some pretty rough hooligans and from this encounter I began to think that some of them had made the trip. I wondered if he might have started something if he had not been with his girl or if there had not been three of us. I may have read him wrong, how many hooligans travel with their girlfriends, but do not think so. The look on his face communicated that if circumstances had different, he was ready for a fight.

I did not dwell on him long and walked off again, down the road where the cab should approach. At the end of a long block, I saw our colors and sure enough, it was my three lost friends. They were looking quite ragged and were cursing the driver, who had pulled off. I told them we were close to the NASA and this quickened their pace. We picked up Jimmy and Neil and went off towards the bar.

Minutes later we went up the single flight of stairs and entered the cool, air conditioned, and spacious NASA. Despite our difficulty in finding it, we were among the first to arrive. We collapsed onto two sofas set up in a sort of booth, with a table between them. We ordered two pitchers of beer that when delivered were smoking! The pitcher had a chute that contained dry ice. It was a mouth-watering sight, steaming, ice-cold beer. Those of us who drink the stuff took turns kissing the pitcher like it was the Cup. In truth, we were probably as happy to have this glorious, refreshing beverage, as the eventual winners will be to kiss the precious and elusive Cup.

Mark, from D.C, joined us at the table. He was with his group, but as we sat down, Vladimir had found out that they were only showing the Japan game, so he and his other friends set off to find another bar so he could watch Russia, who only needed a draw to advance. Andy Mead also sat with us after Big Dog left us to sit with some other friends. The waitress appeared with menus that were in English. We were all hungry, and after Mark and I talked it over and ordered octopus fried rice, all the others did the same! I was somewhat concerned to see what they would bring us, but Mark was confident that it would be good. I was surprised that everyone else followed our lead, but we proved we were an adventurous lot.

After the waitress took our order to the kitchen, a cook came out and tried to discourage us, saying that our order was "very hot, very spicy." However, we were having none of it, and we all said that was the way we liked it. He was surprised that we wanted spicy food.

We were really guzzling the beer when the Japan-Tunisia game came on the very large screen. We continued drinking as the dull game unfolded. Finally our meal arrived. White rice covered with a red sauce that had bite-sized pieces of tentacles in it. I was hungry and dug right in. It was spicy, but not terribly hot, and it was very good. As expected, the octopus was chewy, similar to calamari or even clams. We all enjoyed the dish, though not everyone ate the side dish of *kim' chi*. If you are able to get over the fact you are eating octopus, this is an outstanding meal and cost only W4,500, or about $3.60; less than a Value Meal!

While we were eating, Mike came in and pulled up a seat, took one look at our food and ordered the same thing! On the opposite side of the coin, Big Dog informed us that we were nasty and he hoped we would all have to spend hours in the bathroom.

The NASA was filling up and people began singing, and when the NY Crew showed up, the place really came alive. We did the requisite, *America the Beautiful* as well as some soccer songs. They also led us in a verse of, "Won't you take me to, the second rou'ound! Won't you take me to, the second round!" This really pumped us up as we realized we were only hours away from the big match and what was sure to be a glorious victory.

We drank and sang. Jimmy left the table when he saw Amanda come in and found a quite table with her as we serenaded him with, "One Pierce Brosnan! There's only one Pierce Brosnan! One Pierce Brosnan! There's only one Pierce Brosnan." Jimmy, as always, played along and mimed conducting us, while Amanda grinned as if she knew what we were singing about.

Amidst our revelry, I saw Vladimir coming back in. He had a very sad look on his face. Japan had beaten Tunisia, 2-0 to win the group, but Russia had lost 3-2 to Belgium, who had needed the win to advance. I sensed there was more rioting in Moscow at the moment.

"Sorry, Vlad. At least we can go through for you," I said in an effort to console him.

"Yeah, hopefully," he answered in a depressed voice. I poured him a beer and he brightened for a moment. Soon, the group I was with decided to go catch the shuttle bus. It was still early, but I did not want to leave anything up to chance. This was such a huge game, I would have been pissed if I missed even a second of it. A group of about 12 of us set out. We had not gone far, when someone suggested we were too quiet. They were right and Monty led us in song.

He began with, "Everywhere we go-oh!" Which we repeated. "People want to know-oh!" He continued, and we repeated again. "Who we ar-are." Echo. "So we tell them." Repeat. "We are the US!" Which we shouted out. "The mighty, mighty US!" We were all singing with gusto and attracting a lot of attention on the street.

We did the funny Clint Mathis song, "Show us your Clint, show us your Clint, show us, show us, show us your Clint!" And we even did the YMCA Poland song. Many of the Koreans on the street applauded us as we passed by, while others simply stared.

We continued singing, "Super Power, Super Power, U!S!A!" And then, "Won't you take me to . . .the se-cond rou-ound! Won't you take me to . . .the sec-cond round!"

It was about ten blocks to the train station, where we met a long line waiting on the buses. Many in the line heard us coming blocks away and cheered as we joined the line. After waiting a few minutes, I saw Mike running up to us. I wondered where he had been, because he and been singing with us on the walk. He reached into the bag he was carrying and gave Monty and I a beer. Then one to Andy Mead.

"Where did you get those?" Andy asked.

"In the station," Mike answered. I never would have thought to look in a train station for beer, but was sure glad Mike had. They were OB's and tall ones at that. He had at least a 12 pack with him. When I started drinking mine, I realized that this was the first game of the Cup that I had drunk for. At the others, I had had one beer at the most. Tonight, I was feeling very good.

We were all feeling very good for that matter, and our merriment continued as we boarded a bus. We were among the first aboard, and I led us straight to the long, back seat. As we went down the aisle, we broke into song, "Back of the bus, back of the bus, back of, back of, back of the Bus!" There were five seats in the back and were quickly occupied by Mike, Andy Mead, Monty, Big Dog, and myself. There we were transformed into typical backseat school kids. Scott and Neal sat nearby, but Jimmy and Amanda kept their distance, which was good, as we made a few off color jokes.

The entire trip was spent with us either singing or trying to get those in the front to sing with us. We were all having a great time and had obviously already begun celebrating the second round. The numerous beers and other fans had done away with the fears I had earlier in the day. A loss, at this point, was out of the question.

We quickly entered the stadium. It was a great place to see a game; there was virtually no room on the sidelines. Jimmy and my seats were on the fourth row, behind and just to the right of the goal. They were as good, if not better, as those we had in Suwon for the Portugal match were. However, as other Yanks filtered into the stadium, most were seated, standing would be a better word, in the next section over, a bit further to the right of the goal. Around us, were a few Americans, but also a lot of others. Without speaking, Jimmy and I left our prime seats, to stand with the rest of our crowd.

The section filled up quickly and we sang and continued drinking. We did not even need the game; we were having so much fun. On the sidelines to our right, there was a large Polish section and they, too, were in full song. The anthems came and went and the game was about to start. I had finished my beer a few minutes earlier and, not wanting to miss kickoff, decided not to go to the stand for more. Just then, Mike squeezed in next to me holding two beers. He handed me one and said something about singing while in line for them. I could tell he was loaded and realized that I was too. Then he gave me the other beer.

"I had a great time in line, I'm going back!" he told me with a huge grin. Before I could say anything, he was gone. Moments later the game began. A big cheer went up, and as I looked around, I noticed the stadium was nearly filled. I remember I heard someone mention that no Koreans would come because they were all staying home to watch their match. I had heard a rumor that they had considered showing that match on the scoreboard. While I would have liked that, I knew that it could not be done.

I was holding two beers and trying to drink one of them. Though I was really feeling good, I noticed that Poland's starting goalie, Jerzy Dudek was not in the lineup.

***

We attack right away, sending notice that we are not out to hold for a nil-nil draw. Poland comes down and Jeff Agoos concedes a corner. The corner is served and the ball is in the net.

"Shit!" people around me scream. It was sudden and after a moment to recover, I yell out, "That's alright. You'll get it back! Come on Boys!"

We kick off, and in a flash, at the far end, there is confusion, then the ball is in their net and Landon Donovan is celebrating. Our section goes nuts! Yes! We can score! We can and will run with them! Their goal was a fluke and we set things straight right away! I think that we are going to be all right. But my happy thoughts and cheers are interrupted by more profanity. I look up and see our boys arguing with the referee. He is disallowing the goal! Nobody seems to know why. There is no replay screen that we can see, so we are all in the dark. "The Chinese referee is going to screw us and help Korea!" I hear someone yell. In my state, that thought makes sense, and I am disheartened.

However, before I can contemplate this, Poland advances on our goal. A cross comes in from right in front of us and before I know what was happening, they score again. I am suddenly very sober. The chain of events is astounding. I was happily singing with the others, then Poland scored, but we answered and before we had time to truly celebrate, it had been disallowed. While the confusion spread and we tried to make sense of it all, Poland had scored again. Everything happened so fast. We are stunned, dumbfounded, and silent. It is crashing down around us.

I am unable to even shout support. It takes us a few moments to rally but then we begin to chant, "U!S!A! U!S!A!" We are back, pleading our boys to answer. As the minutes go by, we become desperate, but reality is settling in. We need to score two goals or hope for a miracle in Incheon. The game is being played right in front of me, but my mind is racing. I curse the stadium for not allowing me to see the replays. I curse this referee who looks more and more like he is against us. I curse our fate. How can this happen?

The Korean fans are cheering for Korea, *"Tey-Han-Ming-Go*!" Some of us join them. Then someone yells that Korea has scored! Can it be? Can Korea save us by beating Portugal? I am encouraged with the goal, but think Portugal will come back. Surely they are aware of our situation and they know that they only need a draw. No, our situation is dire. I am cheering for our boys, but am wondering how we can exploit the slow Polish defense when they have fallen back to protect a two goal lead.

We have chances, but nothing is coming from them, although a few are very near, including a Mathis drive and a McBride header. However, their second choice keeper is on his game and it does not look like our night. Suddenly a huge cheer goes up in the crowd. Word quickly travels that one of the Portuguese has been red carded! Is this possible? Korea is a goal and a man up? Now it seems possible. I try to confirm both, but nobody around me knows for sure. "Come on Korea!" I scream.

Most of the action is at the far end, but in front of us, the Poles come forward enough to keep our defenders Tony Sanneh and Frankie Hejduk honest and to draw a pair of amazing saves from our great keeper. After one of their attacks, Agoos is subbed out, bringing on Beasley. I am not sure if it is an offensive move to add an attacker or if Agoos is injured. A few in our section curse Agoos and are blaming him for the Polish goals, though from where I sit I have no idea who is at fault. In any case, I feel badly for Goose. Should it end this way, his much-anticipated World Cup has been a nightmare. The own goal against Portugal. The penalty against Korea, and then being beaten on their goal. Then whatever happened here, ending in a first half substitution. This is what he will be remembered for, rather than his otherwise solid play.

I have mentioned before that I am a big fan of his and really hope it will not end this way for him, but even more, I hope it will not end this way for us. I hope that Beasley will cause the Poles the same trouble he had the Portuguese. The Poles, though, are packing their zone, and we are taking a lot of shots from the outside, desperation shots.

We continue singing, but I do not think our hearts are in it. I know I feel sick. I am hoping halftime will come quickly and we can regroup. Finally the referee signals the end of the half. "Come on boys!" I yell, over and over until the last of our players is off the field. "Come on boys!"

At halftime, I walk among our supporters. Those who had sung so joyously less than an hour ago now ware long faces. I try to find someone who can confirm the Korea score. Eventually I come upon someone on the concourse who has a radio. He is not American, but speaks English. "What is the score?" I ask.

"No score, no goals," is his devastating answer. My heart sinks. I am barely able to ask if Portugal is down to ten men. "Yes, a red card to Portugal." This does little to encourage me, as I am bemoaning the loss of the perceived goal.

Back in the stands, word has gotten around that it is 0-0 in Incheon. The mood is gloomy. Some are despondent while others are trying to rally us. The second half begins, and I hope we will come out strong and get a quick goal. However, Poland attacks right away and the action goes back and forth. The Poles are chanting "*Polska! Polska!*" They are in obvious good humor.

There is exciting play on both ends, but I do not have the feeling that we are close. One goal will be difficult enough, much less the two that we need. The Poles are all professionals in Europe. They know how to hold a lead. This may be a part of the game we have yet to grasp. We killed the final minutes off nicely against Portugal, but we may have attacked too much. "Why am I questioning us now?" I wonder. "Why is this causing me to second-guess strategy in other matches?" I think back to 1994 when, in the third match against Romania, we only needed a draw to be assured of advancement, but lost 1-0. I remember John Harkes saying something to the effect of our mentality was wrong, that we should have packed it in and etched out a 0-0 draw. Should we have done that tonight? I hate to second-guess Arena, but when England only needed a draw the other day, they sat back and got their point. It had been boring and ugly, but they were through.

Just before the hour, Joe-Max Moore comes in for Brian McBride who is obviously spent. This is another blow. I do like Moore, but McBride is our anchor up front. He is so valuable, winning headers with his height and bravery. I feel it is out of our reach. We are attacking, but our shots are blocked. It is like shooting in a forest; there is no opening leading to the goal. Other times, we just miss on the final pass. A corner is barely missed by flying heads. Other balls are just out of the reach of our would be shooter.

We sing the *Immigrant Song* to the beat of the drum and sing "Ole, Ole, Ole-Ole-Ole-Ole, Ole-Ole!" Trying to inspire our boys, trying to will them to a goal. Then there is a cheer and word circulates that Portugal have lost another player! It is 11 on nine! At first I do not believe it, but I see Koreans celebrating and feel the news is accurate. Just then, Poland scores another off a corner.

"That seals it. We need Korea to score." I say to nobody in particular. In front of us, their keeper makes a great save and Mathis scoops a shot just over the bar. Arena makes his final sub, Cobi Jones for Earnie Stewart. The crowd erupts! A deafening cheer goes up. I look around, confused, but hear Korea has scored! Now we are cheering. I, again, look to the Koreans and they are out of their mind, celebrating, and I know they news is accurate.

"*Tey-Han-Ming-Go*!" The cheer goes up and we Yanks are singing it as loudly as the Koreans ever have! My heart is pounding. I am only vaguely aware of some frantic action in front of the goal just a few yards in front of me. I am cheering with everything I am worth for Korea. "*Tey-Han-Ming-Go*! *Tey-Han-Ming-Go*!" We are willing the Koreans to hold on. I am hopeful. As great as the Portuguese are, they are down two players. Surely they know that we will lose, and they only need one goal. As loudly as I am cheering for Korea, I am holding my breath, hoping not to get any news from Incheon.

The referee blows his whistle at the other end and awards a penalty to the Poles. We do not so much as blink or curse the referee. However, when Big Brad stops his second penalty of the Cup, we hold our Korean cheers for a moment to belt out what has become a very popular cheer, "Free-dul! Free-dul! Free-dul! Free-dul!"

The stadium is alive. I can see the Poles cheering, but cannot hear them. The Koreans and we are singing those Korean songs. "Ohhh, *Pil-seung* Ko-Re-a. Ohhh, *Pil-seung* Ko-Re-a. Ohhh, *Pil-seung* Ko-Re-a. Oh-oh-oh-oh-oh! Hey! Hey! Hey!"

144

Mathis blasts a ball solidly into the post, but we scarcely flinch. Moments later, Donovan scores. There are no celebrations, just a few cheers for our young star's first World Cup goal. The clock reads at least eight minutes left. A lot will have to happen and I do not think it will, but that does not stop us from jeering as a Pole is substituted out and walks slowly all the way off the field before the referee finally books him. "A lot of good that will do us," I think.

Come on Korea! Please hold on. I am praying and am now wishing we had gone with the missionaries to church. Anything to help. We are desperate for news from Incheon, but hear nothing. "No news is good news," I tell someone who asked if I knew anything. We are now beyond cheering for our game and even the cheers for Korea have dried up. We are all holding our breath. This is so cruel. Our fate is being decided hundreds of miles from here, and I do not have so much as a radio to know what is happening. Is Portugal in an all out attack? Is Korea controlling the play with their two-man advantage? We have no idea.

A loud cheer goes up! I look to the Koreans to our right and they are celebrating. I look toward our bench and see a lot of action. Word has arrived! Korea has won! We are through! We are through! We are all screaming and yelling. Some others and I are yelling to our players, though I doubt they hear us. We chant some more Korean chants. It is surreal. The team I have come halfway around the world to see is running around on the field, losing 3-1, yet I am celebrating, celebrating two unlikely outcomes. I do not care that we are losing. We are through and that is all that matters.

The referee blows his whistle, and we cheer our losing side as if they have won the game. The players on the bench run onto the field and our boys look relieved as they exchange jerseys with the Poles. A few of the players come over to applaud us, most notably Hejduk and Friedel. We are singing, "Ole-Ole!" Hejduk claps and sings with us.

Elsewhere in a few sections in the stadium, the Poles are singing and celebrating a wonderful victory by their team. They, too, are accepting the applause of their players. The rest of the stadium is also in full voice, a Korean voice. I have never seen a stadium where everyone was so happy after a game. Three sets of fans are basking in a tremendous moment.

***

Someone near me shouted, "We want Mexico!" Immediately our entire section joined in, "We want Mexico! We want Mexico! We want Mexico!" Somehow things had worked out as I had hoped, though it had not followed my script. We were going to get Mexico!

We continued singing our songs. I was walking around our section, high-fiving and even hugging some of my new friends. Monty, Big Dog, Scott, Neil, Kaela, Mike; I had known these people less than two weeks, yet, in this land, we had

145

bonded quickly and through this gut wrenching 90 minutes, I knew we were sharing something very special. They were now my good friends. We had danced after Portugal, sang after Korea, and now, after dodging the bullet, we celebrated the second round.

I was looking for others when I noticed, in the section just above us, three Polish men. They were singing and waving their flag. I went to them. "Congratulations!" I yelled to the first one.

"This is for you," he answered, handing me a Polish jersey. I was stunned and flattered. I was not sure what to do.

"Do you want my shirt or flag?" I asked him.

"It does not matter."

I thought for a split second and pulled off my Sam's Army shirt and handed it to him. As I was doing that, he took hold of the jersey he had just given me and took off his own shirt. He handed it to me, rather than the original jersey. I don't think it was a slight, perhaps it was protocol, the shirt one wears for another. In any case, it was a Polish shirt, but more of a t-shirt than a jersey. It was red with short white sleeves. Just under the collar was the Polish badge. The only words on it said "Active Wear."

I pulled on my new red shirt and he did the same. I looked down and saw many of the Americans cheering us. Together, the Pole and I sang, "Ole-Ole", along with the Yanks below. Then a few of them came up and began trading shirts. I shook the man's hand one last time and went back to our section.

After about ten minutes, we left the stadium, only to find ourselves in the midst of another celebration. The drummers had congregated and a predominately American crowd danced to their beat. Everyone was singing and dancing. I saw some more fans exchanging shirts. I looked at my new one and while I liked it, it was a bit too Arsenal looking for me, with its red body and white sleeves. No matter, I thought, the way it had come to me was fantastic, a memory I will cherish forever. As I was thinking this, a tall American in a Clint Mathis jersey asked if I wanted to trade shirts.

"No, I'm American." I told him, but as he walked away, I had second thoughts. The practical side in me came out. The trade would be a Sam's Army t-shirt, valued at about $10.00 for an expensive jersey. Had I owned a team jersey, I doubt I would have done it, but as I did not . . . I spun around and ran a few steps, catching up with the guy. "Trade?"

He was delighted, and we made the exchange. I thought that he would probably regret the trade. The Polish T was just my size, but no doubt, tight on him. I pulled on the Mathis jersey and felt proud to be wearing our colors. Then I noticed my new shirt was enormous. It was probably big on the tall young man I had traded with, but it engulfed me. The number 11 on the front was huge, bigger than the number on the back should be. I concluded that not only was the jersey way too big for me, it was a bad fake. I was the one on the short end of the trade.

However, the tent-like shirt did not hinder my celebrations. I continued to dance and sing along with everyone else until the crowd eventually began to thin. Some of my friends said they wanted to get back to NASA to start the party there. Just as we were about to go to the buses, I noticed a group of about ten Poles, sitting on a wall, watching our revelry.

"Hold on a minute guys," I told my friends and quickly walked to the Poles. One was standing and he made eye contact with me as I approached. Without a word, I tugged on the front of the Mathis jersey and he nodded. We exchanged shirts. I shook his hand and said, "Great game." I turned and ran back to my friends with a Polish Jersey. It was very plain but was made out of an interesting material that made it's whiteness look almost glossy. The badge was in the middle, directly under the V-Neck. The number ten was on both the front and back in a very vivid red, which was outlined in black. It was plain yet beautiful in it's simplicity and color. It also fit perfectly.

On the way to the bus, we shook hands with many Koreans. All I could say to them was, "Thank you." They all smiled and laughed and were "happy to meet" us. I only said, "Thank you," and I am not sure I ever meant those words more.

The bus ride went quickly and soon we were back at the train station and heading back to NASA. We were still in such a state of frenzy that we had failed to realize that the Koreans were as excited as were we, but with each passing block, we began to notice more and more red shirt wearing, flag waving Koreans. What had began as a nearly solitary walk from the train station had become a parade as we entered the downtown area. By the time it had dawned on us that the Koreans has taken to the streets to celebrate, we were in the very center of it!

About a block from NASA, all traffic on the busy, four-lane road had come to a crawl as the street had filled with rejoicing Koreans. Then the singing began, "Tey-Han-Ming-Go!" And all the cars honked in unison. Trucks were overloaded with college age revelers. Every SUV had it's back door open and held at least eight people, at least two of whom stood waving the inspiring Korean flag.

As we reached the corner where NASA was, we realized that we were in the town center. "Times Square on New Years," I heard someone say, but I am not sure that was accurate. There were people everywhere, thousands of them, yet it was not overcrowded, and we could walk freely and easily. The patriotic element was astounding. Nearly everyone wore a red shirt and many waved the flag. Others played instruments to tunes that all of Korea, as well as visiting Yanks, knew by heart.

For a while, Jimmy, Amanda, and I stood and stared. After the game, I was certain that I was one of the happiest people in the world. Now, about an hour and a half later, I did not think that I was among the happiest in this city! The Koreans were putting on a show, a show of joy and patriotism.

Suddenly some in the crowd rushed a car and began to rock it, then they moved to the one behind it. "Uh-oh. They are beginning to riot. We should get out of here," I said and we all hurried up into NASA. The bar that we had ruled earlier in the day was a madhouse. It was mostly Americans, but there were a lot of Koreans inside. I drank a quick beer before following Jimmy and Amanda back out.

We took up a spot on the sidewalk that looked as safe and as out of the way as any. They were still rocking cars, but that was it and it went no farther. Even the drivers seemed to enjoy it. The street was overflowing and only one lane contained traffic. Then I saw something that I am sure I will never see back home. A police car inched slowly along, caught in the same jam as the other vehicles. About ten Koreans rocked the car in front of him. When they finished, the mob turned to the police car.

"No way will they rock him," Amanda said and moments later, they began rocking him! They did not care. But then, a very bad thing happened. The lights atop the police car were knocked off. I prepared myself to watch a LA style police beat down but was stunned as two of the rockers calmly picked the lights from the ground and reattached them to the roof of the car. When they were secured, the cop waved to them and continued on!

Jimmy and I were speechless. From that point on, I realized that I was in no danger at all and began to mingle with the crowd. I shook hands and offered congratulations and thanks. Koreans lined up to shake my hand. Many of them offered their team's motto, "Fighting!" They would say in a way in which the "F" was nearly silent. I answered this with the same accent, "Fighting!"

The many moments were overwhelming and I realized that although Tokyo and Brussels may be partying down and Seoul was much larger and had many more people in the streets, I was in the one place in the world I wanted to be right then. There was a bar full of die hard American fans about 100 feet behind me, and in front of me were thousands of locals pouring out joyous emotions that their culture requires them to keep in. It was as if everything good that had ever happened to them was let being let out at once.

In all this excitement, I began to miss Ivy. I wished she were here to witness this, as it was a spectacle I will never forget. Then I noticed a few pay phones across the street. I remembered I had a new phone card with me, so I crossed through the sea of red, working my way between the rocking cars to the phones. Unlike the other day, the card worked perfectly on the first try. Ivy was at work, and I yelled so she could here me. Her reaction caught me off guard.

"That sucked," she said, "What's wrong with our team?"

It took me a few moments to realize what she was talking about. I guess I had forgotten we had been beaten, and beaten badly, but that is not what I wanted to talk about. "So what, we are through. But you should see what I am seeing! There are thousands of Koreans in the street going crazy! Can you hear them? Hold on." I held the phone out, facing the street and the cacophony of sounds; singing, horns, instruments. "Can you hear that?"

"Yeah. Are you all right?" She was concerned for my safety. Had I been on the other end, I would have advised her to run away, but being there, I have never felt safer in a crowd.

"No problems at all. They are just going crazy!" I did not know how to describe what I was seeing and told her as much, then said I would give her a play by play. "Now there is a little station wagon with eight people in it and a guy standing on the roof waving a flag. Next is a mini van with five girls hanging out of the side windows, high fiving everyone they pass. Their back is open and two guys are shooting bottle rockets out of it. Now there is an over loaded small car, with a guy sitting on the hood, leaning back against the windshield with a bull horn, leading songs." I was not making this up!

We soon said our goodbye's and I love you's and I decided that Mark needed to witness this, so I called him at work. He came on much as had Ivy.

"Dude, we suck! That was horrible," Bushman was disgusted, and I began to wonder if we were the only ones celebrating.

"I've never been happier after a game!" I yelled to him, lying because nothing will ever surpass Portugal, but this had been very close. "We are partying like crazy, but you should see the Koreans!"

He did not want to hear about it. "How could we do that? We didn't come to play. It sucked!"

"Dude, we're in the second round! Listen to this." I once again held out the phone to give him a quick listen to the sound of victory. "This is crazier than winning the Super Bowl! They are rocking cars and going nuts!"

We talked a little while longer, but he was depressed at our play. Maybe he would have been in a better mood if he was in the one place in the world to be at that moment. That place was a city in Korea called Daejeon.

After the calls, I stood on the side of the road and watched. A few times I went into NASA, but although there was a lot of joy in there, it did not come close to the electric atmosphere outside. Each time I went in, I quickly went back out, usually with a few others who wanted to soak in the moment.

I shook hundreds of Korean hands, thanking each one. Their energy was amazing as hours later, they were still going strong. I have seen scenes from cities that have won the Super Bowl or colleges that win the National Championship. Those scenes looked wild and crazy, but there was something different here. I guess it was a unique form of patriotism. When your country was shit on for years (by the Chinese and Japanese), occupied (by Japan and now perceivably by us) and told that it does not figure into the grand scheme of things and then your countrymen go out in front of the whole world and defy all expectations, you celebrate in a way in which we Americans are not familiar. And you do it ALL NIGHT!

I do not know how they kept it up, particularly when they only had three songs that they sang constantly, one after the other, for hours on end. It was very late and I had had enough. I returned to NASA one last time to see if anyone else

149

was ready to go back to the hotel. It was 3:30 in the morning! At the door, I was shaking hands with still more Koreans when one of the young men offered his flag for trade. Monty was with me and shook his head to the guy. The Korean looked at me. I really did not want to give up my flag, but quickly realized that an American flag hanging in a dorm room in Korea could do a lot of good. I untied Old Glory from around my neck and proudly handed it over and then tied on the large Korean flag. I now wore a Polish shirt a Korean flag but still my ACC Basketball cap.

Only Big Dog was ready to go. He and I made our way a few blocks away where the crowd was thinner. Along the way, I commented to him that generally if I was in a foreign country and a group of natives ran up to me yelling "Fighting!" I would start handing over my money and looking for an escape! Here, I return the motto and shake hands. It was a crazy night.

We found a cab and I told the driver, "Hole in One Hotel." He nodded and took off. Big Dog and I were exhausted and we slumped back in the seat.

"I can't believe everyone is still there, especially Jimmy." Big Dog said and I agreed. This was the first night since arriving here that I was the first one to leave, however, I could have gone to sleep right there in the cab. It was such a long day, not to mention how much I drank before the match and that was seven hours ago!

As we drove on, I commented that I thought we were driving too far, but Big Dog said he had no idea. Our driver looked confident, not talking on his cell phone, just driving and making decisive turns. I was starting to worry that we were way out of the way, when he pulled to the curb and said, "Hole in One."

"Whew," I said and was relieved that in less than five minutes I would be asleep. We paid the driver and went in the hotel. "Room 604," I told the middle-aged man at the counter. He was behind plexi glass and nodded.

However, a moment later, he shook his head and said something in Korean that did not sound good. "604. Room 604," I repeated it slowly.

He fired his answer back and we had no idea what he said. I saw a pen on the counter and wrote "604" on a small piece of paper. He took it and shook his head. It dawned on me that he was trying to get more money out of us. I told Big Dog that he was extorting us. My mind rushed, but was too tired to think clearly.

Big Dog had enough, "Come on. Give us the key!" he yelled, but the man behind the glass just stared at us. Then I remembered that I had folded the receipt and put it in the back pocket of my shorts. I pulled it out and handed it to him.

"This proves we have paid," I told Big Dog. "He didn't count on us keeping it!" I was proud of myself for out smarting this would be con man, and my big friend and I exchanged triumphant smiles and nods.

The reaction from the deskman was not as we expected. Rather than humbly handing over the key, he fired more Korean at us. He was speaking a mile a minute at us. "What are you saying?" Big Dog yelled at him. The Korean then began to speak slower, much slower. I have seen Americans use this tactic when speaking to foreigners, but if they do not know the language to begin with, it does not matter at all how slowly one speaks.

I shrugged, showing him we could not understand. Then he stopped, gathered himself and then spoke two words that we made out to be, "Wrong hotel." We were stunned.

Then Big Dog, in a booming voice said, "No! Hole in One. Give us Key!"

The man held up two fingers and said, "Wrong hotel."

"Two Hole in One Hotels?" I asked holding up two fingers.

"*Nay*," he replied and we had both been here long enough to know that in Korea, nay means yes.

"Son of a bitch!" I cursed and took a moment to look around. I realized that he was right; this was not the hotel we were in earlier. It did look similar, so I did not feel like a complete idiot, but it was different. "Let's get a cab," I said, disheartened. "We are sorry," I said slowly to the man, *"Com sam nee da,"* thanking him with one of the very few phrases I knew and we walked outside.

Outside did not look good. We both sensed we were not in a good neighborhood. We walked quickly to the street we had been driven up on ten minutes earlier. It was deserted. Big Dog led us across it to a convenience store. "I'm starving," he told me, but I was trying to gather my bearings. It was difficult because we were surrounded by tall, dilapidated buildings. The only lights were coming from the store. I thought I knew the direction to downtown and suggested we just walk in that direction, but Big Dog rejected that idea.

In the store, he bought a drink and a candy bar, and I got a bottle of water. The situation sucked. We decided to go back to the hotel and ask the man to call us a cab. On the way back, I thought we were propositioned by two hookers, the only two people on the street, but did not really know for sure.

Inside the hotel, I mimed making a phone call. "Phone," I said slowly. "Taxi." He nodded and dialed a number, had a brief conversation and dialed another number. He talked for a while on this call. Upon hanging up, he led us outside. He spoke in Korean, so we did not know what he said, but it soon became apparent. He opened a car door and motioned us to get in. He then proceeded to drive us away. We only could assume he was taking us to our hotel.

Big Dog was in the front, and I was in the back. Somehow, the big guy struck up a conversation with the man. I was too tired to even try to figure out what they were saying, but Big Dog, in his joy at the ride, seemed to understand. After a few minutes, he informed me the obvious, "He's taking us to our hotel! What a great guy!"

We headed in the direction of downtown and after about five miles, begin to pass groups of Koreans making there way home. They looked tired but waved at our car as we passed. The ride lasted about ten minutes before we pulled up to what I recognized as the real "Hole in One Hotel." *"Com sam nee da.* Thank you. *Cam sam nee da,"* I heaped it on this guy, our savior. Big Dog pulled out his wallet and handed over a fistful of *won*, but the driver declined, waving his hand. Big Dog thanked him and heartily shook his hand.

"What a nice guy. He didn't have to do that." Big Dog was astounded by the man's kindness. I was not surprised, as I have heard others tell similar stories of Koreans going out of their way for them. It is simply another way in which the Koreans have opened themselves for us. I have never met more gracious people.

At the desk, we had no trouble obtaining the key for Room 604. The clock read 4:34 as I collapsed onto the mat on the floor. It had been an amazing day; losing to Poland yet still achieving the second round; and the celebration by the Koreans is something I will remember forever and doubt I will ever see it's equal. Yet, as I fell asleep, the only thought in my head was the profound words spoken by a tall kid from Seattle, "Addresses rule and no addresses suck ass."

Tom, me, Mark, and Jimmy at the Nashville.

Leo and Brent of the New York Crew...
Always Singing!

Ethan Zohn interviewing fans at Nashville

Scott, Neil, Doug, and Tanya enjoy the cheerleaders before the US – Portugal game.

Koreans jump on our bandwagon before the Portugal game.

A great seat to witness history.

"If these people would leave us alone..." Jimmy and Amanda think from Old Blue.

Me, Monty and Kaela shortly before my ankle injury.

Jimmy, Monty, Lamar Hunt and Big Dog wait for a bus in Suwon.

Me and Soccerhead on the train to Daejeon.

Scott, Neil, and Jimmy as NASA.

Fans before the Poland match.

Members of Kiss celebrate the Second Round.

Polish supporter and I exchange shirts.

Thank you for beating Portugal!!

157

Drinking with the Irish.

Me, John, and his
bottled beer.

President Kennedy keeping out
the Spanish.

Me, John, and the Irish ninjas.

Jimmy, Mark, a Mexican, me, and Tom before the game.

Jimmy, Mike, and the ball after we beat Mexico.

We could not find the Rose Garden, but we drank for free here.

I found the Rose Garden...and the Kings.

A young fan and I are proud of our team after the Germany game.

Koreans take to the street as fireworks explode after beating Italy.

Two sisters, one stuck in time.

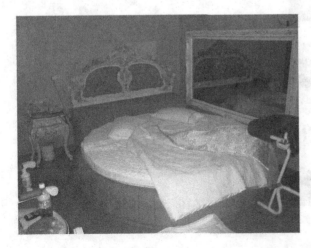

Our room...the Honeymoon Suite at the Valentine Motel.

The world knew we were there.

Day 14
Saturday, June 15

Luck of the Irish

When I woke up, I found the others in the room packing. "How long did you stay out?" I asked, having not heard them come in during the night.

"We got here just before five o'clock." Jimmy answered me. Our room was filled with all six of our group and they were urging me to hurry and get ready, but before doing so, Big Dog and I told them the story of the other Hole in One Hotel. Of course they got a kick out of it.

While waiting for the train, Jimmy bought a small bag of shrimp flavored potato chips. I had to try one and was sorry I did. They tasted like, well shrimp, only not in a good cocktail way. It was more of a fishy, sucking on the shell, flavor. Somehow, Jimmy ate them all and actually said he liked them.

The train back to Seoul was uneventful. The four others got off in Suwon, but Scott and Neil had said their Home Stay was over and we made plans to meet in Itaewon to watch the day's games, after which, they would come back to the *Dong-Il* and check into the great, cheap little place.

When Jimmy and I got off at Seoul Station, we saw Mike who was also disembarking and looking rough. When we commented on his tired look, he told us a great story. He said that after the game he was talking to a bunch of American soldiers. He ended up following them to the line for the buses and boarded one with them. After about an hour or so on the bus, he realized it was not taking him back to the city center. When he brought that up, the soldiers told him they were headed back to Seoul! Somehow, he convinced the bus driver to let him off, however he was in the middle of nowhere. He began walking back and eventually a farmer picked him up and drove him back to Daejeon. They arrived just in time for him to checkout of his hotel and catch the train! We tore into him about it, but he was too tired to fight back and just took our abuse.

After our many jokes, he told us he had a reservation at the Seoul Hotel, but did not know how to get there. We were stunned as this was the large hotel next door to the *Dong-Il*. He followed us there and said he would meet us in Itaewon later.

I was hungry for some spicy soup, so after Jimmy and I dropped our bags in our rooms, and I was delighted to see my clothes had been washed and folded by the two women while we were gone, went to my favorite little restaurant.

After we ordered, an Irishman sat down at the next table and looked over the menu. He asked us for some help and we invited him to sit with us. His name was John and he was a Law professor at a university in Limerick. He had studied at the University of Maine and we spent a little while discussing the differences in Irish and American law.

163

John was a funny little guy with thick glasses and a crew cut. He looked like anything but a Law professor. When he spoke, I could not place his accent to be Irish, which trouble me because I am usually pretty good at that. My sister married an Irishman, and I had spent a long week there once. However, John had, what I heard to be, a unique accent. I laughed under my breath every time he said *"ye"* rather than "you." "Where are *ye* staying?" he asked. "How long have *ye* been here?"

After eating, I said, "I wish I could see your game tomorrow."

I was stunned when he said, "I can get *ye* a ticket. We can go to the hotel and I can buy *ye* one. I am going to buy one for a friend."

We left the restaurant and he led me to the Cowboy Bar, right across the alley from the *Dong-Il*. John was staying in the more luxurious Seoul Hotel next door. In the Cowboy Bar, he introduced me to three other Irishmen he had met earlier in the day. He said he would be back in a few minutes, and we would go to the team's hotel where he would get me a ticket.

Jimmy, who did not want to spend the $100 for the ticket, and I sat down with the Irishmen. They said they were from Coventry and supported the Sky Blues. I said that I thought it was a shame they had been relegated the year before and hoped they would get promoted back to the Premiership next year.

A waiter came over and I ordered a round for the guys and was surprised when Jimmy asked for a glass and poured himself some Hite beer from my 22 oz bottle.

Somehow we got on the subject of Coventry's Swedish goalkeeper, Magnus Hedman. One of the Irish started laughing and asked if we would like to hear a funny story. Of course we did.

"It's a game last year, and we've been losing a lot," he began in his Irish/English accent that I had to concentrate on to get every word. "And we have this friend, a real timid guy, teaches school, never starts any trouble. So we are watching the match and we're down two-nil and this guy runs onto the pitch and punches Hedman in the back of the head. He just hauled off and belts him. Of course the stewards grab him and when they are carrying him off, we recognize him as our friend, the schoolteacher! This guy is so meek and timid, we were stunned." The whole table was laughing, particularly the guy telling the story, who was in tears.

I asked, "Why did he do it?"

"That's what we asked him and he said, 'I just couldn't take it anymore, losing and all.' He then confessed it was the first time he had ever hit anyone!"

We were all laughing and I was trying to picture this weak little schoolteacher punching the big, athletic Swede, when John came back in. "I need a passport," he announced. The three others, reached for their pockets, but only one had his on him. "I'm going to the hotel to get Andy here, and another friend a ticket, but they will only sell a ticket with a passport."

It was amazing to me that the guy at the table, quickly handed over his passport to John, whom he had only met this morning. I am all for sticking together with countrymen, and I would do a lot for any American over here, but I am not sure I would give them my passport. Fortunately for me, this guy trusted John enough and in moments, John and I were hailing a cab and on our way to the Irish team's hotel.

It was a short ride and the driver found a place to park while John went in with the $100 I had given him. While waiting on him, I thought it funny that I had just given this guy that much money and for a few minutes wondered if I had just been scammed. Shortly, I had my answer as the little man exited the large hotel with a big grin on his face. He climbed into the cab and handed me the ticket, "You're right in our section, behind the goal," he proudly told me.

Back at the *Dong-Il*, I secured the ticket and thought about the day's first game, Paraguay-Germany. It was to begin at 3:30 so Jimmy and I, along with our new friend John caught a taxi for Itaewon.

There, we went to the Seoul Pub. As we entered, the owner gave me a thumbs up. I was not sure what that was for, but Jimmy pointed out that I was wearing the Seoul Pub T-Shirt that I had bought a few days earlier. We went to the back and saw the NY Crew there. I shook hands with them but moved to the other side of the bar for a better view of the TV. I ordered a pitcher, but when I went to pour John a frosty mug, he shook me off and said he only wanted bottled beer.

This Irishman had something about him that caused me to return to the bar and buy him a bottle of Hite. I had a pitcher to myself, so I went over to the NY Crew and topped off their mugs, lightening my load. Soon the first game of the Second Round kicked off. We were all rooting for Paraguay, thinking that we stood a better chance to beat them that we did of beating Germany.

Before long, Neil and Scott came in. The game was dull which gave me hope that Paraguay would pull the upset, but it became so boring, that we all lost interest. At halftime, it was nil-nil and Jimmy and I discussed what we would do should we lose to Mexico. The quarterfinal match was to be held in Ulsan, which is on the southeast coast of the country. Seoul is in the northwest corner. We read that it is a six hour train ride to Ulsan. We came to the decision that if we lost to Mexico, we would travel to Ulsan only to see Germany. Thus if Paraguay won today, we would only go to the game should we be the ones playing.

That left me with a dilemma I hoped would not come to pass. If it did end up Germany-Mexico, for whom would I root? These are the two teams I hate most in the world. They had met in the second round of the 1998 Cup and Mexico had taken the lead, but Germany came back to beat them. I think I had pulled for Mexico, if only for the respect it would bring our region. However, if they eliminated us, it would be hard to cheer for them. They are our biggest rivals and a team we love to hate. I hoped this scenario would not play out.

The second half was not much better than the first. Both sides missed a chance or two. We were all hoping that puffed-up Jose Luis Chilavert could keep the ball out of the net. However, just before injury time, Oliver Neuville hammered home a cross and the Germans celebrated. "Looks like we're going to Ulsan," I told Jimmy, praying it would be to see us play and not the Mexicans.

Mike, who had taken a log nap, joined us, and after the match the five of us set out to find a PC Bang. We had about three and a half hours before the England-Denmark game began. John had long gone; where, I was not sure.

On a street that ran parallel to the main drag, we found a PC Bang. This one was larger, and smokier than most. The cloud did not hang in the air, rather, it began on the floor and maintained its thickness up to the ceiling. It was less a cloud of smoke than it was fog. My eyes burned as I read the screen and wrote about the previous night in Deajeon. I wrote a long letter to my friends, trying to relate that experience to them.

Though we were polluting our lungs, none of us were in a hurry to leave. I read all the reports in the *Washington Post*. Steven Goff and Liz Clarke were doing a wonderful job reporting from over here. *USA Today* also had great stories. Big Soccer was in a frenzy, both criticizing our team and coaches as well as hyping themselves up for the most important match we have ever played against our hated rivals. A US-Mexico friendly brings out all the crazies on Big Soccer, a qualifier and the site has been know to crash from all the fans logging on. Now we were less than two days from playing them in an elimination round of the World Cup Finals! I doubt I could have read all the posts had I not stopped reading until kickoff!

While reading some of the hype, I looked up and saw Mike emerge through the haze. "Bathroom that way?" I asked.

"Yeah, but you don't want to go there," was the San Franciscan's answer.

"Damn, I really have to go," I said, to which he shook his head as if I had made some sort of monumentally bad decision, like I was going to begin smoking crack.

Cautiously, I pulled back the curtain, which was all that separated the bathroom from the large smoky room filled with Koreans playing video games. The smell was horrific, and I realized I was in trouble for not taking a big breath before entering. It looked the same as most Korean bathrooms. There was no toilet, just a rounded-rectangular sink-like hole in the floor. Women squatted over it while we used it much like a trough. The floor was wet and I had no choice but to step into the filth.

When I came out, I must have had a terrible look on my face because Mike was laughing out loud. We stayed a little while longer before leaving, but before we went, Scott said he had to use the bathroom. Mike and I exchanged a knowing look and pointed him to the squalor. Moments later he came out, his face red and twisted. It was my turn to laugh at his grief.

We still had over an hour before the game and we split up, deciding to meet back in the Seoul Pub. Mike and I paired up and went to the food stands where I purchased a chicken pita from the Turkey stand for W3,000. It was good, marinated chicken with cucumbers and onions, but left me hungry. We found ourselves in the KFC and I got the chicken wrap; W3,900.

We met the others back in the Pub that was much more crowded than we had left it. There were green shirts everywhere and when England kicked off, they began singing for Ireland. "Come on you boys in green, come on you boys in green, come on you boys, come on you boys in green," etc. . .

It was inspiring as they sang in a strong, unified voice. Clearly, every Irishman knew this song and was unashamed of belting it out. They had not sung long when they were silenced by an English goal. Rio Ferdinand headed to the Danish keeper, Thomas Sorensen, who fumbled the ball into the net. The game was decided before halftime as the Sunderland keeper allowed two more goals. England sat back in the second half and were not troubled. It was a surprisingly easy win for England who are facing a quarterfinal match with Brazil, should the Samba Boys not slip up against Belgium.

Jimmy, Scott, Neil, Mike, and I caught the subway back to our place, and Scott and Neil had no trouble getting a room at the *Dong-Il*. Jimmy went to bed, but the other four of us were not ready to see this day end. We had a few beers at the Cowboy Bar and then decided to his some baseballs.

There was a batting cage next to the Cowboy Bar, on the roof of a small parking lot. I led us up the creaky wooden steps and was surprised to see that a round cost only 500 *won* or just 40 cents! They did not have a good selection of bats. In fact, they only had one bat, an old aluminum one. I went first, in the fast cage. Whether from the beer or years of playing softball, it took me a few pitches before I made contact. However, by the end of the round, I was hitting ropes all over the place. Mike went next and hit some good shots, as did Scott. Neil, it seemed, was not much of a player and only got a piece of a few balls. We laughed as he constantly swung and missed. Mike and I each hit another round, and I was sweating as we went back down the stairs.

We agreed to meet at my favorite place to eat at 11:00 the next morning and headed off to our rooms. It was 1:00, and I found a replay of the Korea-Portugal match on TV. It was in the 60th minute which allowed me to see the second sending off of a Portuguese player, and then the wonderful goal. It was scored by Park Ji-Sung. The goal was brilliant and reeked of skill, savvy, and class that I did not think the Koreans possessed.

After the goal, nine-man Portugal attacked and had many chances. They blew a few and Lee Woon-Jae, the Korean keeper, made a huge save. Although I knew the result, my heart was pounding and my blood pressure was high. It was so dramatic and nerve wracking that I am not sure if I could have watched it live without suffering a breakdown.

After the replay was off, I lay in bed and silently thanked the Koreans for taking us to the second round. I also knew that I had an answer when I would be asked who my favorite Korean player was. Park, Park Ji-Sung.

Day 15
Sunday, June 16

Come on You Bhoys in Green

I woke up around 10:00, picked up Jimmy, and headed for the PC Bang. I only wrote a short note home and spent about a half hour reading about tomorrow's game with Mexico. Despite the anticipation that was overcoming most U.S. fans, I was having trouble focusing on that game. Maybe I was slightly concerned that I did not yet posses the tickets to the match. Jimmy and I had planned on picking them up in the FIFA offices near Seoul Station later today. Although we had bought and paid for them and held the conformation, something in me was making me nervous until I actually had them in my hands.

Also distracting me was the game I would be attending tonight. If the U.S.-Mexico match was a battle for CONCACAF supremacy, the Ireland-Spain match was a European affair and though these were not the continent's best, they were both very interesting to me.

Spain plays very attractive soccer and has some of the world's best players. I was excited to see the pair of Real Madrid forwards, Raul and Fernando Morientes; world class midfielders from massive clubs such as Barcelona's Luis Enrique and Lazio's Gaizka Mendieta; and two tough defenders from Real (is it any wonder they won the Champions League?) Madrid Fernando Hierro and Ivan Helguera.

Ireland, on the other hand, having had their only true world class player, the great Roy Keane, sent home after a row with coach Mick McCarthy, are made up of gritty, hard nosed players who all earn their living playing in England. They play with the heart and determination that is on display in the Premier League every week. Their best-known players are the young star forward Robbie Keane, and the ageing, tall forward, Niall Quinn. Their goalkeeper is one of the best in the Premiership, Newcastle's Shay Given. Defender Ian Harte of Leeds is a free kick specialist and young winger Damien Duff, Brad Friedel's teammate at Blackburn, has had his first-round play widely praised.

Not only was I looking forward to the game, but also I was excited about standing and cheering amongst their fans. I had heard them singing on television during the first-round. Joe, the New Yorker who had left after the Korea match had been at Ireland's first match and told me about the incredible atmosphere they created. This was my first chance to really cheer along with seasoned supporters. I was hoping to learn a few tricks to bring to Sam's Army the next day.

At 11:00 Jimmy and I left for the restaurant with my favorite spicy soup. The walk took about 20 seconds. The Seattle brothers, Scott and Neil, arrived at the same time, and we all sat down and were soon joined by Mike. I ordered the hot soup, as did everyone else but Neil, who opted for a beef and rice dish. Scott and I also ordered the sushi. I felt better about trying it along with someone else. If I did not like it, somebody at the table would finish it.

Everyone enjoyed the soup, though Scott was sweating and his face turned red. The sushi ended up being very good. It was pieces of shrimp, octopus, an unidentified fish, and something that I think was calamari, but that Scott said was some sort of fish. There was indeed soy sauce, to my utter happiness as well as a dollop of wasabi. The only thing it was missing was the pink leaves of ginger that I love, but there were these things that looked like pearl onions, but had a sweet, clean flavor, similar to ginger.

After lunch we all returned to the *Dong-Il*, except for Mike who was enjoying his luxury room next door and said he was considering going to the sauna that was hidden behind the *Dong-Il* and was popular with Buddhist Monks who wore the traditional robes.

Inside the *Dong-Il*, we encountered another American that we had not seen before. He was younger than us and had out of control dark hair with sideburns. He introduced himself as Tom and said he had just flown in from Thailand. He had seen how well our team was doing and had decided he should make the trip and lend his support. He had recently graduated from the University of Virginia and had spent the last few months traveling around Asia. He had had a great time thus far and encouraged us to see more of the continent.

This was his first time in Korea and he was concerned with what he called "high prices."

"How can $23.00 for a room and $3.00 for a good meal be high?" I was curious.

"In Vietnam and Thailand it's $4.00 a room and 50 cents for food. Laos is even cheaper. Yeah, I'm not sure how long I can stay here, money is starting to get tight as it is," he talked like a California surfer and I was surprised that he was from Annandale, the city where I live in Virginia.

We told him we were going to the train station to get train tickets to Jeonju as well as to pick up our game tickets. He decided to tag along and travel to the game with us.

After he had dropped his bag in his room, the three of us made our now familiar subway ride to Seoul Station. Once there, we went to the window that had been set up for foreigners to purchase tickets.

There were two windows labeled "English."

I went to one and bought a train ticket to Suwon for 3:40, which would give us plenty of time to find the game tickets. Ticket in hand, I shuffled over to the other window.

"Three tickets to Jeonju for tomorrow," Jimmy said to the agent. We had decided to only buy one-way tickets and decide after the game if we would try to return right away or find a hotel. Before leaving the states, I was concerned that all hotels would be booked. For that reason, I had made the expensive around the world phone calls to reserve rooms for the two U.S. games in Daegu and Daejeon. Having been here for over two weeks, I have realized that those fears could not have been more misplaced. There are rooms available everywhere. We had no concerns whatsoever about finding rooms in Jeonju.

The game was set for 3:30 in the afternoon. Should we loose to the Mexicans, we would probably get back to Seoul as soon as possible. However, should we beat our hated rivals and advance to the quarterfinals, we did not want to miss the party afterwards and would probably stay the night in Jeonju, a city only a two hour train ride from Seoul.

We joked with one another as the agent typed on her computer, but our carefree attitudes were quickly lost as she replied after a few moments, "No tickets."

"What? No tickets? No, we *need* three tickets to Jeonju, tomorrow," I was now doing the talking. Does she not know that we are playing Mexico there tomorrow?

Dutifully, she went back to her computer, but still found nothing. "All sold out."

Not believing her, Tom went to the other window for a second opinion, but was given the same answer. We walked away to regroup. Tom was stunned and told us that for the months he had been in Asia, he had not been turned away from any form of travel. I was trying to make sense of how this could be happening. Everything had run so smoothly until now. Korea had done a fantastic job organizing this Cup. How could it be that now, in the second round, they come up short on trains.

Jimmy suggested that we find the FIFA building and pick up our game tickets. This was a good idea, because it gave us a task on which we were forced to focus. A cursory search around the sprawling station found no FIFA building. We asked around awhile and had a few false leads before we located and made our way through the heat to the building.

Inside a cool lobby, we had no trouble obtaining our tickets, much to my relief. The tickets looked just like those from the first round, and I was pleased to see that those for tomorrow's game had printed on them, USA v Mexico. The Quarterfinal tickets simply read "Quarterfinals."

Feeling better that we had the tickets, we turned our attention back to getting to Jeonju. Jimmy remembered that that was the city where he had seen the Spain-Paraguay game. He said he had taken a bus there and had no problems doing so.

It was now after 3:00 and I needed to get to my train to Suwon. "Jimmy, Tom, you are in charge of finding transportation to Jeonju. If the bus thing works out, great. If not, start asking people to drive us. We should be able to convince someone to drive us there; we can pay them."

"Yeah, we'll go to the bus stop and that should work," Jimmy said confidently.

"Good, but if it doesn't, you have to get creative. I am entrusting you with getting me to Jeonju. The game, my book, my sanity are all in your hands."

Tom chimed in, calming me, "Dude, we'll get you there. Don't worry."

"Cool, just leave me a note telling me what time we have to leave. See ya," I said and took off to the station. I was not worried. Jimmy has traveled alone in Europe and Tom has been all over Asia. I was very confident that they would figure something out.

About ten minutes later, I boarded a train for Suwon. There were a number of Irish boarding as well, but I was disappointed as there were none in my car. I quickly realized that this was the way to travel to Suwon. The ticket had been about $3.50, compared to a 60 cent subway ticket, but it was saving a half-hour. The train only made one brief stop before pulling into Suwon Station. The seat had been comfortable and I disembarked feeling refreshed, very much unlike the two subway rides I had taken here, once sitting on the hard plastic seats, the other time standing as the subway made countless stops.

"Suwon!" I thought as I walked out of the station and my mind went back 11 days. I thought about how we exited into what was then the unknown. After that wonderful night when we had stunned Portugal, things changed for us. Or was it only for me? Before that game, I was not sure I belonged here. After 1998, the U.S. was not given much thought by the rest of the soccer world. I had a feeling that I was here more as a witness, much like I had been when I attended two Arsenal matches. Their supporters ruled the grounds and they had fun interplay with the visiting supporters. I just watched. I was rooting for the away teams, but just had a feeling that the game was not for me, that somehow I did not belong.

All that changed when John O'Brien hammered in that rebound. From that moment on, we were a part of this event. The world would have taken little note of us had we lost to Portugal, as had been expected, and gone on to not qualify for the second round. We would have been nothing more that a footnote in the story of this Cup. But our boys saw to it that we would be remembered. They forced the world to take notice. We had become a player here. From the shocks we had sent in beating mighty Portugal to Brad Friedel making history by stopping two penalties to the guy from Newcastle who told me, "I can see you in the finals." The world was talking about the U.S soccer team. Knowing this, I walked taller. I was a part of this. I did belong here, not as a witness but as a participant.

Suwon brought these feelings to a head for me. As much as I have come to love Seoul, Suwon will always be special to me. It was here that we announced our presence on the world stage.

Before I reached the street, I encountered an Irishman selling the green jerseys and scarves. I had been sure to wear the only green shirt I had, but felt I needed to do more. The jersey was too expensive, but the scarf was only W10,000. That was much less than the street vendors wanted in Itaewon, so I handed over the largest denomination in Korean currency. In return I was given a green scarf with white and orange trim. "IRELAND", it proclaimed and then in smaller letters, "The Emerald Isle" and "Irish and Proud" there were two shamrocks on either end. I wrapped it around my neck and made off toward the marvel of modern city building combined with ancient roads that is downtown Suwon.

For some reason, I walked directly to Orgasm, the bar that had been closed before the Portugal game. It had advertised viewing for the matches. I had hoped to meet some Irishmen and party with them, but I also wanted to catch the early game, Sweden-Senegal. I calculated that it was probably halftime as I walked down the narrow road and entered the dark bar.

From the sounds emerging from the downstairs room, I knew the Irish were there. Amazingly, the first person I saw was John, the short, stocky law professor who had obtained the ticket for me! He was wearing a triangular straw hat, which was very Asian in it's look. He was one of the few Irishmen not wearing either his country's jersey or that of Celtic, but instead, he sported a simple green knit shirt. Covering only the top of his legs were short green shorts. A green shamrock was painted on his forehead and on each cheek was the tri-colored flag. He was a leprechaun.

The room was filled with Irish, and I pushed my way through and tried to order a pitcher, but they would only give me a bottle. I thought this strange because others were drinking from pitchers, but had to settle for a bottle of OB. I returned to where John was sitting and stood next to his table. I was able to see the TV and noticed the players were returning for the second half, but I could not see the score. An Irishman told me it was 1-1.

John told me he had been in Suwon since 11:00. He said they had been drinking all day. As I was talking to John, I heard others complaining that they were not being served pitchers. This complaint soon exploded and in minutes, I had to chug my beer down because everyone was leaving.

Once outside, the green mob was not sure where to go, so I took the lead. Almost directly across the alley was a place with the words, *Hof & Soju*. Having been in Korea much longer then the Irish, I knew *Hof* meant beer and *Soju* is a Korean liquor. I told everyone this and that we would find beer in there. Almost immediately, the group of about 12 entered the bar.

There was one large television and only a few Koreans in the place. The Irish did not hesitate in rearranging the tables, against the wishes of the overwhelmed owner. His mood did improve when we began ordering beer. I went to the bar, but one of the Irishman who had been sitting with John told me to sit down. I did as instructed and sat next to John, with a great view of the television. A very short time later, the young man returned with a pitcher, handed me a glass, and poured the cold golden happiness. John refused the glass, saying he only drank out of bottles and the guy did not hesitate in returning to the bar to buy John a large bottle of Hite, which John said was his favorite Korean beer.

I settled in to watch the match, while talking with the green-clad fans. The game was exciting, but I was sure Sweden would pull it out. As the game went on, more and more Irish poured onto this large, well-lit bar. A few of the groups entered, singing. I sang the song I had learned the day before, *Come on You Bhoys in Green*, with them.

One group had a great song that I am not sure if they made it up or if it is out of their songbook. It was to the tune of The Beatles, *Yellow Submarine* and was about their center fullback, Gary Breen. It went:

We all dream of a team of Gary Breen
A team of Gary Breen
A team of Gary Breen
Number one is Gary Breen
And number two is Gary Breen
And number three is Gary Breen
We all dream of a team of Gary Breen
Etc...

This song cracked me up and I tried to think of how I could put a U.S. player's name in there, but none really fit. The best I could come up with was Eddie Pope, but it just did not work. I thought it was too bad that Charlie Sheen did not play for us.

Some others sang a song about Niall Quinn's disco pants, which, according to the song, "go from his toes to his chest."

The game went to extra time or Golden Goal, the first game this tournament to do so. More and more Irish were coming in the bar, some with incredible outfits. There were some dressed as Leprechauns. Many had crazy green or orange wigs and there was the requisite face paint. Green dominated everything.

The Irish were split in their support, but John was vocal in his support for Senegal, so I cheered loudly for the guys with last names like mine. Extra time was very exciting. Both sides went on the attack. Sweden hit the post.   Then, seemingly out of nowhere, a Senegalese player went in on the Sweden goal and sent in a shot that found the corner of the goal. Stunningly, just like that, the game was over. The room erupted and even I smiled at the celebrations of the Africans. As disappointed as I was for the Swedes, I was overjoyed for Senegal. Having eliminated France, they were continuing to put their mark on the Cup.

I went to the bar and bought two pitchers, which I poured for those sitting near me. John simply said, "I'll have a Hite." It is amazing the spell he has over people, but I went back and bought him his own bottle. The Irish around him seemed to defer to him. I was not sure if it was his position as a professor that earned him this reverence, but everyone seemed to respect him and his wishes.

As I was returning with his bottle of Hite, I passed by a young Irishman who was handing the owner a CD and asking him to play it. The owner agreed and took it to the back. I was worried that this was some mix of techno and those goofy songs the English always play. Happily, I was wrong. It was a mixed CD, but the only thing on it was what I consider the best band of my generation, U2.

I paused for a moment to take in the surreal scene. Bono was belting out *Where the Streets Have No Names*, which was appropriate for this country of no addresses. In front of me were about a hundred soccer fans dressed in all sorts of green outfits. I was drinking Korean beer and was preparing to go to see Ireland play Spain for a spot in the quarterfinals. Excluding the U.S. games, this was the best moment of the Cup for me so far. The scene itself was amazing and I had a pretty good buzz from the beer, but the presence of U2 truly made the moment. I have a love affair with this band. I had seen them for the first time in concert earlier this year and when they walked on stage, it was a religious experience for me. Listening to them with their countrymen, added yet another dimension to them.

While in this pub, I had made a couple new friends. As my favorite U2 song, *Bad*, came on, I told them how great I thought the band was. They agreed and said there is nothing like seeing them play in Ireland. Though my sister is married to an Irishman, and I spent a short time there, it was this connection to U2 that makes me feel Irish. I took off my new scarf and pointed to the phrase that said "Irish and Proud". My new friend smiled and nodded and then said, "You are Irish today." In response, I did what I thought a real Irishman would do. I filled his mug with beer.

As I looked around at all the Irish and not one Spaniard, I wondered aloud at how strange that was. "It's not strange. We hung a flag outside," a green-faced supporter said.

"What, an Irish flag?" I asked.

"Yes. A big one. With a quote on it. A famous quote by an American."

I was not entirely sure what he was saying, but then he asked me to guess the quotation. I had no idea what American quote would be on an Irish flag, but he would not tell me.

I walked around and had my picture taken with many of those in wild costumes. As I was doing this, John and the others in our small group told me it was time to go. I downed my beer and followed them outside, where I had to fight through the flag.

It was huge, probably 10 by 15 and was hung covering the door. I had no doubt why no Spaniard had dared enter. I laughed when I read the quote: "Ask not what your country can do for you, but what you can do for your country."

"Kennedy, a good Irishman," one of them said.

Before getting in line, we stopped at a convenience store to buy more beer. I bought two large cans of OB, which I drank outside the stadium with three guys dressed as Ninjas, except that instead of all black, they were in all green.

Inside the stadium, our seats were at the opposite end that I had sat for the US-Portugal and Brazil-Costa Rica games. I realized that from this end we could not see a video replay screen. The only one was in the upper deck directly above us. This made me even happier about the seats I had for the Portugal match, as I could see that screen from them.

I found my seat and John followed me there. A few minutes before the game, I quickly ran to the bathroom and on the way back, ran into Andy Mead and his friend Wade. They said their seats were in the upper deck and asked where mine were. I pointed halfway down the lower deck, slightly to the right of the goal. I said farewell to them and said I would see them in Jeonju tomorrow and returned to my seat.

Just like the U.S. games, everyone was standing and singing. Just as the anthems were to be sung, I felt a tap on my shoulder and turned to see Andy and Wade. Andy was out of place, wearing a red shirt. He quickly pulled my scarf from around my neck and draped it around his. Their presence was not noticed as everyone was standing and though it was a bit crowded, we were not packed in.

As the game kicked off, a curious thing happened. The moment the ball was touched into play, everyone sat down! Everyone except for Andy, Wade, and I as we had assumed we would stand the whole time. The three of us looked at one another and quickly looked down behind us. There were two empty seats. He was much older than us and it has probably been a lot longer since Wade had played musical chairs. His rust showed as Andy and I quickly sat down, claiming the only vacant seats. Wade looked around for a moment and without a word, walked away.

Andy told me that the two of them were averaging a game a day and they had an agreement that if one was able to upgrade his seat, he could leave the other behind. He told me Wade would have no problem with what had just happened. I watched as Wade did find a seat some eight to ten rows from us.

On the field, Ireland attacked, but Spain grabbed the lead in the eighth minute when Morientes headed home in front of our section. We were quiet for the first time. Spain decided not to press to widen its lead and was content to counter attack. Both sides had chances, but nothing came of them from reasons ranging from terrible finishing to wonderful goalkeeping.

Halftime came and went and I learned a new song. It was the song of Celtic and an old Irish song, *The Fields of Athen Ry*, a wonderful song that can be described best as Irish. Pure Irish, with words about a free bird and imagery of green fields, mountains, and a prisoner held on a ship.

When the second half started, we all stood. Spain continued to defend and the Irish seemed to rely on Duff to cause trouble, which he did, drawing a penalty. Our side went wild, but quickly settled down as the spot kick was right in front of us and there was concern that we would distract the kicker. As Ian Harte placed the ball on the spot, a few supporters were yelling not to take pictures. The few that had pulled out cameras put them down.

Harte's kick was bad and Iker Casillas saved, but pushed the ball right to an onrushing Kevin Kilbane who should have buried the follow, but miss hit it wide. Despair settled in.

Ireland began sending high balls into Niall Quinn whose height allowed him to win nearly all of them. Ireland was attacking and playing as hard as they could. It was an exhausting pace and for a moment, I leaned back and enjoyed the action. The fans were desperate and one yelled, "Get stuck in!"

I kind of shook my head and said to Andy, "They are as stuck in as they are going to get." Andy nodded agreement as both sides were leaving it all on the field.

The stadium was growing louder and very near the end, another ball was played to Quinn, but this time, his defender nearly pulled off his jersey. Making the gutsy but correct call, the referee again pointed to the spot. Robbie Keane demanded the ball. I got my camera ready, but was scolded. Actually scolded is to tame a word. The fanatic in front of me screamed, "No picture!"

I nodded and held it down, saying out loud, but certain he could not hear me, "It's for the celebration."

Keano made no mistake and sent our section into rapture. Extra-time came and went with Ireland cursing having missed a few golden opportunities. It went to penalties. Everyone held their breath.

The players went to the far end and we realized they would be taken a long way from us. We cheered as Keane got things off to a great start, but Spain answered. We despaired as Ireland missed their next three, through Matt Holland, David Connolly, and Kilbane. Spain made two, then missed two, but put it away when their last shooter, Mendieta scored. It had been sloppy, but Spain won, 3-2.

Our section sang a rousing verse of *You'll Never Walk Alone* as most of the Irish team made the long walk over to applaud us. It was inspiring to hear them, having only moments ago suffered a crushing defeat, quickly rally in support of their lads.

It had to have been about 11:30, so I offered my condolences to John and the others around me and headed out. The Irish fans all wished me luck for tomorrow.

As I neared the shuttle bus, I noticed a familiar face. It was Daniella, the girl who had interviewed Jimmy and I the first night at Nashville.

I reintroduced myself, and we had a good conversation on the bus back to the station. She was wearing a green Ireland jersey and orange soccer socks, pulled up over her knees, which was a very hot look.

As we talked, she told me she had traveled all over Asia this summer and said Laos was her favorite. She said it was lost in time, and she simply enjoyed the people and the way they make their lives.

At the train station, I suggested that we take a train, but she told me to "Suck it up and ride the subway with me."

How could I resist her? Against my better judgment, I bought a cheap subway ticket and we were able to find two seats together. During the long ride, I learned that her assignment here was simply a summer internship.

About 45 minutes into our ride, a voice came over the speaker and announced that the train we were on would not be going all the way to Seoul. We were advised to get off. There was a large crowd on the platform waiting for the next train.

The minutes went by and Daniella grew frustrated. "Where the hell is the next train?" she demanded.

I think I upset her even more when I told her to, "Suck it up." All I could think was that I would probably be in bed had I taken the train. We were on the platform for at least a half-hour before a train came. There was a stampede to get on and she and I were separated. I rode the rest of the way standing in the crowded car. I did see her getting off, and she waved as she was herded out of the car.

Eventually I made it back to the *Dong-Il* and found a note shoved under my door. It said, "We have bus tickets and should leave here at 8:00. Jimmy"

I set my alarm for 7:45 and was distraught to see that it was currently 3:00 A.M.

Day 16
Monday, June 17

Somebody Stole My Sombrero

I think U.S. soccer fans have waited all our lives for this day. Due to the lack of coverage the sport receives, we have had to go through many things. We have driven and flown far to see our team play in friendlies. We have bought expensive European magazines to learn more about this great game. We have ordered Pay-Per-View to see meaningless exhibitions. And we have been forced to do what would be unthinkable elsewhere in the world; we have been made to huddle over our computers and stare at a seemingly unmoving screen in order to read scattered and unreliable reports as our team play important qualifying matches! I will never forget nearly going blind as a ten man U.S. side fought bravely to hold an attacking Mexico to a vital nil-nil draw in 1997. At least I read that they fought bravely and that Mexico attacked. I do not know for sure because it was not on television where I lived.

Yes, we have suffered many indignities while awaiting this day. For this is a day in which the U.S. has a good chance to advance beyond the second round in the World Cup. In fact, in my 32 years of life, we have only had this opportunity once before. In truth, playing Brazil on the Fourth of July in 1994 was not much of an opportunity. Brazil was the best side in the world, and we were still very naïve. Couple that with the suspension of John Harkes that day and only the most optimistic gave us a half chance. Even at halftime, with the score 0-0 and Brazil down a man, I was not hopeful. Of course, Brazil did find the goal and went on to win the Cup.

Today is very different than 1994. We play Mexico, a team we know so well. Of the 14 other countries in the second round, I doubt any would intimidate us less. The only others that would not outright scare us would have been Paraguay and Senegal with the possible exceptions of the two hosts, were they not holding the home field advantage. For us, the draw was perfect. Somehow, in all the drama of three nights ago, we had avoided Italy and been matched with our fiercest rival, the hated Tri-Colors of Mexico. We know them, and they know us. We hate them, and they hate us. We crave their respect, and they give us none.

Today, we will play Mexico, a team with whom we have won many a game in the last few years, but no one seems to notice. Today will be different for so many ways. The game will not be held in the intimidating Azteca Stadium or on the frozen field of Columbus or in RFK Stadium, nor will it be held in front of 70,000 obnoxious Mexican fans in the L.A. Coliseum. It will be played in a place called Jeonju. The winner will not simply earn minor bragging rights or three points toward qualification. No, today the winner will exalt in advancing to the quarterfinals in the most important sporting event in the world while relishing in the knowledge that it has banished the humiliated loser from the Orient, back to North America where it will be many years, if not decades before they will have a shot at redemption. It will be different in one other aspect. Unlike all our previous meetings that go largely unnoticed elsewhere, today the entire world will bare witness to our border war. The eyes of the football world will be focused on us, leaving the loser nowhere to hide. I pray that will not be us.

It seemed only minutes ago that I offered these prayers, before my alarm clock buzzed and I wearily rolled out of bed. One would never know how long I had waited on this day from looking at me. This was by far the most tired I had been all trip. I was so tired that a small part of me wanted to get back into bed and forget the game, but I fought off that foolishness and slowly showered and dressed, choosing to wear my new white and red Poland jersey.

Everyday, the first thing I had done, even before getting out of bed, had been to turn on the television. Today, I had forgotten, and after dressing, finally realized the room was too quiet. I bent down to pick up the remote and stretched a few seconds while doing so before turning on the set. I was devastated by what I saw on the screen. It was the time and it said, 7:38! Somehow, my alarm clock had been set about 45 minutes fast. I thought about climbing back into bed for seven minutes more of sleep, but realized that this sudden awareness of the time had caused my heart rate to increase to the point that sleep would be unlikely in the next few minutes.

Instead, I went into the hallway and found Jimmy almost ready to go. A quick trip upstairs revealed that Tom had made himself a shirt for the game. He had painted USA in red on a wife beater. We collected Jimmy and were off.

We caught a cab to the bus station. Once there we saw a bus leaving at 9:20 for Jeonju. We had thought it was 9:30 and I had to forego the decent breakfast that I needed. Rather, I quickly grabbed a chocolate donut for W800. After buying it and hurrying to the line, we realized that there was both a 9:20 and a 9:30 bus, for which we held tickets. I easily finished the donut before we had to board. Once onboard, we spread out, each setting up camp in our own aisle of two seats.

The first thing I noticed was that there was no bathroom. As comfortable as the seats were, I feared this would become cause for concern. Mercifully, we stopped well before things became serious at about 11:00 at a rest area very similar to those on the Jersey Turnpike. There were bathrooms and a number of small restaurants. I really wanted something Korean, but did not want to be eating noodle soup on the bus, so opted for the fast food looking Lotteria, where I ordered the Chicken Burger Set, consisting of the burger, fries, and a Coke all for W3,000 or just under $2.50. On the way back to the bus, I passed a large grill on which the two "chefs" were laying out living squid.

A little over an hour later, the stadium came into sight. Jimmy leaned over my seat and pointed to it and said, "Too bad we can't get off here, the bus stop downtown is a good ways away." But once again, things worked out. The bus driver pulled to the curb and opened the door. Tom, Jimmy, and I hurried off, thanking the driver on the way out.

It was three hours until game time and there were only a few people around. The sun was blazing, but we noticed a large tent set up near the stadium. We stood under it and waited for the rest of the Yanks to arrive. There was a refreshment stand nearby, and I bought a Coke, as did Tom who reached into his backpack and pulled out a pint-sized bottle of *Soju* he had purchased in a convenient store earlier in the morning. It had cost about a dollar. I took a large sip, but really only to see what it tasted like. I immediately wished I had not. It was clear and hot. It brought back college memories and the taste of grain alcohol. I gulped down about half of my Coke to get the taste out of my mouth and the feeling out of my throat and stomach. Tom decided it was better to mix it with Coke than to drink it straight. I avoided it all together.

People were arriving in droves, and there was some action nearby. A crowd surrounded a man juggling a soccer ball better than anyone I had ever seen. The man turned out to be Coach Woo, the coach of the University of Hawaii soccer team and record holder for longest continuous juggling session. He put on a fantastic display of juggling as well as balancing the ball on his head.

Soon, we were joined by Mark, the lawyer from D.C., who had seen Vladimir and his other friends leave after the first round. Mike also met up with us. They both were drinking the cans of Budweiser, the only choice of beer at the stadiums and were chiding me for not imbibing. But that shot of *Soju* had been enough for me. I wanted to remember this game with a clear mind. I did not need anything to get me more up for the game. In addition, it was so hot that I was concerned about dehydration. We were going to be in this sun a long time and I wanted to make sure I could last the whole game.

Our group of five enjoyed ourselves, and we talked more about our experiences here than of the day's game. Perhaps we were nervous. As great as a victory would be, a loss would hurt so much. From time to time, a few Mexicans would approach us. They were very different than the Mexicans I have encountered at matches in the U.S. Generally back home the Mexican fans live in the U.S. For some reason they feel the need to be extra loud and obnoxious. The phrase, "If you like it so much, why don't you go back?" is heard often from American fans.

These Mexican fans were very much like all the others we have encountered here: friendly, humorous, and fun. It was a refreshing change from the usual Green Shirts we encounter who are profane, combative, and threatening. One of these "new" Mexicans stopped by to offer us a sample of what he promised was the best tequila in all of Mexico, a brand called Don Julio. After watching him take a swig (you can't be too careful, he was wearing a tricolor jersey) the four of us, all but Jimmy of course, took a mouthful. Not being a tequila connoisseur, I could not differentiate it from the cheap stuff I had once drank way too much of in college.

Other Mexicans stopped by to shake hands and make their predictions on the game. They were confident, very confident and that pleased me. They were looking past us, perhaps looking for revenge from Germany from 1998. Their confidence also showed the lack of respect they have for us. In the previous four World Cup Qualification matches, both countries had a win, a loss, and two ties. Yet, despite our even record as of late, they still considered us their whipping boy.

With an hour left before game time, Jimmy and I left the group and walked the few hundred yards to the stadium. There we were quickly searched and sent inside. When we got to the entrance to the stands, we noticed our tickets pointed us up into the upper deck! Unhappily, we trudged up the steps to find ourselves at the bottom of the uncomfortably steep upper deck. We found our seats about eight rows up. There were other Americans there, and we were glad that we were not alone.

As the minutes went on, more and more Yanks came through the entrance and nearly everyone complained about FIFA sticking us up here. A few of us walked from row to row, trying to determine if we should make a move to the lower sections. A lot of support was gathered and the NY Crew took the lead, and decided that if there was an open section, we would all go there once the game began.

It was still a half hour before game time, but for some reason, the security guards around us were trying to get us all in our seats. This was not sitting well with us as we were leisurely visiting the new friends we had made. At one point, I was returning from a trip to the restroom and was behind a few Americans I did not know. As they began their way up the steep steps to their seats, one of them spotted a friend sitting in the middle of the second row. The young man yelled to his friend and made some small talk. The security guard grabbed the guy, who was right in front of me, and shoved him up the steps. Before he could react, and I could tell he was going to, I inserted myself in between them and motioned with my hands for the guard to calm down. I did it in the way that referees do, with my palms down, forearms moving up and down.

"Easy, easy," I said.

The American fan yelled, "Calm down. This is the World Cup!"

One of us must have gotten to the guard, because he simply turned and walked away. I think his over reaction came more from a nervousness on his part than any real animosity. I think that whenever the U.S. plays, tensions are higher, not so much from a soccer standpoint as we just do not have hooligans, but from a national standpoint and the politics that follow our country everywhere.

As the players completed their warm-ups and left the field, Tony Meola turned toward us and punted a ball that flew up into our section. We all cheered him. Kasey Keller turned and did the same, though his ball fell short of the upper deck. A few minutes later a smiling Mike came down the aisle to where Jimmy and I were standing carrying the ball!

"Is that the one Meola kicked up here?"

"Yeah. I skied to get it!"

Soon, the teams were back on the field and we cheered and sang for them. The lineups were announced and Arena had made an interesting tactical move. Jeff Agoos was injured and out for the rest of the tournament. Frankie Hejduk was suspended for this match. With those two starters out coupled with the fact that reserve Steve Cherundolo had been injured just before the tournament, we were short on defenders. I was certain that David Regis would be inserted into the left back position vacated by Hejduk. It was a position that had been his until the Portugal game. At some point in the last month of training, Arena had lost confidence in him and had moved Hejduk to that spot. From today's lineup, it was clear just how much confidence Arena had lost. All of it.

We read on the scoreboard that we were only playing three defenders, Gregg Berhalter, who was seeing his first action of the tournament, and mainstays, Tony Sanneh and Eddie Pope. There were four midfielders, Pable Mastroeni, John O'Brien, Eddie Lewis, and Claudio Reyna; and three forwards, Brian McBride, Landon Donovan, and Josh Wolff.

I doubted we would line up in a 3-4-3 but could not figure what we would do. Certainly Donovan would play in the midfield, but where would that leave Reyna?

Before we had time to discuss all this, the anthems were played. The teams ran to their positions, the U.S. defending the goal below us, giving us a good look at Arena's tactical lineup. We were in a 3-5-2. The midfield had Reyna on the right wing! I was aware that he had played that position, as well as right back, for Rangers when he was there, but never thought that he would not be our creative midfielder. That role was left to Donovan. Lewis took up the left wing, which left O'Brein and Mastroeni at defensive mids.

As soon as the ball was put into play, we headed for the exits in droves. The stadium was maybe just over half full. We had speculated that many Koreans had snapped up these tickets, guessing that they would see their beloved Reds, never thinking they would have won the group and headed to Daejeon. There was a nearly empty section below us, in the corner to the right of the goal. That section was our destination.

"Oh when the Yanks, Go marching in, Oh when the Yanks go marching in, Oh I want to be in that number, When the Yanks go marching in!" Hundreds of us sang as we, in an unbelievably orderly fashion, made our way down the steps, through the concourse, into an entranceway, and down to our new seats at field level. In all honesty, to simply watch the game, our original seats were much better. From the perch high above, we could see everything quite well. It was, like most in Korea, a small stadium, and we were not too high. They were fine seats. However, watching the game was not what we had come to do. We had flown nearly 20 hours to be involved, to encourage, inspire, and support. That cannot be done effectively from the upper deck.

We were now squeezed tightly together, two of us for every one seat, though we would never use them. We were low and in the corner, not an optimal viewing location, but we were close to the field, which is what we wanted. The players now knew we were here.

***

As I finally situate myself, squeezed between Jimmy and Tom, I see on the scoreboard that I had missed the first 2:10, but there had been no goals, nor had I heard any loud cheers, so I doubt I missed anything. The play is away from us. These new seats have inspired us and we are making a lot more noise than we did before the game.

Mexico attacks and wins a corner, but a dangerous looking cross from their best player, Blanco, crossed the end line and we breathe a sigh of relief. Though it is not full, the stadium is loud and many are chanting the familiar, "May-He-Co! May-He-Co!" But, we respond in a language that they will understand, *Estados Unidos! Estados Unidos!*" To our right, along the sidelines, we see the three Elvis. They are in a section with a few green shirts in big sombreros. We can see them in a friendly exchange with the Mexicans and we chant for them, "Elvis!"Clap-clap "Elvis!"Clap-clap.

Suddenly Reyna is running down the right wing. He lays the ball off, I see McBride streaking in, the ball comes to him. I have a very good feeling which is proven correct as McBride hammers a shot into the goal!

We erupt! I am jumping up and down, hugging Jimmy, Tom, and a few others. The clock reads under eight minutes! What a fantastic start! The big flag is unfolded and we wave it, but it only stays out a few seconds as nobody wants to miss anything. We chant, "U!S!A! U!S!A!" It had dawned on me earlier that there are a lot fewer of us here, many have gone home after the first round. To make up for our missing friends, we sing louder than before, "Oh, Oh-Oh, Oh-Oh, Oh-Oh-Oh-Oh, Oh-O-O, Oh-O-O, Oh-O-O, Oh-Oh-Oh, U!S!A!" And then, the *Immigrant song*, mostly drums, but then, "U.S. A.Aaaaay! U.S.A.Aaaaay!"

The replay shows that it was Wolff who dropped the ball back to McBride. It was a wonderful back pass. The play went Reyna, Wolff, McBride.

We taunt the Mexican's. They have a chant that goes, "May-He-Co, May-He-Co, Ra-Ra-Ra!" We chant, "May-He-Co, May-He-Co, Ha-Ha-Ha!" They hear us and return fire. The excitement is building, but I am glad we are the ones with the lead. I do know that there is a long time left, and Mexico will not quit. If I had not known that, I am reminded in the 15th minute, Moralas cuts to the middle and finds space. He shoots and Friedel seems beaten, but the ball scoots just outside the post nearest us.

The Mexicans cheer their good play, and we wonder how he found that much room, that near the goal. There have been a few shaky moments in front of our goal and this worries me. I love Friedel, and he has been wonderful this Cup, but we cannot continue to rely on him.

184

Mexico has an awful lot of the ball, and we are falling back, not bunkering in, but defending in numbers. Four of our five midfielders are helping our three defenders. Mexico is having trouble getting near our goal as we continue our singing. It is hot out and humid. We are in the sun, and it is draining. My body is tired and does not want to stand and sing, but I am not listening to it. This is the U.S and Mexico in the World Cup! I would never forgive myself for sitting this one out.

Out of nowhere, Blanco hits a 35 yarder that Friedel does not handle well, but we make the clearance. Moments later, Pope draws a yellow card. Many of us ask if that is his second. It would be terrible to not have him for Germany, should we hold on here. There is disagreement, but most say it is his first. Others say it does not matter, that they are wiped away after the first round. In any case there is confusion, and we will have to wait to see.

A few minutes later, Mexico makes an absurd move, substituting out Moralas, the player who had the close miss. Obviously, their coach, Aguirre is unhappy with him. However, the player they bring in is Luis Hernandez. We laugh at first, but then begin to chant, "MLS reject! MLS reject! MLS reject!" As we do this, I wonder how terrible it would be for him to be the one to beat us.

Mexico continues to posses, but the game is being played mostly in the midfield, which is fine with me. Mexico looks dangerous, but is failing to make the final pass. They are pressuring, but we are holding. We sing to let our boys know we are there for them. Pope makes a bad pass just outside the box. Sanneh blocks the shot, but it caroms toward the goal. Friedel seems to have trouble and weakly pushes it out, but it goes right to Blanco who is alone at the penalty spot. I do not want to look; I am sure he will bury it. The play unfolds like many of the U.S. goals for me, in slow motion. Blanco brings it down with his chest but not where he wanted to. He still has a shot, but puts it right to Friedel, who is just able to push it away, but to an onrushing Hernandez. "Oh no, not him! Anyone but him!" I think, but the angle is too acute and he shoots into the side netting.   Disaster averted. I have no idea how Blanco, whom I consider a fabulous player, blew that one. We were lucky.

We look shaky for another minute, but then a Mexican gets booked for a foul on Lewis. This calms us and on the restart, Wolff is sent in alone, but shoots right at their keeper, and he knocks it out for a corner. This fires us up, and we are back to matching the Mexican's intensity.

Mexico goes back on the attack, but again fail to get the last pass through. There is a scare as Friedel and Borgetti collide, but the tall Mexican striker is offside.

Now it is into injury time and I pray we will not give up a late one. A great chant begins, a first for this one. We do the Tomahawk Chop, made famous by Florida State University and then the Atlanta Braves. It is a natural soccer chant as every American knows it. I love doing it and am sure the players hear us. We survive a couple corners and the whistle is blown. Halftime, 1-0 to the U.S.

At halftime, I find Monty. "Too bad your passport was stolen!" I yell to him. Grinning, he says, "Yeah, that sucked."

185

"Where would you be?" I ask.

"Probably in a bar in Boston. Damn those bastards who took it," he says with more than a bit of sarcasm.

"Are you staying for Germany?"

"No, my boss knows I get it back tomorrow. I will get back just in time for that game." We exchange cameras and take each other's picture while standing next to the field. Halftime goes quickly and as we are taking pictures, the second half begins and I find my way back to my standing place.

Mexico is now attacking the goal away from us, and I am worried that all the action will be way down there. Mastroeni is booked and just afterwards Friedel has to make a big save which is followed by a foul, just outside the box. Blanco will certainly shoot and does so, but right into the wall. "That's a lot of pressure this soon in the half," I say to Jimmy and notice that Tom has moved and I have a little more room. Finally we get the ball down to our end, but Wolff is booked, I think for delay.

Mexico gets another free kick just outside the box and Friedel does not look confident as he puts it out for a corner. Confusion ensues on the corner and Berhalter is booked. We survive another corner but do not look good doing so.

The Green Shirts continue to attack and win another corner, but we clear again. We are singing but are worried. Most of the play is at the other end, but we counter. McBride whiffs on a shot, but the ball continues to Reyna. We all position for a better view and Reyna hits it hard, but right to the keeper.

We are doing a lot of fouling, and I am not sure if it is out of desperation or if the ref is calling everything their way. It is just before the hour, and Arena subs in Earnie Stewart for Wolff. Mexico continues to press and Friedel is quick off his line to punch away a dangerous cross. Then a shot goes high and wide. We are urging our boys on as are the Mexican fans. "*Estados Unidos*!" we chant.

Mexico wins another 22-yard free kick, but it sails a few feet wide. We try to attack, but Mexico shepherds the ball out for a goal kick. We do little pressing in the Mexican end, rather choosing to pick them up near midfield. This produces a turnover. O'Brien finds Lewis who is flying down his wing, rushing right at us. He has room and sends in a cross. Anxiously, we look towards the goal and see Donovan there. The cross is perfect and the youngster meets it with his head. In a flash we are celebrating a two-goal lead! This may be our best celebration since that first magical goal against Portugal. This goal will send us to the quarterfinals!

There is disbelief in our section, which makes our cheers all the more intense. In all the scenarios I had played in my head, I had really never looked past the first round. Everything had centered on advancing out of group play. Even the few times I looked to this game, we put up a brave fight against Italy to earn respect. Once or twice, I had considered us playing Mexico, but for some reason, I never played that game in my head. I always left it as a tremendous place to advance our rivalry.

These few hundred Yanks had flown thousands of miles to support our countrymen, but I doubt many of us thought we would still be supporting them in the quarters. This turn was stunning. There was no rhyme or reason to this celebration. We are all screaming, some of us unable to form words, such is our mindset. We are jumping up and down and, again, hugging strangers. They are strangers, but they are Americans, and we are rejoicing that. I think I hear drums beating, in the midst of high-pitched screams combined with deep, guttural urgings. This, I realize, is the sound of joy.

We are in the 64th minute. Our party will last all night. Or will it? The Mexicans attack and as I look up, I see Hernandez fall in the box. The referee blows his whistle and it grows silent around us. "Dear God, no," I say aloud. Again, my prayers are answered. The ref pulls out a yellow card and books *El Matador* for diving. This sends us into another frenzy. They tried to beat us but failed, so they tried to trick the ref, but that did not work either. Victory is close.

We fall back even more, but counter. Stewart has a bad touch in the box, which causes him to not be able to shoot, but he lays off to O'Brien who blazes a shot just over the bar. Things are looking very good for us, and we sing with the energy of teenagers. Then Blanco is assessed a yellow.

McBride pressures them in their end and a back pass skips over their keepers foot and out for a corner for us. Stewart volleys the cross off the bar and we go wild. But Mexico is not finished and the ball is dangerously sent across our goalmouth.

Mexico is really pushing forward which is giving us many counter opportunities. Mexico takes a long shot which Friedel pushes over, but, once again, their corner comes to nothing. We have a little possession, and we sing perhaps the best song yet. I am sure it is a NY Crew original. It goes like this:

> *I Yi-Yi-Yi-Yi-Yi*
> *Somebody stole my sombrero*
> *A dirty old rat*
> *Has taken my hat*
> *And now I have nothing to WEAR-O*
> *WEAR-O*
> *I Yi-Yi-Yi-Yi-Yi*

I think some of the Mexicans in other sections are able to understand it because a few suddenly have become very angry, and we see the Elvises taking some abuse. But they are fine because they know the score.

Mexico makes a substitution and we follow shortly by bringing on Cobi Jones for McBride. Cobi immediately gets knocked down and stepped over. A minute later, in the 81st, he draws a yellow by taking a brutal tackle.

We sing on and on, but I have a bad feeling, like we could give up two goals and have to play overtime. I think I am thinking about something I had once heard one of my youth coaches say late in a two-goal game, "They are only a lucky goal away from a one goal game."

A Mexican player is injured and is carted off. On the ensuing kick, Mexico fouls in their box. The ref blows the whistle well before the ball comes down. When it does, a Mexican fires it at our goal. Friedel volleys it back and for some reason is given a yellow for delay. I am furious! The ref has obviously not seen the Mexican shoot the ball at him. I am really mad, but Jimmy calms me down, telling me there is less than eight minutes left.

Another Mexican is booked for hammering Donovan and we can tell that they are out for blood.

"*Estados Unidos*!" we chant so they can hear us. We win a corner and take our time. We fall back to defend and Cobi takes another shot; this one a combination of a flying kick and headbutt from their captain, Marquez, who is sent off for it. Cobi is down for a while and gets up looking woozy. But for us, that has settled it; there will be no comeback for the Mexicans. We are through. Our only concern is for the safety of our players as the Mexicans have abandoned hope of a goal and are intent on making us pay in other ways.

Just before full time, we break into *The Goodbye Song*. I sing this with as much gusto as I have ever sang anything. "Na-na-na-na, Na-na-na-na, Hey-hey-hey, Goodbye!" We are loud and proud, and the Mexican fans know they are beaten and sit quietly.

Cobi is once again drilled, this time in the corner right in front of us, but though his back was to the two Mexicans that plowed into him, he is charged with the foul.

Into injury time, Carlos Llamosa comes on for Mastroeni. I am always so proud to see Llamosa play for us as he is the epitome of the American Dream.

Cobi breaks down the wing and sends a great cross, again to Donovan, but this time, the youngster shoots over with the goal at his mercy. That would have put the cherry on top. Mexico quickly goes down and wins a few corners, but finally we get a goal kick. As Friedel puts the ball in play, the referee blows the whistle, and we are in the quarterfinals of the World Cup!

***

We celebrated as expected, singing all the while. I went down to the first row, closest to the field, as did many others. We were crammed tightly together and below us, a bunch of cameramen were taking our picture. More of the players than before came over to acknowledge us. Cobi, Friedel, and Hejduk, who had not played, spent the most time and seemed much more into it than the others.

We sang and danced in the stadium for about 15 more minutes, before security told us it was time to go. Just like the Poland and Portugal games, we simply moved the celebration to an area just outside the stadium. This was a lot of fun. People were playing drums, the rest were singing and dancing. Somebody had a sign that said, "Friedel=The Human Wall." Later two guys carried a large sign that said,

"USA: Let's Roll!" I thought that was the best one I had seen. A few others proclaimed, "USA Team Fighting!" a takeoff on the Korean team's slogan. I think we are all fans of Korea now. Not only did their victory over Portugal put us through, but their hospitality had been simply wonderful.

Then I saw a few guys with a replica of the Cup. I quickly found Mike and posed for a few pictures with the Cup and the official ball he had caught earlier. Everywhere was Red, White, and Blue. Eventually, we began to break up. We had heard the party would be at The Rose Garden. Nobody was sure where it was, just that that is where we would all be. Somebody said it was near the university, which really meant nothing at all to me.

I walked away from the stadium with Jimmy, Monty, Kaela, Mike, Scott, Neil, Chuck, and an older gentleman that I think knew Chuck. Just as we were off the grounds, I turned for another look at the stadium when I noticed a group of Korean girls wearing the neon yellow Steward shirts. They were exchanging them with some Mexicans. The first time I had seen these shirts, I wanted one. They are sharp looking, with the World Cup logo on the sleeve and STEWARD written across the back.

I ran off to them, but only one girl had hers left, the others were wearing the now disgraced green shirts. I offered her my Poland jersey. She thought for a second before shaking her head, no. Her friends tried to talk her into it and I used all my sales techniques, but she would not budge. I was about to give up, when another of their friends ran up. They said something in Korean to her and she took a quick look at my shirt. She then pulled off her Steward shirt. I did the same and we made the exchange. "Com-Som-Nee-Da," I said, and they all giggled as I ran off wearing my new souvenir.

We made our way to the shuttle bus stop, but decided we would take a cab to The Rose Garden. Most of the group ran across the street, and I was about to follow when I heard Scott yell at me. I turned and he said that he and Neil had to get back to Seoul. Their flight leaves early the next morning. We said our good-byes and shook hands. As I ran off, I thought that I would really miss those two brothers from Seattle. I hoped that we would keep in touch.

As I caught up to the group, I found Monty and a Mexican yelling at each other. This Mexican was much more like those I am familiar with at game in the U.S. He was loud and argumentative, very much unlike the other Mexicans we had met earlier who shared their tequila with us.

This guy and Monty were having a heated exchange and it took a few of us to pull Monty away before fists flew. As we walked away, this guy yelled in almost perfect English, "Go home to your jobs! You will be working next week! Me, I don't work."

I could not resist. "We know!" I yelled back. Then we all broke into a patriotic song and left the sore loser behind in the heat. Soon we found two cabs. Monty, Mike, Jimmy, and I jumped into one, leaving Kaela to ride with Chuck and his friend, a fact that was not lost on any of us. If looks could kill, we would have buried Monty right there in Jeonju after Kaela made her feelings about the cab situation known. We all ribbed Monty about leaving her with Chuck.

Of course, neither driver knew where The Rose Garden was and our cab followed the other around for a while, Kaela glaring out of the back window at us the whole time. We could see Chuck talking away, no doubt complaining about something. Eventually we came to what had to be a college. Our driver rolled down the window and asked some students. After talking to them, he made a U-Turn and we emerged from the campus setting into a happening part of town. After going through a few lights, he pulled to the curb and let us out.

We assumed we were there, but we were wrong, there was no Rose Garden in sight. Jimmy said he recognized this place from his earlier trip to Jeonju and said we were near the bus station. Somebody asked a helpful older woman, but she did not know. As I surveyed the scene, I noticed there was a sign that said, "Coffee and Beer." I suggested we go in and cool off. Our group, joined by the old lady and another Korean she had been talking to, trudged up the steps. I entered first, followed by Mike who let out a yell announcing our arrival. His broadcast was heard by the only person there, the bar owner, a good-looking Korean woman who had been sleeping at one of the tables! Mike's scream had shocked her awake.

The room was small, just a bar and a small glass coffee table surrounded by some leather chairs and a sofa. There were a few large plants and on the walls were pictures of American lingerie models. We ordered a pitcher and were in surprisingly good humor about everything. Not even being lost could suppress our joy at the day's game. When we finished the pitcher, I went to pay, but the old lady told me it was free because, she said in broken English, but with great enthusiasm, "Congratulations! To U.S.A. Team!" she sang out the words and the barkeeper smiled at me.

I told Monty and we decided we should order another, so she would make some money off us, but once again, there was no charge, because, "Congratulations! To U.S.A. Team!" the old lady repeated to our amusement. I told Monty we should just stay here and drink for free all night. However, the old lady announced that the Korean man knew where The Rose Garden was and he would lead us there.

We all threw some *won* on the table and left on foot. The sun was beginning to go down and it had cooled off quite a bit. After about a ten-minute walk, we were at The Rose Garden. As we went in, we heard loud chants of, "U!S!A! U!S!A!" We joined in, and then realized they were for us. There was only a small group of fans there and they were happy to see us, thinking they were in the wrong place. Before we even approached them, the DJ played The Eagles' *Hotel California*. There were maybe 15 Americans there and we all sang that great song. It was a magical moment, singing along with my countrymen on this wonderful day.

Soon others found the Garden, including the three Elvises. One of them turned out to be Dave, one of the guys I had met at the Brickskeller in D.C. before leaving. He told me he had replaced one of the original Elvises who had returned home. The DJ put on Hound Dog and we all danced with the Kings. Within an hour, the place filled with Americans, and we danced and toasted for hours.

Monty, Kaela, and I went out for dinner and ate a wonderful chicken and pasta dish. The noodles were clear, and we had to cut them with scissors. It was spicy, and we drank a few large OB's with it. The restaurant had a TV showing the Brazil-Belgium match, which Brazil won 2-0. Both Rivaldo and Ronaldo scored meaning both of them had scored in all four of Brazil's matches. I actually thought Belgium outplayed them, but in any case, on the day we play Germany, Brazil will face England in a dream match up.

Returning to The Rose Garden, we found there to be many more people inside. The fun American classics had been replaced with techno and we saw some stewardesses dancing on the tables. Many Yanks joined in with the stewardesses, but I ended up talking with a guy in a Celtic uniform. I told him Ireland had been unlucky and he agreed. I then told him that I loved singing *The Fields of Athen Ry*. He told me that it is the song of Celtic, so I asked if Rangers have a song. "Yes," he said, "*The Sash*, it's called." I asked him to sing it, but predictably, he refused, saying he would never sing the Ranger's song.

Mike, Monty, Kaela, and other Yanks all told Jimmy and I that their hotel had vacancy and we could follow them back if we wanted. We thanked them and said that we would do so. Mike and I wasted some time kicking his new ball around on the dirty floor.

We drank a lot and had a great time all night. Monty came to me and said he was leaving and asked if Jimmy and I wanted to go to his hotel. I was having too good a time to leave, so I told him goodbye and said we would get together in the States. I told Kaela I would see her in Ulsan. They left and another good supporter was on his way home.

I went back to the Irishman in the Celtic uniform. I filled his glass and again asked him to sing *The Sash*. I guess he had drank a lot, because he did so! I was stunned watching a guy in the green and white hoop shirt singing the Ranger's song. When he finished and I questioned him about it, he shrugged it off.

It was late and the club had thinned out. Slower music was played. Mike said he was leaving. He was going to Japan for the rest of the Cup. Jimmy and I declined to go back to his hotel, and we told him and his World Cup ball goodbye, but promised to look him up in San Francisco if I ever get there. We shook hands and he left.

Jimmy and I looked around and it suddenly dawned on us that we were the only Yanks there! A bit of panic struck. It was about 1:30, and we were in a strange city with no room. Jimmy suggested we go to the bus station and see if we could get back to Seoul.

There was a cute Korean girl sitting near me and I turned to her and said, "Do the buses go back to Seoul this late?"

Her almost unbelievable answer was, "I would go back with you, but I have a class tomorrow."

I was dumbfounded. I had no idea what a great pickup line that would be. I collected myself and asked again, "Can I go back to Seoul at this hour?"

She answered that she did not know. Jimmy and I decided it was worth a shot. Remembering the buses have no bathrooms, I went to use the one in the bar. As I was leaving, the song *Always*, by Bon Jovi came on. Ivy and I love Bon Jovi. In fact we had managed to get backstage passes to their concert in D.C. a few months before and had met them. This song made me homesick, and I wished that she had been here with me to dance to this song.

Before leaving, I asked the Korean girl to dance. She agreed and we danced to this cheesy, yet classic, Bon Jovi song. I kept telling her how we had met him, but she just sang along, which was pretty funny, with her accent. As soon as the song ended, I told her goodbye, and Jimmy and I left for the bus station.

Miraculously, Jimmy knew exactly how to get there, however after the roughly 15 minute walk, we found the station locked. The streets were empty, but I saw in the distance, a building with the symbol for hotel on it. We went in and were grateful to find a room for W20,000. Somehow, I ended up in the bed and Jimmy slept on the floor. The TV was showing *The Ace*, or *The Great Santini*, starring one of my favorite actors, Robert Duval. I watched this great movie as long as I could, but was so tired that I did not make it far.

Day 17
Tuesday, June 18

Are You Watching Japan?

Somehow we were up just after 8:00 and got to the bus station to catch a 9:40 bus to Seoul with five minutes to spare. I thought the ticket was expensive, W15,200 or just over $12.00, but maybe it was the cobwebs in my head.

We rode back to Seoul as Champions of our region as well as one of the final eight teams in the World Cup! Not even a bad lunch of a Chicken Burger, cold fries, and a Coke from the rest area could dampen my good humor. Jimmy ordered and ate a shrimp burger, which, from what I could tell, was one shrimp that had been flattened until it was the size of the bun and then fried.

From the station in Seoul, we rode the subway back, and it was a long ride. At one point an older Korean came aboard and began preaching. I am sure that is what he was doing because he sounded just like some of the evangelists we see in America preaching on the street and on television. I could not understand a word he said, so after watching him for a few minutes, I returned to the newspaper I had been reading. Occasionally I looked up at him, and he would shoot me a look. I thought that somehow he had recognized I was a Christian and was happy for me. At times, he pointed at me and I thought he was saying that if I was a believer, anyone could be. However, near the end of his sermon, he hit me. I had my left foot resting on my right knee and he took his hand and really smacked my foot. At first I thought it a friendly gesture, but after taking a moment to consider, I changed my mind. I began to think that he thought that I was a heathen, an evil American, and he was using me as an example of what not to be. Before I could figure the whole thing out, he had moved to the next car.

Back on the streets near the *Dong-Il*, we immediately noticed a difference. While we had been gone someone had turned the city red. We soon realized it was the street vendors. They now lined the street and were selling those Be the Reds T-Shirts that seemed to be the only proper mode of dress. They were also selling flags, scarves, and towels. Jimmy and I were in a good mood and were excited about the Korea-Italy game later this evening. We each bought a "Be the Reds" t-shirt for W8,000. I also picked up a Korea Team Fighting towel and a Red Devil Mask, each for W4,000. No one was going to accuse me of not having the proper spirit.

Back at the *Dong-Il*, I put on my new gear, complete with the mask and went downstairs to show off for the two ladies. One of them was in the hallway with her back to me. I tapped her on the shoulder. Unfortunately, I do not think she had ever seen a devil mask before. She let out a shriek and nearly fell over. I quickly pulled off the mask to assure her that her soul was safe. After a few moments she calmed down and laughed at me.

193

Jimmy and I went to the PC Bang and Damian greeted us with congratulations on the big win. He then presented me with the game I had previously spoken about with him, *Padduk*. I thanked him and forced him to take W10,000 that he said it had cost.

Jimmy and I spent a long time there. The first thing I did was to open my E-Mail. I was curious to see a letter from Ivy whose subject was, "Holy Handball, Batman!" In reading it, I realized, for the first time, that John O'Brien had punched a ball clear in our box. It had occurred at the end away from us, and none of us in the stands had any idea it had happened. In reading other reports, I learned that they had made a big deal out of it on the telecast, and rightly so. While it certainly does not have the importance of Diego Maradona's "Hand of God" goal in the 1986 Cup, I told Jimmy that it must have been, The Hand of Uncle Sam.

I read a lot of reports on the game and sent a long E-Mail to my friends detailing yesterday and last night. As soon as I sent it, I realized I had made a terrible mistake. For some reason I had included the part about dancing with the Korean girl. I had also included Ivy on the long list of recipients. I quickly sent her a note saying not to worry, that it was no big deal, that I had left right after the song, and that I did not even know her name. I then prayed she would understand.

As I was reading and writing, I was aware that the Japan-Turkey match was on the small television, but I was not too interested in it and paid little attention. So little attention in fact that as I was about to leave, I realized they were in injury time and Turkey was leading 1-0. I felt a little disappointed that Japan and their fans were going out. However, when the whistle blew, the 20 or so Koreans in the PC Bang cheered loudly.

"You guys really don't like Japan, huh?" I said to Damian.

He was grinning ear to ear as he told me that they sure don't. He related to me that Koreans are taught early and often of what the Japanese did during World War II. How they forced the Korean women to be sexual slaves for the Japanese troops among other things. Damian also told me that this same history is not taught in Japan, and they are mostly ignorant of it. He said that many Japanese come to Korea to shop, being that prices are much lower here than in Japan. He said Koreans poke fun at them, and the Japanese are blissfully unaware of it.

I asked Damian where City Hall was. That is the place that an estimated 500,000 Koreans gather to watch their games on large screens. I thought it was nearby but was not sure where it was. Keep in mind that this was the first chance I have had to watch the Koreans with Koreans. For their first match, I was at the U.S. party at Nashville. I was at their second match, rooting against the red mass, and their final first round game was played the same time as ours with Poland. Thus I was excited about the game. I wanted to see their fanatical fans in person and cheer with them.

Before the tournament, I would have never thought they would have any chance against Italy. However, after seeing them live and the way they run like

194

crazy, and the surprising technical skill they have combined with the unbelievable support they enjoy, I think they have a good chance. In fact, I wrote to Ivy, "I am hoping they win and can't believe I am saying this, but I think they really can!"

Damian told me it is down two blocks and turn left and go one block. I was stunned it was that close. Down two blocks and turn right is the U.S. Embassy. I tried to clarify the directions, but he said, "Just follow the crowd."

When Jimmy and I finally left the PC Bang, I was stunned at the scene outside. There were thousands of red shirted Koreans all heading toward City Hall. Jimmy and I decided to eat a good dinner first, so we returned to the restaurant where we had eaten the first night. We pointed to the same Korean symbols on the wall as we had done over two weeks earlier and ate the same delicious beef cooked at our table and wrapped in lettuce with garlic cloves, onions, red sauce, and other toppings; and, of course, *kim' chi*.

At 7:30, an hour before the game, dressed in red and carrying the Korea Team Fighting towel, we headed off to City Hall. We only made it as far as the street where we were to turn left. This wide boulevard, the very one where we had survived the taxi wreck, was jammed with people. 99 percent of them were wearing red and nearly all of them were sitting. Jimmy and I walked for about five minutes, looking for a spot to sit, before finally finding one well over a hundred yards from the screen.

As we were about to sit, a Korean teenager gave us each a piece of newspaper on which to sit. I marveled at the scene, there were people as far as I could see. From the air, I am sure we resembled a giant red ant colony. There was an old lady making her way through the crowd selling a dried squid. The atmosphere was electric and I stayed for about 15 minutes.

I was really excited about this game and wanted to watch it with the Korean mob, but even more, I wanted to see the game. I was sure that from where we sat, I would be able to make out very little. So, I left. Jimmy remained in the sea of red.

I decided to find a bar and drink a few beers while watching the game. I was going against traffic and had to dodge the thousands still making their way to the scene, but eventually I turned onto our little road. It was much less crowded and I felt I could finally breathe. I had only taken a few steps, when I had to stop as I broke out in laughter. In front of me was John, the Irishman who had got me the ticket. He was wearing a "Be the Reds" t-shirt and had the Korean flag painted on both of his cheeks. It was a fantastic sight and I snapped a few pictures of him, before advising him not to go where he was headed. I tried to convince him to watch with me, but he had none of it and ventured off into the red after offering his congratulations on our win.

I went a few doors past the *Dong-Il* and entered the empty Blues Bar. I sat down right in front of the TV and ordered a pitcher of OB. As if people were afraid to be the first ones in, the cool, dark club filled up soon afterwards. Some Irishmen sat at the table behind me and then a couple of their friends came in and I welcomed them at my table. The rest of the bar was filled with Koreans.

None of the Irish gave Korea any chance, except for one, who was being ragged on by his friends. I filled his glass and told him not to worry, he and I would be the ones laughing after the game. I got to know the Irishman who sat next to me. John was from Galway, as is over half of the Irish I have met and is a Queens Park Rangers supporter.

The Koreans, who had filled the recently deserted bar, cheered at the kickoff. They went mad just minutes later as Korea was awarded a penalty. They made so much noise, I was scared the roof would come down. John and I exchanged shocked looks as the referee pointed to the spot. I was happy that it was Ahn, their most popular player, who would take the kick, and not Lee, who had missed against us. Ahn has the rock star good looks that cause the girls to scream whenever he is on the screen. He also plays for Perugia, in Italy's Serie A and is the one who scored the equalizer against us. However, despite those credentials, Gianluigi Buffon saved his spot kick. The mood inside the Blues Bar was, oddly, blue.

It got worse about 15 minutes later when Christian Vieri headed in a corner. I feared the game was lost and the classy Italians would blow out Korea. The Irish all smiled their knowing smiles. As is their nature, which is the only way I can explain it, The Azzuri sat back and defended their one goal lead. They applied their infamous, "Bolt" defense when, I feel, they could have added to their lead.

As is the case with most teams, Korea could not solve the defense. As I drank beer after beer with the Irish, our minds drifted from the match. Korea was not able to create any chances and Italy was not interested in doing so. Rather than concentrate on the, somewhat boring match, we talked about our experiences in the Far East. They had all been to Japan and said Korea was much better. It was much cheaper and the people were more into the Cup.

We snapped back into the match as time was running low on the home team. A nifty move by the Koreans was repelled and John said to me, "The Italians are just too smart for Korea."

I agreed and said, "When it really counts, Italy does not give up a goal." Seconds later we were out of our seats, cheering a goal. The bar erupted and I heard noise drift in from the street. Korea had done it! They had equalized in the 88th minute. Replays showed that defender Christian Panucci failed to clear and Seol Ki-Hyeon had pounced and calmly beat the Italian keeper.

We were still on our feet, clapping and chanting with the crowd (even the Irish joined in the celebration) when Vieri missed an absolute sitter. I am not sure what was more stunning, the complete lapse in the Korean defense or Vieri, one of the world's great goal-scorers, missing from less than five yards.

Everyone cheered as the game went to the Golden Goal, the third of the eight second round matches to do so. In the extra time, the player who I had predicted would launch himself to greatness during the tournament, Francesco Totti, was given his second yellow card and sent off. He clearly dove in a failed attempt to trick the referee into giving him a penalty. Italy's coach, Giovanni Trappatoni was shown angrily banging his fists on the clear plastic behind his bench at a FIFA official, who only shrugged at him. We all had a good laugh at his antics.

Down to ten men, Italy again applied the lock in front of their goal, preferring, it seemed, to take their chances in a penalty shootout. However, those hopes were dashed just three minutes from time when Ahn rose over the best defender I have ever seen, Paolo Maldini, and headed into the net. My hands went to my head in disbelief. Stunned, I turned around to see five Irishmen all holding their heads in their hands with a look of shock on their faces. I will never forget that look, and I know I was wearing the same one.

As we recovered from the shock, the Irish sang "Are you watching Japan." I joined in, but am sure none of the Koreans understood or even cared for that matter.

Meanwhile the Koreans were in rapture. I told the Irish goodbye, ran to pay my tab and headed out into the street that was rapidly filling. The small narrow road had been deserted minutes before. Then, it was as if someone had yelled, "Fire!" in every building there. The red-shirted people could not get out fast enough. In the direction of City Hall, I heard fireworks. I sensed that not one Korean was unaware of what had just happened.

I ran to the *Dong-Il* to congratulate the two women. They were, as always, sitting on the floor of their office, watching it on TV. They were grinning from ear to ear. I pulled them out into the street so they could revel with the others. They did not join the march that was headed out into the main street, but rather stood smiling with a look of unsurpassed pride on their faces. My heart warmed to see them take some happiness in what seemed to me to be an unbearably boring existence.

Soon, I joined the march. I thought we would turn right onto the main street and head down to the huge road that held both the U.S. Embassy and City Hall. However, it was clear that everyone who had been there was marching the other way going, I knew not where. I decided to just stand at the entrance to my little street and watch Korea pass by.

This celebration was different than the one in Daejeon. To begin with, the street was closed, so no cars were rocked. Secondly, many vendors were selling bottle rockets. I never inquired about the price, but they must not have cost much at all because thousands of them were shot off. My arms burned from falling powder and my hair was full of the stuff.

They sang the familiar songs and waved their flag and they shot off bottle rockets. Again, most everyone that passed by me stopped to shake my hand. The conversation was nearly always the same. Them: "Where are you from?"

Me: "Washington D.C."

Them: "Ohhh. Nice to meet you."

A few had a little more knowledge of English and many of them expressed hope that our two teams would meet again, in the semi-finals. They were also, surprised when I greeted them with "*Ayn-ya has-E-oh!*" I may not know ten Korean words, but "hello" is one I do. They are genuinely flattered whenever I utter a word in their language, as if I spent a lot of time learning it. Well, I guess I did!

At one point, I struck up a conversation with a very large and old German. He did not speak English very well, but he was able to say that he was worried about playing us. He said we have new, younger players and this concerned him, because "Thomas Dooley is no longer there." That statement caught me off guard and I laughed out loud.

Eventually Jimmy showed up and we spent hours shaking hands and posing for pictures. An endless stream of Koreans passed by, waving flags, singing songs, and shooting fireworks. The scene was unbelievable. I have seen those old pictures of the party in Times Square when WWII ended, but in all honesty, I do not think it compared to this. Certainly I am not comparing defeating a fascist enemy to winning a soccer game, but the intensity of this celebration is such that I cannot comprehend it's equal.

The way the game played out was astounding. They scored an unlikely equalizer two minutes from time and then the winner was a Golden Goal. The emotions they went though had to have been wrenching, yet they showed great stamina and continued singing and marching hour after hour.

At about 12:30, I went to the PC Bang and check my E-Mail. The streets were still going strong and I needed a break. I opened a letter from Ivy, as I picked the firecracker powder from my hair. "Uh-oh," I said aloud as I read her note. It seemed that she had not taken my dance in Jeonju very well. She was not happy about it. It had not helped, she wrote, that she had watched a movie about an engaged man dancing with a girl and then ditching his fiancée for her just before reading my note.

I did my best to set her mind at ease. I told her that all the girls here are very shy and, we have discovered, they all live at home until they are married. From all reports I have heard, even the single guys who have tried have not had any luck. In any case, I reassured her, and then wrote about the incredible game/celebration I had just witnessed.

After spending about an hour on-line, I went back outside. The street was back open and many Koreans had taken to it in their SUVs, once again, crowding as many into it as possible and then waving the flag out of every window. The crowd on the street had thinned and I watched the cars go by, from time to time clapping along to their rhythmic honking.

Jimmy and I stayed out for a long time before calling it a night as the last of the celebrants headed home. It was 3:30 when I got to my room. For fun, I turned the channel and found a replay of the match on ten different stations! Ten stations at 3:30 in the morning were showing the replay! I choose a channel that was in the 80th minute and when the game ended, I went to sleep.

Day 18
Wednesday, June 19

Free Day

I slept very late for two reasons today. I did not get out of bed until 11:00 because, 1) I had not gone to bed until very late the night before and 2) Today was the first day, since we have been here, that there were no games.

Being we had absolutely nowhere to be, all day, not even in front of a television, Jimmy and I had decided to do some sightseeing. Actually, I feel guilty for doing next to none so far. I am not sure if I will ever be back here and if that is the case, I will have missed a golden opportunity to see this countries best attractions. One thing, in particular that I am surprised that we will not see is the DMZ. Most other Yanks have gone and recommended it. The problem is that it takes the better part of a day, even for the half-day tour. I would really like to go; how many times can you stare at a soldier, who is technically at war, pointing a gun at you. However, Jimmy and I never looked far enough ahead to book the excursion.

Rather than take a bus trip to the DMZ, Jimmy and I decided to go to the Military Museum. We left soon after I was up and caught the subway to Seoul Station where we bought tickets to Ulsan. The sight of the Germany game is on the complete opposite side of Korea. We are told the train ride will be six hours. The ticket cost W28,000, nearly $23.00.

Once that important task was out of the way, we turned our attention to lunch. I really wanted noodle soup, but as half the day had been slept away, we decided on a quick Burger King lunch. I had the same thing that I have at BK in the U.S., a Number 1, Whopper Combo. It was just about the same price, W4,500 ($3.80) and tasted just about the same.

After scarfing down the burger and fries, we jumped on the subway and rode a couple stops to the museum. From the outside, it was impressive and I was glad to see many armored pieces on display outside. We spent nearly an hour looking at U.S., Korean, and even Soviet artillery, tanks, and planes. As military history is my favorite, I had a ball. I was able to climb on some of the tanks and could have stayed outside longer, but it was very hot, so we went inside.

Jimmy liked the inside better than I did and he took his time, slowly reading every placard. I was content to simply look at the display. Thus, I spent most of my time waiting on him.

I must say Korea has had quite a history and I learned a lot of it at this museum. I will not bore you with it other than to say that they had some very advanced weaponry. For example, around the time of Columbus, they were using a machine that shot dynamite arrows, 20 some at a time. Predictably there was a lot of information and displays on the Korean War, which I found very interesting. I had no idea that it seesawed back and forth so much, before eventually bogging down to the point that a cease-fire was called. Incidentally, that cease-fire is still in effect today and because terms have never been decided, the two Koreas are still technically at war.

When we left, we passed by two amazing statues outside. The first was of two soldiers embracing. They represent two brothers who fought on different sides. It reminded me of our Civil War, though I told myself that this one was only 50 years ago. The second was of two sisters, each holding a clock. One clock keeps accurate time, the other is frozen. It displays the date of June 25th, 1950 and the time reads 4:00 A.M. The exact moment in time North Korea invaded the South. They say that once the two are reunified, the second clock will start again. The two statues are a dramatic reminder of how the Cold War and politics separated a people.

We spent about five hours there and then left for *Namdeamun* Market. Chuck had told us that this was the largest market in Seoul and had said that it came alive at night. We arrived around 6:00, but there was no crowd at all. A few shops were closing. A Korean shopkeeper pulled us into his shop and said they were closing and were having a going out of business sale. I was not sure I believed that line, but did buy a set of five Soju glasses. They were basically shot glasses and only cost W2,000 or about 32 cents each. He then walked around with us.

He said he would be our guide. I did not need a guide, but he did come in handy when I came upon some soccer jerseys. I told him what I would pay and he did all the talking. I ended up not buying any, but was glad for the help. Then I mentioned that I wanted to buy a leather bag for Ivy and he immediately took me to a friend of his who had a small shop of them. However, after looking for a few moments, realized he did not have anything I wanted. I told them this, and they led Jimmy and I up to the warehouse.

This was a little scary as they took us into a deserted building and up an elevator. I feared the worst and never took my eye off them, nor turned my back to them even while looking through the many bags in a large room full of them. I found one Coach bag I thought looked good, but it was about $100 and I did not want to spend that much on something I did not know if she would like. I thanked them for the effort and was happy that they did not pressure me to buy anything. They said no big deal and led us down the elevator and we all shook hands goodbye.

Jimmy and I caught the subway to Itaewon where I ate that delicious curry bread while Jimmy ate two small pizzas from the Italian booth. I had decided to have a suit made and we went into a shop. In Itaewon, the vendors are much more aggressive then elsewhere in Korea. I picked out the fabric, a nice dark blue with some black in it and began negotiating a price. I had been told that I could get the suit, a shirt, and custom made shoes for $200.

I stated that price and the vendor nearly fell over. "No way," he said. I called his bluff and started to walk out, certain that he would stop me. I lost confidence as I reached the door and finally realized I had asked for too much as I got half way down the block and saw that he was not coming after me. So, I went into another shop.

This time I picked out a nice dark green color. This guy said, "$250 for the suit." I had decided I did not need the shirt or shoes.

"$180 is all I can pay," I said, holding to the price I had been offered a few weeks ago. He came down to $200, but as I started to walk away, he stopped me, agreeing on $180. He took a lot of measurements and I told him I would be back Monday to pick it up. That would be no problem he assured me.

We spent a little more time in Itaewon as Jimmy wanted to buy a blanket with Snoopy on it. Just as he found one, I spotted a David Beckham England jersey. "35.00 dollars," the vendor told me and I walked away. He came after me and shuffled me into a shop where he began to whisper to me. I really do not know what he was saying, but I think he did not want the other vendors on the street to know what he was doing. He showed me a different Beckham England jersey and he continually pointed to the Umbro symbol on it. I think he was telling me that it was real and not a fake like the ones on the street.

He told me $30, but I said I did not have any dollars and only had W20,000, $16.00. Finally he relented, and I ended up with a tight fitting # 7 England shirt.

In the meantime, Jimmy had bought the blanket, saying that he loved Snoopy and it was very cheap. We had walked a long way and were tired so we went back to the *Dong-Il*. I stayed up until 2:30 watching television, in particular Survivor and yet another replay of the Korea game.

201

Day 19
Thursday, June 20

Master Baker

There were no games again today, but our day was not nearly as leisurely as yesterday. I woke up at 8:00. On TV they were still discussing, actually gloating would be a better word, their victory over Italy. Two days later and there are still a few stations showing the game.

We left around 8:30 and told the two ladies that we would be away two nights and would return on Saturday. Actually, I showed them this by pointing to the calendar and saying, "Ulsan." They nodded and repeated after me to show they understood. For the third time this month, they carried our heavy luggage downstairs to keep for us so that we neither had to carry it with us nor pay for a room. During the other two "away" trips, they had done our laundry, so I had made a special bag containing my dirty clothes. These ladies had been wonderful.

At Seoul Station, I ate a chocolate donut from Dunkin' Donuts and boarded the train. The ride was five hours and I wondered how I would pass the time without Monty. I read the paper until we reached Suwon. There was a story about the owner of the Italian Club Perugia. He said he was going to release Ahn Jung-Hwan, the Korean who scored the golden goal. Unbelievably he called Ahn "the ruin of Italian football." Silly me, I thought their dull, boring, take-no-chances tactics did them in.

After we had pulled out, I headed to the bar car, without my Indian beer buddy. Paying homage to him, I ordered the curry rice. As I waited, I pulled out my notebook and did a lot of writing.

After I had eaten, I sat back and watched the country go by. This was one of the few times I had here to myself, and I used the time to reflect on what had been a wonderful trip. Outside, the scenery passed by at high speed. The country looks a lot like Southwestern Virginia, without the rolling hills. The land, for the most part, is either flat or a mountain. Interestingly enough, every bit of it falls onto one of three categories. It is either farmland, a city, or a mountain. There are no empty fields or forests. Every bit of flatland is farmed. There are many rice paddies, but I am told they grow a lot of cabbage and peppers.

As I was enjoying my time alone, a familiar face entered the bar car. It was Tom, the U.V.A. grad with whom Jimmy and I had traveled to Jeonju for the Mexico game. Even though he had been at the *Dong-Il*, I had not seen him since just after that match ended. I had assumed he had resumed his Asian travels.

"Jimmy told me you were here," he said, taking a seat next to me. "You drinking?"

"No, just had lunch, haven't started drinking yet," I said. "What happened to you after the Mexico game? We had a great party."

"I didn't know where everybody was going, so I just got the bus back to Seoul." He looked over the menu that the waiter had given him and asked my opinion. I recommended the curry rice, but he did not want curry. "What do you think about Ox Tail Soup?"

"I've never had it, but I think it is really the tail of an ox," I told him, doubting he would order it, but he surprised me, and I was anxious to see what it looked like.

He was disappointed when it arrived. It was just a few hunks of beef in what looked to be hot water. However, after a few bland tastes, he realized not all the ingredients were in the soup. He added a dollop of red sauce, *kim' chi*, and some salt. He stirred the large bowl and finally declared that it was very good. When he offered me a taste, I took one, just to say I have eaten Ox tail.

When he finished, I returned to my seat and passed the time both reading and trying unsuccessfully to sleep. At around 2:30, we pulled into Ulsan Station. During the ride, Jimmy and I had decided to buy return tickets rather than playing it by ear. We hoped to get back to Seoul early Saturday afternoon in order to cheer on our second favorite team, Korea. Their quarterfinal match against Spain was to start at 3:30.

In the station, we saw Mark, the lawyer from D.C. who was still traveling alone since Vladimir and company had returned home. We told him to wait for us to buy the tickets, but he told us that they were sold out. He told us that we would not be able to return until Sunday. We decided that we better get them now, before they sold out as well. When we reached the ticket window, we asked if there were any seats on Saturday. The agent smiled and said, "9:30, 11:00, 2:30, or 5:00?"

Jimmy and I looked at her and said, "9:30." She punched it in and produced our tickets, much to the astonishment of Mark who had observed the whole thing.

At the station's exit, was an old woman asking if anyone needed a hotel. She just happened to be from the one Mark had a reservation for, so we decided to follow. In all, she collected eight travelers. Mark, Jimmy, Tom, and I were joined by Andy Mead and Wade, and two guys none of us had seen before. We soon learned why we had not known them, they were not American. Joe was from Singapore and spoke excellent English, with a British accent. The final member of our group was Rod, an Australian who had just arrived from Japan, where he had followed England.

If Suwon had reminded me of Coruscant, the city-planet from Star Wars, Ulsan was Tatooine. Though not a desert, it was the color of sand. The Pacific was not far, but this did not resemble a beach town. Between the train station and the city, lay a large empty lot that stretched for a quarter of a mile. It really was not a lot, rather just a wide open space, rare in Korea, that, at it's end, rose into a large city. Everything was the dirty yellow color of sand.

As we made our way to the Valentine Motel at the far end of the emptiness, I could not help but to think of Obi-Wan and Qui-Gon as they set out across the desert for Mos Eisley.

We worked up a good sweat before finally reaching the motel, but our frustration was about to kick into high gear. Of the eight of us, four of us were paired off and wanted to share a room. Jimmy and I would shack up together for two nights as would Andy Mead and Wade, though they did not need a room tonight, but only wanted to reserve a room for tomorrow. The other four, Mark, Tom, Rod, and Joe each wanted a single room for two nights, except for Joe, who only wanted it for tonight.

Have you got that? Clear on who wanted what, when, and for how long? Now imagine if you spoke no English, as was the case for the two women who ran the Valentine Motel. Confusion ruled for nearly a half hour. We were still trying to explain what we needed when Andy Mead and Wade decided they did not need to make reservations for tomorrow and left. They would be spending this night with a host family with whom they had stayed earlier in the month.

That left six of us and we all needed a room for the night. One of the ladies opened a room, holding two fingers so Jimmy and I claimed it, which left only the singles. Shortly things were sorted out, though things were not perfect.

Korea has what are called "Love Hotels." We had all read about them and the guidebooks had advised against staying in them. They basically serve Koreans for one-night stands, but do provide a good value for the tourist on a budget. I am not sure what qualifies as a Love Hotel but am pretty sure the *Dong-Il* is one. Just by the front door is a large rack of soft-core pornographic videos that were free for the guests. Other than those videos, there is no evidence that the *Dong-Il* is a Love Hotel.

The Valentine Hotel in Ulsan, on the other hand, screams Love Hotel. From it's outer coating of pink paint to the must be seen to be believed vending machine of, um, toys, there is little doubt to whom this place caters. However, had there been any doubt, one would simply have to peek inside our room.

I can only assume that the ladies thought Jimmy and I were together in the don't ask, don't tell kind of way because none of the other rooms were like ours. We were given the Honeymoon Suite. The room was done in two colors that strangely complimented one another, pink and orange. The first thing we noticed was the round bed. The sheets were pink and a large orange padding surrounded them. There are two kinds of people I could envision desiring this bed: drunk couples looking for love and kids who could use it as a trampoline without fear of injury!

To the immediate right of the bed hung a huge mirror that ran the length of it. To the left hung his and hers shiny robes. At the foot of the bed was a contraption over which we all debated for a long time. At first glance, it appeared to be some sort of workout device. On closer inspection, it too, turned out to be some sort of kinky toy. That after about a half hour of climbing on, over, and around it, Tom discovered it's proper usage.

"Your feet go here and she does this and you face this way!" he exclaimed as if he had solved the Riddle of the Sphinx. Tom loved our room and was upset to learn that for some reason, it was W28,000; 2,000 less than his "normal" room across the hall.

Outside, there was trouble as Mark did as Jimmy had done on our first night at the *Dong-Il*, and locked the inner door to his room. It took us nearly ten minutes to explain this to the two ladies at the desk. Finally, we were all satisfied with the rooms and decided to go out and find some food. First, however, Tom discovered that his room only locked from the inside. Again, we all took turns explaining the danger in not being able to lock the room while he was away, but the two ladies never saw the problem with it.

Eventually, we all set out, except for Tom who wanted to take a nap. It was Jimmy, Mark from D.C., Joe from Singapore, Rod the Aussie, and myself. We walked toward town and soon came across a fantastic sight, a seafood market. It was covered with a large wooden roof, but was without walls, and it was enormous, covering an entire city block. Inside, we saw all sorts of seafood from crabs to shrimp to squid and all sorts of fish. We were all excited and set out to find a good stall at which to eat.

Much to our dismay, we quickly realized that though we could buy nearly anything from the sea, there were no places cooking it. It was a market that catered to those with ovens, pots, and pans at home. We hungry tourists were left in the cold. I was upset at this turn of events as I had initially believed that this was similar to Fisherman's Wharf in San Francisco where I had once eaten clam chowder, calamari, and crab for lunch. Here, I could only look and not eat.

Then came word that Rod had found a stall that would cook for us! It was set in the corner of the market. There was a table that reminded me of a picnic table and behind it were two burners and frying pans. With visions of a feast, we set out to choose our meal, but word got back to us that they would only cook what they sold to us. As we returned to the stall, we saw only an aquarium with some eels swimming around in it. No crabs, fish, or even octopi. Only eel.

We stood around, unsure what to do. None of us had ever eaten eel, and we were not sure we wanted to start. Eels are the most unappetizing animals I have ever seen. Near the *Dong-Il* there was a shop that had them in tanks and I did not want to go anywhere near it. They have ugly fish heads and scaly snake bodies.

At the table, sat three Korean men. One of them handed Rod a bite sized piece from his plate. Rod ate it and pronounced it good, and before I knew it, we had sat down.

Within seconds large bottles of Hite beer were placed in front of us. Then the lady in front of the stove reached into the tank. She pulled out an eel, quickly chopped off it's head with a knife, slit it open, and pulled out it's spine. Then she chopped it into bite-sized pieces and threw them into the pan. She repeated this two more times. It took her maybe ten seconds for each eel to go from swimming in the tank to cooking in headless, spineless pieces in the pan.

I was horrified and quickly took a large gulp of beer. To my right, Rod had taken up a conversation with the Korean who sat closest to us. The Korean spoke almost no English, but was trying to communicate with Rod. He introduced himself as Mr. Lee.

Soon the eel was cooked and was put on a large plate in the middle of the table. It was surprisingly white, almost like sea bass or another whitefish. Mr. Lee instructed us on how to eat it. It was very similar to how the beef is eaten at the restaurant near the *Dong-Il*. The eel was wrapped in a piece of lettuce, then spicy red sauce, onions, garlic, and even *kim'chi* was added. We ate them like a cross between a taco and a burrito.

I took a bite. The taste was not bad, in fact it was good. However, the consistency bothered me just a little. The eel was very soft. Mark called it delicate, but I thought of it more like Jell-O or tofu. Just after I finished my first bite, Mr. Lee told me that eel is very good for virility. He did this by making a fist with his right hand and gripping the forearm with his left hand and growling. Soon we were all making the virile sign and growling.

As I continued eating the eel and drinking the Hite, it became apparent that Mr. Lee was obsessed with the male member. Not only did he continue to make the virile sign, but without any English, implied that because Rod had a big nose, he must also be big downstairs as well.

When Mr. Lee was not making phallic references, he was pouring soju and showing us the correct way of doing so. Apparently, the tradition is that the pourer pours with one hand with the other over his heart. The other person extends the cup with the right hand while holding his arm with the left. Upon drinking the firewater, one holds the free hand over their heart. Do to the Hite and Soju, I never understood which hand went where and was constantly corrected by Mr. Lee and the two other Korean men. I tried to get it right, but ended up drinking too much soju.

Somewhere between eating, making my eel tacos, and pouring Soju, I heard from Rod that the three Koreans were bakers. This did not make sense to me because they did not look anything like bakers. They were young perhaps mid thirties, well dressed, and seemingly hip. Yet they maintained they were bakers.

We English speakers debated this for a while and decided that they were not backers. I tried to clarify and said, "Bread."

"Yes. Bread," Mr. Lee said.

After more beer and Soju, we realized that they wanted us to go to their bakery. Our conversation went something like this.

"Do you think it's a bakery?"

"I don't know."

"I think it's a brothel. These guys are pimps."

"You might be right.

"Yeah, that one is awful curious about Rod."

"It might be a strip club."

"Should we go?"

"I want to, we have to find out what they are talking about."

"Where will they take us?"

"Either to a bakery, brothel, or strip club. Either one is fine with me."

I decided to make one more attempt to discover the truth. I found Jimmy's phrase book in his backpack and looked up the work for bakery. I pulled out a pen and paper and drew, the best I could, the Korean letters for bakery. I handed it to Mr. Lee.

He studied it and then passed it to the other two. They said the word that sounded like the one the dictionary described. Mr. Lee looked at me and nodded. "He says it's a bakery," I said to the others.

Except for Jimmy, who had not drank, the rest of us were feeling good, and we were all up for an adventure. We paid the tab, which came to W10,000 each and headed out with the Koreans bound perhaps for a bakery, maybe a brothel, or maybe even somewhere else. Each of them had a car, and I went with Mark with Mr. Kim. Jimmy rode with Joe in a fancy looking Hyundai with Mr. Park and Rod the Aussie went alone with his friend, Mr. Lee.

As country music played on the stereo, Mark and I talked about what we were getting ourselves into. The bottom line was that we had no idea. We rode for at least 20 minutes before pulling up to an odd scene that seemed to answer the question of where we were going.

We parked just across the street from the shop. On either side of the door was a small stage, more like a large box. On top of each box was a pretty, young woman in a blue cheerleader type outfit, dancing to blaring music. Though my attention was drawn to the girls, I also noticed a bunch of balloons and flowers.

Soon Mark and I were just outside the door. I took a deep breath and followed Mr. Kim inside, still unsure what I would see. Inside, I was stunned at the sight. Rather than the stage and more dancing girls that I had suspected, my eyes took in more pastries and breads than I had ever seen. It was a bakery! It was full of people and my mouth watered at some of the treats.

Mr. Kim sat us down just as the others arrived and sat with us. We learned it was the bakery of one of their good friends and today was the Grand Opening. In moments we were introduced to the owner, and after shaking our hands, he left. He returned moments later with trays of goodies, which he proudly set on our table.

Mr. Lee said something in Korea to him and he spun around to a cooler and produced more large bottles of beer! "Eat! Eat!" he said and we did. The treats were good, but different. I thought something was a chocolate cake, but it turned out to be bean cake. It was not very sweet, and I did not care much for it. I did like the balls of dough. They were green and white and very doughy and sweet. There were other assorted bakery items, and we tore them up!

It turned out that Mr. Lee was one of only 50 Master Bakers in Korea. They had all studied in Paris. Apparently baking is serious business in Korea, and we were with one of the best.

After at least an hour of eating and drinking, we were stuffed. The Koreans ushered us out, presumably to take us back near the hotel. Once outside the bakery, they posed us in front of the dancing girls and filmed us as we sang the name of the bakery to the tune of everybody's favorite "*Tey-Han-Ming-Go*!" I think they I heard them say something about a commercial.

After the filming, they pointed us toward "bars" and sent us on our way. We walked a few blocks, having no idea where we were going or what we were looking for. We stopped in a convenience store and each bought a can of beer, except for Jimmy. Soon we saw the Cuba Bar and went in and found a table in the empty second story pub. We ordered stout.

As we drank the dark beer, Joe pulled out some papers from his backpack. "These are United States players," he told us. Joe turned out to be an autograph collector and had done amazingly well at the Cup. "Tell me whose they are." The first was clearly Eddie Pope. The second was Joe-Max Moore, then John O'Brein. The last one he had, we did not recognize. Both names were short and it had a # 6 next to the signature.

"Who is number six?"

"John Harkes," I said and we laughed. "I can't think of who it is." The beer had gotten to me.

Then Joe provided another clue. "He is a black guy."

"It's not Tony Sanneh or Beasley."

"It's definitely not Llamosa. It looks like Eddie Pope," I said.

"No, he's 23," Mark said of his favorite player.

We were stumped and left the question for a while as the subject changed as the waitress checked up on us and we went back to drinking Hite.

After finishing off our third round, we paid the bill and left. On the way out, someone said, "David Regis!" How quickly they forget, I thought. Going into the Cup, he was slated to be the starting left back now he was so far down the depth chart, we could not even pull his name. It seemed that Arena had forgotten about him as well.

We walked for a little while towards the town center and soon found the Royal Crown. Inside, it was quiet, but there was a nice large screen television. We had not yet heard where the pre game party would be and decided to tell the others, through the Yanks in Korea Yahoo Group, about this place.

After we had had a beer, an American came in and announced he had wondered if any Americans would show up for the game. His name was John, and he was an English teacher living in Ulsan. He was happy to see us, and I bought him a beer.

It was nearing the end of my trip, and I had yet to find anyplace serving dog. I asked John and he gave me directions to a place. He said they would not want to serve me but to be persistent, and I would get it. I recited the directions back to him but doubted I would have the time to go.

Then he asked if we had eaten silkworm larvae yet. When we told him we had not, he jumped up and said to follow him. We did so and he led us outside and down to the end of the block. There was an old lady behind a stand on wheels. In New York she would be serving hot dogs. Here she peddled bugs.

The smell was awful as she removed the lid from a large pot. She scooped a large spoonful out and let the water drain before pouring them into a large plastic bowl. John ate one to prove they were edible. Rod, Jimmy, and I each took one. I examined mine. It was just larger than my thumbnail and was brown. It looked like a rollie pollie, only bigger. I ate it, chewing slowly in attempt to place the flavor. It was not bad, with an earthy taste, perhaps resembling dirt. I ate a few more and then some more.

Just outside the Royal Crown, we met some Germans. One of them spoke good English and we began talking. He was not excited about the game. I played the weak sister part and said, "What are you worried about? You are Germany, you will kill us."

"No," he said. "I am worried." He was maybe in his late 20's.

"You are crazy. I predict Germany 4, U.S. 0," I said, hoping to send him into a false sense of security, much as the Portuguese had been in that night in Nashville.

He was not buying it and actually laughed at the suggestion. He was really worried and I kept saying, "Come on, you are great Germany. We are little United States. You will kill us." Again, he simply shook it off. I changed the subject and asked what club he supported."

"Bayern Munich," he said.

"Do you travel to watch them?" I asked.

"Yes, sometimes."

"Did you go to the Champions League finals?" I was hoping for the answer that I got.

"I went to Barcelona."

"Yes!" I almost screamed. "You were there when Manchester United scored those two goals?"

"Yes," he said, not nearly as excited as I was.

"I don't think I have ever met anyone who was at that game. What was it like?" I shook his hand, and was excited to be talking to him. That day was one of my happiest sports moments. Man United was trailing 1-0 nearly the whole game. Just as it went into injury time, they tied it. I jumped all over my apartment in joy. I was glad I had taken the day off from work and was ready for overtime when they quickly scored another! Moments later the referee blew the whistle and I fell to the ground and actually cried. I am even tearing up while writing this, so happy was that moment.

"It was the worst night of my life. It was terrible." I could see the memory was painful for him, but he continued, "Even when we won the championship two years later, it still hurt and the victory did not mean as much."

I was trying not to smile at his vivid recollection and before I could say anything else, his friends pulled him by the arm and they walked away.

I had a few more beers and ate a few more silkworms, though they had cooled off and I found that a cold silkworm is not a tasty silkworm. Around 12:30 we caught a cab back to the Valentine Hotel and I made a bed on the floor while Jimmy enjoyed the lover's bed.

Day 20
Friday, June 21

Respect

There were two games scheduled today. The first, a game anticipated by the whole world. England-Brazil. The country that invented the game vs. the country that perfected it. Arguably the games two biggest stars, David Beckham and Ronaldo will carry their nation's hopes. When this match kicks off at 3:30, I suspect it will draw the largest television audience of the tournament, save for the final. It is a match up of epic proportions. I am excited about this one.

The late game is ours. The United States vs. Germany. Hardly a match that would inspire the rest of the world. It would be seen as an afterthought to the earlier clash of the titans. Although I have read that back home, the success of our boys is causing excitement and bringing in new fans, I doubt that most folks have circled this date on their calendars. In Germany, there may be more fear than excitement. In years past, a match with the U.S. for the right to advance to the semi-finals would have been looked at as a Godsend. However, this Cup, the Germans did not have their usual, dominate team and there was deep concern that they would be embarrassed by the lightly regarded Yanks. For those of us here, this match is huge. It is a chance to prove that we belong. A chance to beat a world power in a game that means an awful lot. For me, today would bring two emotional, important, and meaningful games.

I began such a momentous day by sleeping until noon. Jimmy and I dragged ourselves out of the Valentine Hotel into the bright sunlight and hot humid weather not knowing where we were going. Our first task was to find a PC Bang and determine where the rest of the Yanks were meeting. Then we needed food.

We walked into the fringe of this large city and began looking for the familiar PC Bang symbol. It took a bit longer than anticipated, but we found one. This one was quite different than all the others. I believe it was new because it was not the color of cigarette butts, but rather the walls were gleaming white.

Once on-line, we read that the pre-game party, as well as the England-Brazil watching party, would be at The Junco, which, we read, was close to where we were. Jimmy and I were happy about this as it gave us longer to relax in the cool computer room. I bought a Coke and sat back in the comfortable leather chair that also seemed out of place here. I read reports of our big match and I wrote long e-mails to friends detailing yesterday's excitement of eels and baked goods. I wrote to Ivy, assuring her of my love and that I would be home soon, though depending on the game, maybe not as soon as we had planned. I told her that I would not leave if we were playing in the semi-finals.

Jimmy spent a lot of time writing on the website. Word had spread that our site was offering reports from Korea and we had had, by far, the most hits since onthesidelines.org had begun. Jimmy had done a great job updating it nearly everyday. I hated not contributing anymore than a few stories as I was saving my writing for this book, but Jimmy understood and not once did he press me to write for him.

Somehow in our relaxing early afternoon, the time got away from us and we quickly fled the PC Bang in search of The Junco. We followed the directions and reached the spot where it should have been, about four blocks from the PC Bang. We looked up and down and in most every building, but there was no Junco. We walked around the block a few times, but could not find it. I was becoming frantic because it was after 3:00 and I would have been very upset to miss a second of the game. We asked a few Koreans, but they had never heard of The Junco.

"Three more minutes and I'm getting a cab for The Royal Crown," I told Jimmy. I did not want to go to Plan B because I feared being lost in a taxi again, but I did not want to spend anymore time looking. We bumped into a few Americans who were also looking for it which at least told us we were in the right area. However, after five minutes with still no luck, I spotted a cab and waved to it. It stopped and Jimmy and I hurried to it, but just as we arrived, it took off.

I was pissed and as I looked around, I did not see any other cabs. We decided to walk out to the main street where we would be sure to hail one, but as soon as we took a few steps, Jimmy pointed to a second floor sign that read, "The Junco."

I ran up the stairs and into a very crowded bar. It was large and featured a lot of wood. A quick tour found that all the tables were full. I was able to find a good standing spot right in front of a television set. I leaned up against the back of a booth and told myself that I would be here for a long time. There were a lot of familiar faces in the crowd and I ordered a pitcher of OB to share.

Others came in and took up spots near me and before long the game kicked off. Just in front of me was Super Limey, a Brit married to an American who had been one our best supporters here. He had shaved a Mohawk into his head and colored it red. This was a very popular look over here and for some strange reason did not look as odd as I would have thought.

A few times I asked for a menu because I was very hungry, but the waiter seemed to indicate that there was no place to put the food so I was never given a menu. A Korean girl next to me had the same experience in ordering food and we exchanged pained and hungered looks.

On the screen, the blue shirted Brazilians were dominating possession. The bar seemed 50-50 in its rooting interest, which surprised me. Most soccer fans love Brazil and I have found that most hate England. However, against logic, Super Limey and I were far from alone with our support for England.

212

Then, about 20 minutes in, a Brazilian defender made a horrible mistake with the ball and Michael Owen snapped it up and scooped a shot into the net. "Yes!" I yelled, but not nearly as loud as the Englishman in front of me. For a while, I thought that England would win the game and the Cup as I believed the winner of this game would eventually lift the trophy. They defended and seemed to have a hold on the game when, just before the half, Ronaldinho made a wonderful move with the ball and found Rivaldo who shot into the England goal.

A disappointed England went to the locker room level at one. As the television went to commercials, the Korean girl next to me said she was going to McDonalds and asked if I wanted anything. It was such a nice gesture on her part, I told her that if she went and got the food, I would pay for it. I handed her a W10,000 bill and asked for a combo with some sort of burger. Just before the second half began, she returned and gave me a cheeseburger combo. I thanked her and tore into the burger and fries.

Shortly after the break, Brazil lined up for a free kick from the right wing. It was a good ways from the goal and did not look particularly dangerous. However, Ronaldinho spotted David Seaman cheating off his line, expecting a cross, and put his kick on goal. Seaman struggled in his retreat, but did not get there, and Brazil led 2-1. It did not look good, but less than ten minutes later, Ronaldinho was sent off. He made a dangerous challenge, one that is usually disciplined with a yellow card, but this referee saw fit to show red.

We cheered, and I thought that this was the chance England needed to take the game back, but they never did. Just like against the U.S. in 1994, a ten-man Brazil played as if it had the advantage. England looked tired and never seriously threatened and when Owen was substituted out with just over ten minutes to go, even Super Limey knew the tournament was over for the English.

After the game, The Junco cleared out, and I found a long table against a wall. I spread out on the bench and slowly drank a beer. Chuck was there and was loudly complaining about how some Koreans called him names while he tried to sell the ticket he had for the Korea-Italy match. I tried to block it out, but was unable due to his sheer volume. I gazed at the people mingling in front of my table and suddenly I saw an unexpected, familiar face. It was Mike! He was supposed to be in Japan.

"Hey man!" I said as I jumped up and hugged my friend. "What are you doing here?"

He sat and I poured him a beer. "I couldn't stay away," he told the story. "I flew to Tokyo and was drawn to the south. I got on a train and headed south and kept going. I got way down there and found that they had ferries that came here. I thought about it for a few seconds and decided I had to come."

"Man, I'm glad you're here," I told him. Before we could talk any further, Chuck told him about how some Koreans called him names while he tried to sell the ticket.

A few hours later, Jimmy, Mike, Chuck, and I caught a cab to the stadium. Once there, Mike set about finding a ticket. It was not hard and after turning down a few that were for sale at just under face value, he bought one for about $20.00. Chuck left to go to his side of the stadium, and Mike and I went to the beer stand where we each bought a Budweiser, and Jimmy got a Coke.

As Mike and I opened our cans, a German who was sitting at a picnic table next to where we were standing, leaned over to us and said, "This is expensive water." I thought that was funny and told him that it would be nice to have some good beer.

After downing the Bud, Jimmy and I went to our seats, early as usual. Just like in the Mexico game, we were in the upper deck. Again, the view was great, but we wanted to be closer. Furthermore, we soon realized that unlike the Mexico game, most Americans were not with us. Rather they were in the lower section, behind the goal opposite us!

In our section, there were some Americans and some Germans. Mark came into view and asked why we were stuck up here. He was upset that we were not with everyone else. I had not seen him all day and he said he had gone to The Royal Crown for the Brazil game. An American I did not know said he was going to try to get over to the U.S. section. He carried a flag and we told him that if he made it, to hold it upside down to alert us of his success.

About ten minutes later, we saw his sign. Jimmy, Mark, myself, and four others decided that we would also attempt the move. The four guys I did not know ran ahead, but Mark needed to stop at the bathroom. Jimmy and I left him there and followed the four who said they had a plan. We caught up to them at the entrance/exit gate and they explained the situation. The guards told them that if they left, they would probably not get back in.

None of us were about to risk that and we wondered how the one guy had made it. He must have gone through the barricades set up to separate the different levels of seating. Although there were three price ranges, ours being the lowest, there were only two barricades. They separated the end zone seats we had from the sideline seats. To reach the Yankee Army on the far side, we would have to go through two gates. The first would put us into the more expensive seats along the sidelines, the second would release us back into our price range, but at the other end of the stadium.

Game time was near and Jimmy and I decided to return to our seats. Our section had filled more while we were away, but there were still many empty seats. It was a large mix of Germans, Americans, and others. We sang our anthem and did not like the way we sounded. Without hundreds of others singing with us, we were able to hear each other. It was not pretty.

Our line-up held no surprises. Brad Friedel in goal. Frankie Hejduk was back from his one game suspension. Gregg Berhalter held the position he had claimed from the injured Jeff Agoos. Eddie Pope and Tony Sanneh filled out the back line as they had done all tournament. The midfielders were Pablo Mastroeni, Claudio Reyna, John O'Brien, and Eddie Lewis who was not the first choice beginning the tournament, but had a great game against Mexico. Up front were Brian McBride and Landon Donovan, the two goal scorers from the Mexico match. They each have scored twice this Cup and still left Arena with firepower on the bench in Clint Mathis. As our boys shook hands with the Germans, their lack of height was apparent. Arena had been worried about set pieces and crosses. Seeing the size mismatch, I understood why.

The game began and it was unnervingly quiet. I could see the Yanks at the far end bouncing up and down and I could hear them, faintly but distinctly. I wanted to be down there with them, but as always, I tried to look on the bright side. I was sure I could see better than them. I could also see a replay scoreboard in the opposite end zone. There was not one behind me and I realized that the rowdies did not have the benefit of replay.

***

The U.S. attacks the goal in front of us and I hope we would have most of the action at our end. We do attack and Donovan finds himself one on one with a defender, but is whistled for a foul as he breaks away. We applaud his effort and hope it put a bit of fear in the big but slow German defense. We win a corner a few moments later but it comes to nothing.

As the action moves away from us, I look down at the German keeper, Oliver Kahn. Though I hate to admit it, I consider the Bayern Munich man to be one of the two or three best keepers in the world. I always root against Munich and Germany and Kahn is usually the one to whom I direct my anger. He used to have the worst haircut, a floppy Beatles style bowl cut. Now he seems to be one of the few Germans to have moved at least into the 90's and now resembles The Terminator with his close-cropped cut.

Germany wins a few corners and on the second have a shot go wide of Friedel's goal. Then Reyna wins a free kick just outside the box. Lewis takes it and we hold our breath, but the ball flies harmlessly over the goal. Most in our section are sitting, but Jimmy and I refuse, ignoring a few pleas from those behind us.

A cross comes in and McBride is there, but a defender just does get to it and heads it away. The action goes back and forth, with the Germans having a little more of the ball, but not much more. Then Lewis gets free on the left wing and sends in a cross. Kahn dives and pushes it out. O'Brien is there but is unable to collect the ball for a shot. It is another encouraging sign. Sanneh sends in a cross that does not reach McBride and it looks like we have the Germans on their heels.

A few rows above us a couple of Americans that I do not know are yelling at Kahn. One of them is pretty funny and he screams "Oh Mr. Kahn! Oh Mr. Kahn! You're gonna lose, Oh Mr. Kahn!" Our section is quiet and his voice is booming, "Oh

215

Mr. Kahn! Oh Mr. Kahn! You're going home, Oh Mr. Kahn!" I think he is drunk because he keeps doing it, over and over.

Donovan has the ball, and he runs at the defenders, beating them and firing a shot with his left foot. It is heading into the corner, but Kahn lays out and just gets a fingernail to it, sending it inches wide. "Ohhh!" Jimmy and I yell in unison and I can feel my nerves kicking in. We were inches away from leading, and we are taking it to them. We chant "U!S!A! U!S!A!" A few Americans in our section join us, but there are not enough of us to sustain it for long.

The Germans manage to send in a dangerous cross, but are whistled for offside as they miss the goal anyway. The Germans apply some pressure, but are not able to get a shot off. We attack, and I see the Germans arguing amongst themselves. Lewis whips in a free kick, but Berhalter's lunging header is off the mark.

Play again goes back and forth but not at a fast pace. The Germans are managing to slow the game, depriving us of perhaps our only advantage, speed. But just like that, Donovan takes a long pass and closes in alone on Kahn. Just as he enters the box, he loses the ball momentarily before recovering and shooting with his left foot. The split second he lost allows Kahn to cut down the angle and he is able to block the shot out for a corner. The corner sails dangerously through but is untouched. Wow! Donovan had been so close twice!

The guy behind us continues with his "Oh Mr. Kahn!" song/shout and a nervous German fan has had enough. His team is on it's heels and now an American fan is on his nerves.

In his German accent, he yells, "Why don't you shut the fuck up already? You're annoying everybody!"

He was wrong, he was not annoying Jimmy or I and without so much as a glance at one another, we both start yelling, "Oh Mr. Kahn! Oh Mr. Khan! You're going home! Oh Mr. Kahn!"

We were proud of ourselves, but on the field, Germany is causing a lot of trouble for our defense. First a free kick is dangerously knocked around the box. Then a corner causes a moment of apprehension. Then a few other shots seem dangerous. Finally, we take control and McBride sends in a cross from the left side. The ball finds it's way to Lewis just inside the 18 and he fires a shot that Kahn can only parry high I the air. Germany is able to clear, but we are showing no signs of going away.

Our captain, Claudio Reyna, is working extremely hard, winning balls in the midfield and running everywhere. Then the referee makes what I think is a bad call, giving Germany a free kick from the right side of the goal. The cross bends towards goal and a pack of players rise to meet it. Suddenly, it is in the net. The replay screen shows that Michael Ballack had gotten higher than Sanneh and headed past a stranded Friedel.

Soon afterward, they have an identical kick, as Lewis is booked, but do not convert it. Moments later, Pope is booked at the same place and again they just miss but win a corner. We begin to wonder about the referee. He is Hugh Dallas, and I have always thought he was good. I remember seeing a picture of him in Sports Illustrated, his face bleeding after being struck with an object thrown during a Celtic-Rangers match. Tonight, he does not impress me.

From another cross, Klose hits the post, and we are reeling. I am now hoping we can hold on until halftime, just a few minutes away. But, again, they are awarded a free kick, this one even closer, just outside the box, again, on the right side. Ziege shoots high, and I breathe relief.

Finally, the halftime whistle blows, giving our boys a chance to regroup. Jimmy and I quickly decide we need to get down with our fans. Not only will we be able to add our voice to theirs, but it will also put us behind the goal we will be attacking. Should we get the tying goal, we want to be there.

***

We ran quickly down the steps and across the wide-open concourse. Reaching the first gate, leading to the sideline seating, I approached the guard. There was both a policeman and a security guard there. I said slowly, "We want to sit with the other Americans." The two gatekeepers seemed disinterested and simply unlocked the heavy iron door and waved us through! "Yes," I almost whispered to Jimmy as if I was worried someone would hear me and send us back. "Should be easy now." We were in the expensive zone and I did not think we would have any problem crossing back into the cheap seats.

We walked about 80 yards to the last gate. Once again, I said, "We want to sit with the other Americans." This guard took his job much more seriously. He held out his hand for our tickets. I handed it over and he said, in not the Queen's English, "Wrong way," and pointed back in the direction we had just come.

I thought quickly and said, "That is the German side, we are American. The guard told us to come here." He was unmoved, so I continued, "The Germans were threatening us," I lied, but was not sure he understood, so tried to make it simple for him. "Germans," I pointed the other way. "Germans are angry at us. They want to fight. The security guard told us to come here, to be with the other Americans." I thought this would sway him, but he just shook his head.

I decided another tact was needed. Luckily, I was wearing my "Be The Reds" t-shirt. I held the words so he could see I love Korea and began singing, *"Tey-Han-Ming-Go!"* He smiled, but did not budge. I felt like the foreigners you see on television back home that do not speak English. They offer the few words they do know in hopes of escaping arrest or maybe to get some food. I moved to one of the other phrases I knew, *"Com-som-nee-da,"* I said. I was not sure what saying "Thank you" would do, but at least I was speaking his language.

I was about to sing the other Korean song when another group of Yanks showed up and tried to get through. The guard looked at me and said, "Come back after halftime." That sounded fine with Jimmy and I, and we walked over to a tunnel to see the field. The moment we stepped through the tunnel, we felt the atmosphere. It was still halftime, but the Yanks were singing. They were only a few sections to our left, but a tall, impassable fence separated us.

Just then the players came back onto the field to a large cheer. Jimmy and I walked out of the tunnel and when we were back on the concourse, I saw the guard waving to us. We ran to him and he opened the gate and we hurried through! Behind us, he quickly slammed it shut and I heard other Yanks protesting. I would have liked to help them, but did not want to jeopardize our position and we did not look back. In less than a minute, we were descending the stairs and pushing our way through a Red, White, and Blue mass to find standing room.

It was apparent that there were many more Yanks here than there were seats to hold us. It was tight quarters standing there, but at the moment, there was no place in the world I would have rather been. Just below us, I saw Mark. "Where did you go?" he asked. "I came out of the bathroom and you were gone."

"We didn't make it through until just now. We went back to our seats up there," I told him, pointing to the upper, far side.

"I made it right through! That's what you get for leaving me!" he said and I could only nod in agreement. The second half began and the noise we made was music to my ears. It was good to be among friends.

***

We attack right away, but they counter. In our new seats we feel not only the atmosphere, but also the tension. Then Lewis sends in a cross that a diving Sanneh can just not reach, but we win a corner. We applaud the effort as Kahn collects the ball. We are not as large a group as we had been in during the first round, but we are singing loudly to make up for those who left us here. "Let's go U.S. Let's go!"

Donovan works his way into the box and gets off a shot that is blocked out for a corner. I look away for a moment and when I look back to the field, the ball is loose in front in the six-yard box. A blue shirt hits it and there is confusion in the mouth of the goal. It is Berhalter and he is wrestling with Kahn and Frings. Some players are arguing with the referee. I yell that it was a goal and others are screaming for a handball. The referee motions everyone away, "Go!" I can hear him yelling to our players. "Go!" And whatever had just happened had come to nothing for us. At this end, we cannot see the replay screen so we turn our attention back to the match.

Lewis takes a corner right in front of us, and O'Brien shoots, but right at Kahn. We urge our boys on and they respond with waves of attacks that just end up failing at the end. Reyna is still working hard, and I also notice Tony Sanneh who seems to be everywhere. The Big Cat plays in Germany and is obviously fired up for this match. He is running like mad.

Most of the play is right in front of us, and the Germans call on Kahn a few times to thwart our relentless attacks. Just before the hour, Clint Mathis comes on to our great cheers, but I also fear the loss of McBride whom he replaces. He was one of our few players who was matching the Germans in the air. Playing on three days rest has taken its toll on McBride. I curse the schedule that allowed the Germans five rest days, and I worry that we will not be able to sustain our pressure.

Moments later our other Most Hated German, Jens Jeremies, a brutal defensive midfielder comes on. Every American soccer fan knows how he hammered Reyna in the opening minute of the match in the 1998 World Cup. Reyna never recovered and his ineffective play was a factor in our pathetic performance there. I yell out a few choice words to Jeremies.

We have most of the ball, but Germany has a dangerous counter that Sanneh makes a great tackle in the box to break up. His outlet finds Lewis who sends a long ball too far for Mathis, but Kahn comes aggressively out of his box to clear the ball. He sends a big header up field, but we all tense and lean forward, holding each other for support, as the ball goes directly to Reyna. He is just inside midfield and we realize he has the goal at his mercy. The captain knows it as well and volleys one time. The ball is high in the air and I think that this will be one of the greatest goals in World Cup history. I see Kahn running to the goal like a centerfielder hopelessly chasing a long drive. We are all screaming and willing the ball into the net. It hangs in the air for what seems like minutes. I am watching Kahn, and as he desperately looks over his left shoulder, I see the faintest sign of relief on his face and know that the ball will not find the goal. I do not know by how far it missed, but it did not look to be much.

The near miracle goal fires us up even more and we are louder than ever. "They cannot continue to dodge these bullets," I think. Germany is sitting back, much like Italy did, though in this case, I am not sure if it is by design or necessity.

As the Germans are preparing for a corner, Cobi Jones comes on for Hejduk. An attacking midfielder for a defender and I am sure we will switch into an attacking 3-5-2 formation. Mathis breaks away and draws a yellow, which sets up a free kick from about 30 yards out to the right of the box. As Lewis prepares to take the kick, I see Jeremies try a dirty trick. He grabs Reyna and pulls him to the ground, falling under him to make it look like Reyna ran him over. The referee blows the whistle and runs to them. I am sure he will book both of them, but he confers with the linesman.

While this is going on, Lewis takes the kick and Pope heads into the goal. Of course it does not count, but we give a good cheer and some, no doubt, thought that we had scored. At the end, Dallas calls over Reyna, and I am scared he will send him off. However, he simply books him, even though he had done nothing. For some reason he also books Oliver Neuville, which only insures Jeremies will continue his thugery. By the way, if you do not know what Jeremies looks like, picture the cousin from National Lampoon's Vacation. When the Griswold's visit their relatives in the desert, the boy who does the worm farming looks just like the German.

On the German counter from the free kick, Mastroeni is booked. Seconds later Berhalter is given a yellow card and the Germans take their time putting the ball in play.

The clock has now reached the 70th minute. The Germans have now packed the zone. We continue the possession, but the Germans are looking dangerous on the counter. We are not giving up hope and continue to sing. We know how many late goals have been scored and we believe that we will get one. I pause to consider the meaning of that. We are a goal down to Germany in an elimination match in the World Cup, and we are confident we will score the equalizer. Things have certainly changed a lot in the past few weeks.

Coach Arena makes his final substitute, bringing on Earnie Stewart for Mastroeni. We have now completely committed to the attack. It is now the 80th minute. We press forward but do not have the space for a shot. Germany is content to just blast the ball out of the zone. Sanneh has space for a header from a free kick, but is unable to direct it. At least we got a shot off, I think.

Nearly all the action is in front of us and we are breathless. Reyna and Jones send crosses in, but they fail to produce a dangerous shot. There are a lot of Germans in the box. They attempt a few counters, but only with one or two players and our defense is able to clean up without much trouble.

Just a minute before time, O'Brein sends a cross that is deflected wide by the defense. Mathis collects the ball. It is apparent the Germans are exhausted as Mathis is given a lot of room on the wing. He picks his target, and I see it all the way. He floats a cross to Sanneh who is unmarked just to the left of the goal. The tall defender rises to meet the ball, and I am sure it will be a goal. Sanneh's head meets the ball and I jump into the air, using my left arm on a stranger's shoulder to propel myself higher. I am celebrating as I rise into the air. As I reach the peak of my leap, the ball strikes the net, but as I descend, I realize it is the outside netting. I have deflated by the time I hit the ground.

For a split second, I had felt the thrill of the tying goal before the cruel reality had presented itself. I think that that could have been the one chance we would get. I can hardly curse Sanneh, the player who has been everywhere for us tonight. He has played the game of his life, but come up just wide on his shot at glory. I take a breath and for the first time begin to think we will not score. I look to the scoreboard and see that we are seconds from fulltime.

The fourth official signals three minutes of injury time. Again, I curse this referee. I had thought that we would be given at least five, if not more. There had been two major stoppages and six substitutions. As we discuss this timekeeping error, a German goes in alone from the left wing, but shoots just wide. There is more action in front of the far goal and Reyna is back winning the ball. We send in a few long balls that the Germans repel, but one finds it way to Mathis who hits it hard, on the run. I am sure it would have found the net if a defender had not got there in the nick of time to block it.

Again, Reyna runs the length of the field to thwart another breakaway. We come forward but as we lose position, Hugh Dallas blows his whistle for the last time.

The Germans collapse to the ground. Kahn lies prone in his goal. I cannot but help to smile, seeing the mighty Germans so spent and relieved at beating us. Mathis goes to Kahn, and I wonder if they are talking about being teammates in the near future.

At the far end, we can see the German fans cheering, but cannot hear them over our own chants of "U!S!A! U!S!A!" We are not ready to go home and we cheer for all our team has given us here. I see Reyna hugging Jeremies, and I know that he is a better sport than I.

***

Our players applauded us, and Reyna walked with the flag draped around his shoulders. Our section cleared rather quickly and I saw Kaela. She was sitting and had tears in her eyes. Ever since the ref blew the final whistle, I had been happy. I was pleased at the way our team played and the respect that we had earned. Seeing Kaela's tears made me realize just how close we had been. I tried not to dwell on the loss as I tried to comfort the girl from Boston. In truth, I was not bitter or hurting as is often the case after a difficult loss. I wanted to enjoy my final few minutes at the World Cup.

I stood alone and looked across the long field and for the first time could hear the German fans. "Deutschland! Deutschland!" They chanted. They bounced up and down and were waving flags. I took in their joy and realized how happy they were to have beaten us. It was satisfying. I thought back to that first night at Nashville and the Portuguese guy who had predicted they would beat us 4-0. Three weeks later, the Germans are wildly celebrating a 1-0 win over us. Above all, U.S. soccer fans crave respect. Here in Korea, our team as well as our fans, have earned it in droves.

Finally, we left the stadium for the last time. Jimmy had met up with Amanda and they joined Mark and I as we headed out to find the shuttle buses. When we were near the line for the bus, Amanda thought she saw Rob Stone, the ESPN announcer. She said she knows him and wanted to talk to him. She left and Jimmy followed her.

On the bus, Mark told me of his travel plans. He has to fly to New York tomorrow and once there, catch a bus that will deliver him to Washington at 6:00 in

221

the morning. He will have less than a half hour to shower and leave for work. I do not envy him.

When we got off the bus at the train station, we walked to our hotel for a quick stop before heading back out for The Junco. The mood was subdued as we entered the bar. It is a strange feeling and I realized this is the first game after which we did not party. After the Portugal match, it was a wild celebration consisting of singing and dancing outside the stadium. In Daegu, we partied together with the Koreans at Old Blue, both sides happy with the draw. Even after the Poland match where we had been beaten badly, we celebrated making it out of the first round. Of course there, our celebrations were overshadowed by those of the Koreans whose victory over Portugal had sent us both through. Then there was the incredible night at The Rose Garden after we had beaten our archrival Mexico.

Tonight we had won still more respect from the rest of the world, but that was something that, as grateful as we were for it, we did not want to celebrate. Most Americans were sitting and eating dinner. Mark and I sat with a few friends from Minnesota, but I was not hungry and excused myself.

I went down the stairs and onto the dark street. Depression was setting in and I wanted to talk to my best friend. I circled the block a few times looking for a payphone so that I could call Ivy but could not find one. I wandered around for a few minutes but there were no phones in sight.

I must have looked a sad sight because as I passed in front of a pizza place, I saw people inside waving to me. It was the New York Crew. I went in and sat down. They looked concerned and asked if I was OK. I assured them that I was and after a few minutes I got up and left.

The pizza had made me hungry and back out on the street, I saw Mark. We decided to get some food from a street vendor just across the street from The Junco. We ordered tempura and for only W2,000 each we were treated to lightly fried imitation crab, *kimbop*, and vegetables. We dunked it in the community bowl of soy and enjoyed the exotic food.

After eating, we went back to The Junco. The first person I saw was Joe, the guy from Singapore I had hung out with the day before. At first I was happy to see him, but he soon changed my mood. He was wearing a Germany jersey. I made a quick joke about it, but he responded by pulling up the shirt and kissing the badge. I just said, "Bandwagon jumper," and walked away.

I saw some people gathered around a television and went to investigate. It was showing the incident from early in the second half. Reyna swung in the corner and it was flicked on. Berhalter shot and Kahn only got a piece. My heart nearly stopped when I saw what happened next. The German defender, Torsten Frings, was on the post. The ball was past him, but struck his arm and rebounded out of the goal to safety.

My stomach sank and I felt cheated. It was a clear handball and this damn ref had once again ruled against us. The replay ran a few more times from other angles. It was clear that the only thing that prevented the ball from crossing the line was Frings' arm. The small group became agitated. We were all upset that we had not been given a penalty. All of us except for Chuck. Chuck tried to tell us that it was not intentional, that the ball played him and thus was not a penalty.

That argument holds no water at all with me. Whether or not it was intentional, it stopped a goal. Normally this type of foul would not only result in a penalty, but also a red card for the offending player. I would argue that in this case, a red may not be deserved, but a penalty surely would. Regardless of intent, a handball cannot prevent a goal. In addition, I would argue, that if the ball had been on fire, Frings would have managed to move his arm out of the way. No, he did not move his hand to the ball, but he was well aware that it was the only hope of preventing the goal. He knew what he was doing.

As we were getting more and more frustrated, somebody offered some of the best advice I have heard since arriving in Korea. "Take it easy, guys. Let's have some class and not whine like Mexico," said an anonymous voice. We immediately quieted down and I smiled. I decided that I would not be like the Mexicans and I would not complain about the referee.

Minutes later, Rod the Aussie, came in and approached me. "Tough luck," he said in his accent, "You deserved better. Your team was great." He went on to say that he did not know much about us, but had been impressed. He and I sat at a table with Jimmy who said they had not seen Rob Stone. Also at the table were Mark and the two brothers from Minnesota, Steve and Andy.

At around midnight, Jimmy left to return to the room. I thought I would not be much longer and was preparing to leave when a couple of Koreans came up to our table and asked if we wanted to play a drinking game. We all shook our heads but then Andy said he would do it. He got up and followed them to their table. A minute or two later, Steve said he wanted to check on his brother, Mark, Rod, and I followed him.

The Koreans had a large table. There were four Korean guys and three girls, one of whom may have been the best looking Korean girl I had seen all trip. They were not playing drinking games, just doing shots of Soju. Though I had not had a drink all night, I shot down the Korean firewater when it was passed to me. We each had three or four shots, but there was not much conversation. None of the Koreans spoke much English, in fact only one of the girls spoke any! On our side, Steve actually spoke a little bit of Korean as he had taught English here a few years ago. He said he did not remember much, but was able to get out a few words.

After our fourth shot of Soju, we convinced them to drink beer and ordered two pitchers. A tradition in Korea is that you never fill your own glass. It is considered extremely rude for your friends to allow your glass reach empty. Once a glass reaches less than a quarter full, others will fall over themselves to refill it. Steve taught us a funny Korean expression which meant, "Are you busy." That is what you say should your friends fail to realize your glass is in need of a refill. It basically says to them, "What are you doing that has you so wrapped up that you cannot fill my glass." It is not used often and when it is, it brings many apologies from the others.

We loved this and drank our beer as fast as we could in order to ask, "Are you busy?" The other conversation centered on who we non-Koreans looked like. The Korean girls started by saying Andy looked like Nick Cage, which greatly flattered him. Next up was Mark and he was told he was handsome because he looked like Robin Williams. We all laughed at that and wondered why looking like Robin Williams would make you handsome.

Then it was my turn and the three girls conferred and decided that I looked like Guus Hiddink! Normally being told I looked like a man who was probably in his upper 50's would be an insult, however, knowing the esteem in which they held their coach, I took it as a compliment. After a few minutes, the girls decided I did not look like Hiddink and instead said I was handsome because I looked like Jim Carey! That was a slap in the face, but rather than deny it, I stood up and started talking out of my butt, like the comedian in *Ace Venture*.

For the next hour or so we all drank beer and called each other by our doppelganger names. "Hey, Robin Williams. Are you busy?" After a while, the Koreans left, saying the had class in the morning. The Minnesota brothers and Mark left as well leaving Rod and I.

It was very late, but I was enjoying talking to him. He was a soccer coach in Australia, but was looking for international experience and had looked for jobs in Japan and here in Korea. We talked a lot about cricket and Aussi Rules Football and he asked me about American football and baseball. He told me stories of Japan and I related how great it had been to beat Portugal. He had been bitterly disappointed that his country had not qualified, falling to Uruguay in a playoff. He hoped that his region, Oceania, would be awarded an automatic spot for Germany in 2006. I agreed with him and we promised to meet up there.

I am not sure why, but the bar remained open. For a while I thought we would be kicked out, but as the hours went by, we realized it would be up to us to leave. We finally did so at 6:30. The sun was coming up as we hailed a cab for the short ride back to the Valentine Hotel. We exchanged e-mail addresses and shook hands as I unlocked my room.

Jimmy was asleep on the floor, leaving the round, pink bed for me. As I crawled into it, just before 7:00, I knew that the alarm would go off at 8:30.

Korea, Again

It seemed that I had only closed my eyes when Jimmy woke me. Actually, I had. With a fine one and one half hours of sleep, I was up and quickly packing. I was able to catch a quick shower in the pink bathtub before we left the aptly named Valentine Hotel.

Jimmy and I walked across the wasteland that led from the edge of the city to the train station and caught our train with just minutes to spare. I tried to sleep for most of the five-hour ride back to Seoul, but as before, I was unable.

Whenever I neared sleep, my mind would conjure up images from this wonderful trip. O'Brien's goal still stands out as the greatest single moment, but other, off field events conspired to deny me the sleep that I needed. I remembered entering the restaurant that first night here and realizing none of the staff spoke English, but through the good will of Mr. Hyun, had a great meal. I replayed the party at Nashville, when I had first met so many people that I now consider good friends. For some reason, I thought about Monty and I singing Country Roads while looking for food in Daegu. After that, that song was stuck in my head and I knew I would never sleep.

I passed the time reading the paper and eventually we pulled into Suwon. Only a quick half-hour ride and we would be back in Seoul. Jimmy and I planned to hurry back to the *Dong-Il* and either watch the Korea-Spain game in our rooms or make the short walk to City Hall and try to find a place near one of the large screens. However, as we breezed along, passing one subway car after another, we began to notice that they were very full. It had not dawned on us that all of Korea was headed to City Hall. Once that fact became clear, we remembered that the City Hall subway station was the one directly before the one we use for the *Dong-Il*.

As we passed another subway, it was apparent that it was filled beyond capacity and Jimmy and I realized that we would not be able to simply board the subway once we reached Seoul Station. We knew we would never get onto the train just one stop before City Hall. We also knew that we would not be able to take a taxi because all the roads around City Hall were closed, blocking our route home.

The first thing we did upon disembarking from the train was to go out of the large terminal. We had previously seen a large screen outside, between the train terminal and the subway station. I had hoped we could watch from there, but alas, a few thousand Koreans had that thought sooner than I.

It was nearly 3:00 and not only did I want to find a place to watch the game, but I was also very hungry. I remembered a few small noodle shops nearby. They were a cross between a stand and an actual restaurant. They were each self-contained in their own room that sat perhaps 20. I looked into one that was empty except for two old women. I also noticed a television and so I led Jimmy in and we took a seat right in front of the small screen.

One of the ladies was sitting at a table near the door. She had her shoes off and was picking at her feet. To be more precise, she was digging under her toenails with her fingernails. I winced at the sight that is never really seen back in the States, at least in public. The second of the two women, who had been standing behind the counter, came over and said something in Korean that I took to mean, "Can I help you?"

A few days earlier, I had learned a new word, "Raman." Someone had told me it meant "noodle" which had made sense because in college I sometimes ate Raman Noodles. I confidently said to the woman, "Raman." She gave me a funny look, so I said again, "Raman." Only this time I threw in what I thought was a Korean accent.

It must have worked because she said something that sounded like "Raman" and I nodded, holding up two fingers and pointed to Jimmy. She nodded and walked off. What she did next horrified me. Rather than going into the kitchen and fixing what I hoped would be noodle soup, she went over to the other lady who was still picking her toenails. She bent down, very close to her ear and spoke loudly. The Foot Lady nodded, slowly stood up, and shuffled into the kitchen. The waitress returned to her spot behind the counter.

Jimmy and I were stunned. We did not know what to do. On one hand, we had the perfect situation. We were sitting in front of a television and food was on the way. On the other hand, our soup was sure to be filled with old Korean lady toe jam!

I do not know our logic, but we decided to stick it out. After a few minutes, the soup was served. As I expected, it was noodle soup. It was boiling hot which gave me hope that whatever had found it's way into the bowl would be dead. As it cooled, I began to eat and found it to be spicy and very tasty. Soon, I was able to put the cook out of my head and enjoyed the meal.

I was only a few spoonfuls into the soup when the game began. As the ball was put into play, I heard a roar that swept in from seemingly every direction. All of Seoul was watching. I made a prediction. "Brazil 3 Korea 1 in the finals," I told Jimmy and he did not disagree.

The game neared halftime at 0-0 and Jimmy and I decided to make a run for home. We paid the W3,000 for lunch and ran to the subway. As expected it was empty. We hurried to the *Dong-Il* and found our two ladies sitting on the floor, watching the game. We decided to watch in my room. Spain had the better of play, but could not score. Twice the ball found the net, but neither time did it count and the match went to penalties.

I could feel the tension as the first shooter, Hwang prepared to take his kick and heard cheers erupting from the streets only a story below as he converted. Spain answered and the next four shooters found their mark as well. Korean poster boy, Ahn was true and the Reds led 4-3 as the Spanish youngster, Jauquin stepped up. Korean goalkeeper Lee guessed correctly and made the save. I was stunned and both Jimmy and I let out a loud cheer as Hong scored the clincher. We quickly ran down the stairs and out into the street where, despite the bright 6:00 sun, fireworks were exploding.

For the next six hours, we watched the now familiar scene. Tens of thousands of Koreans went crazy. They were completely out of their minds. The celebration was as large and as loud as the others, but because they have done this at least two other times, I feel it had lost just a bit of it's intensity.

It was still as impressive a spectacle as I have ever witnessed and I spent a few hours standing just off the street and taking it all in. The colors, I should say color, red. The two songs sung over and over. The bottle rockets that exploded not too far overhead. The handshakes and now familiar greeting , "Fighting!" Each of these combine to create a unique and patriotic demonstration.

The people of Korea have been such wonderful hosts and I am very happy for them. If it is not the U.S., I am thrilled that it is these wonderfully hospitable people singing in the streets. It is another moment for them and for all they have done in the years of preparation, and the last month of action, they deserve this. Perhaps, four years ago, in France, the people were as fervent and jubilant, but I do not think so. I was not there so I cannot judge, but it is hard to imagine any people celebrating like this.

After a few hours, I went up to the PC Bang. I congratulated Damien on the win and asked for a Coke. He handed me two and refused payment. "For the big win," he told me.

I read and wrote and was vaguely aware of the last of the quarterfinal matches on the television. At one point I stood up and realized the game was in the 80th minute. The score was Turkey 0 Senegal 0. I watched as regulation ended and then as the two of many Cinderella teams played for a Golden Goal. I did not have to wait long as Turkey scored in the 4th minute of extra-time.

I was both happy for Turkey and sad for Senegal. Both these teams had made it farther than expected, and I hoped that in the streets of Dakar, there would be celebration for the wonderful display of football their team given to the world.

The streets of Seoul were still full of gleeful Koreans when I left the PC Bang at midnight. On the way home, I stopped at my favorite little restaurant and ordered the sushi. As I ate the delicious raw fish, I gazed out the window in wonderment at the wild scene. If you had told me that on the 21st day of my trip, I would be eating sushi at midnight while watching a wild Korean celebration in the street, I would have asked what you were smoking.

This, like nearly the whole trip, has been one awe-inspiring surprise after another. I am honored to be a part of this, if only as a witness. I am also grateful to the game of soccer for bringing so much joy to so many people. The world's game had lived up to that moniker.

The final four teams are Brazil, Germany, South Korea, and Turkey. How I would have loved to have played that parlay.

Day 22
Sunday, June 23

Sometimes Nay Means Yes

In essence the World Cup was over for me, at least the World Cup experience. There would be no more games played while I am in Korea. In fact, I would watch the next game, the Korea-Germany semi-final, from my couch in my home in Northern Virginia. Thus I began my last full day in this wonderful country by sleeping until 11:00.

When I finally made my way into the hallway of the *Dong-Il*, I knocked on Jimmy's door and also that of both Andy Mead and Wade. Both had come to Seoul and upon my recommendation, had found their way to this small hotel.

The four of us went to my favorite restaurant, and I told them about the delicious spicy soup. Andy ordered it and liked it. Wade was not a fan of the spicy stuff and instead got a beef and rice dish that he enjoyed.

I had realized that this would be the last time I would eat here and hoped that I would find something similar to this dish back home. I was sad to leave this little orange restaurant. It was dawning on me that I was doing many things for the last time today. I had been here three weeks, but somehow it seemed longer. Many times I have been anxious to return home towards the end of a trip, however, other than missing Ivy, I had no desire to go home.

The only thing on my agenda today was to pick up my tailor made suit in Itaewon. Jimmy wanted to do some of the sight seeing around our home base that we had been sure we would do, but had never gotten around to.

With Jimmy off, I followed Andy and Wade to the *Namdaemun* Market where they searched for a camera Andy had left behind the night before. We went to the top of a tall building to the restaurant where it had been left, but it was closed until dinner. I was hoping to do some last minute shopping, but found nothing in the large market so we jumped back on the subway and headed for that famous foreign zone, Itaewon.

It was raining lightly, nothing more than a mist when we entered the shop to pick up my suit. The owner of The Swank Taylor recognized me immediately and within a few seconds produced the suit. It still had some stitching on it and I worried that it was not ready, but he assured me that there were only minor adjustments to be made. I tried it on and it was a perfect fit. He told me to come back in four hours, and it would be ready.

Seeing me in the new custom-made suit gave Andy an idea and he asked if he could get a tuxedo. Of course he could, the small, well-dressed Korean told him. It was a little more expensive and Andy agreed to the $200 price. Wade and I waited while Andy was fitted. I actually thought about doing that as well, I pay nearly that much each time I rent one, but in the end, decided against it.

After the fitting, and with a few hours to kill, we walked the long street of Itaewon. At the far end, we bumped into Jim Morehouse, the Director of Communications for U.S. Soccer. We all reflected on what a great run the team had had. I could tell by talking to him that this wonderful surprise had caused a lot of extra work for him and he was tired. He said that he was making arrangements to get some of the players on Letterman and Leno. I thought it was good that the federation was taking advantage of this success to market the players. I was glad a guy like Jim was doing it, though I did not envy his workload.

After he excused himself, we continued with our slow walk and I made a few purchases. It was my last time here and I was determined to get some bargains. I saw a nice wooden jewelry box. It was small and had a Korean scene carved into it. I talked the vendor down from W16,000 and bought it for 10,000. I also got 2,000 *won* knocked off the already low price of 12,000 for a bright orange Hawaiian shirt.

We were hungry and decided to have a nice sit down meal and opted for one of the better restaurants in the area. I lead them to the Monghul Restaurant. They had a wonderful Indian buffet. At W18,000 it was, by far, the most expensive meal I had here. It was well worth it and we all stuffed ourselves and toasted the U.S. team.

Over Tandori Chicken and other Indian goodies, Wade told a funny story that sums up some of the difficulty with the language as well as the friendliness of the Korean people. I had mentioned how the Korean word for "Yes" is *"Nay"* which sounds like "No."

Wade nodded agreement and said it had caused him some trouble. "In Suwon, I was looking for a haircut and asked a policeman where I could find a barbershop. The cop put me in his car and drove me to a salon. He went in and told them I needed a cut. Then, as I am sitting in the chair, the hairdresser asked me if I wanted a scalp massage. I said 'No.' and she started massaging my head! It felt good, but ended up being expensive!"

I laughed at the story and thought that I never would have had the guts to ask a cop where to find a barbershop and that it had to be scary going into a Korean salon. Who knows how they will cut your hair?

We talked about some of the exotic food we had eaten. While I was eating eel in Ulsan, their host family there had treated them to a meal of whale. Wade said it was delicious, very similar to steak. They had also been told of people eating live baby octopus. They said it was something one does over beers. "You pop one of those suckers in your mouth and go to work," Wade explained. "You really have to chew fast and hard before they latch onto you. They say it is a lot of fun, but you have to work like crazy."

I had eaten silkworm larvae and had actually eaten baby octopus a few times at a sushi place back home, but never alive. I am not sure if I would have been able to do that.

After dinner, we returned to the Swank Taylor and found my suit ready to go. The man gave me his card and told me to fax him if I needed another. He told me that if I ever saw a picture of a suit I liked to send it to him and he would make it.

I thanked him and we headed back to the *Dong-Il*. At about 12:30 I was ready for bed, but just as I was turning off the TV, the U.S.-Germany match came on. I watched it until the bitter end and fell asleep for the last time in Korea at 2:30.

Day 23
Monday, June 24

The Sun Came Up Twice Today

I woke up at 9:00 and spent an hour or so packing. It took that long because I was watching a few different morning shows. It is simply amazing to think that the hosts will be playing in the semi-finals and the TV personalities here are making the most of it. I can scarcely believe, along with the rest of the world, I am sure, that Korea has made the final four in the World Cup.

This honor is usually reserved for the giants of the game, but tomorrow the Reds will face off with one of the usual suspects, Germany. I think that Korea can beat them, but fear that playing on only two days rest, after the long, hard fought, penalty decider against Spain may be too much to overcome.

I checked to make sure Jimmy was packed and ready, and he assured me he was. He declined lunch, saying he wanted to do some last second running around. I found Wade, and he and I went for lunch.

It was a rainy day and after circling the block a few times, decided on a place that I had not yet been. We both ordered a Bulgogi Bowl. It was good marinated beef, served very hot along with onions, garlic, and the good, spicy red sauce. We ate it with rice and it was an enjoyable last meal. Again, the price was right at W6,000 or just under $5.00.

Back at the *Dong-Il* we met up with Jimmy, made one last check around our rooms, and headed out. We stopped to hug the two ladies and thank them for everything they had done for us. I do not think I am wrong in saying that we could not have found a better place in which to stay. I am grateful to them for making it that way as well as to Chuck for setting up our stay here.

Wade went with us and we decided we would take a taxi, which dropped us off at Seoul Station. There, we said goodbye to Wade and boarded a bus to the airport that was just about to pull out. As we drove through the large city, I looked out the window and saw the same flags lining the road that I had seen on the way in.

I remember the pride I had felt upon seeing our flag those three plus weeks ago and now, because of our brilliant coach and brave players, that flag seemed to be flying higher, it's colors a little brighter, and the feeling in my soul a bit deeper.

I also noticed that a few other flags had new meaning for me. The Portuguese one was not as intimidating and because of the guys I had met the night before that first match, it seemed welcoming, and I thought ahead to a trip Ivy and I have been planning for the European Championships in 2004. The Polish flag brought back a feeling of brotherhood, as I remembered the Pole who offered me his jersey after which he and I, arms around one another's shoulders, sang in delight.

I saw the Mexican flag and laughed, feeling warm and fuzzy inside. We had beaten our chief rival in our most important meeting, but I also took a moment to

232

remember the Mexicans I had met before that game. They were as nice and as friendly as any I had met over here. The Italian flag made my think of a foolish team who loses because they refuse to change their tactics and then blame everyone else. The Brazilian flag reminded me of everything beautiful about this game, the early Rivaldo incident notwithstanding. They are truly the masters and I am lucky to have seen them. I am certain that they will lift the trophy next Sunday.

We next passed the Irish flag and I thought not only of my brother-in-law, but also of a team that rallied around each other in the wake of the Roy Keane disaster. They played with the passion that makes this game so great. All of Ireland should be proud of the effort given by the *Bhoys* in Green. There was another tri-color flag, this time it was the *bleu, blanc, et rouge* of France. I shook my head, thinking that I picked them to win it all and wondered at how such a talented team, one full of megastars, could be so humbled, not even scoring a single goal. I knew that in a tournament of surprises, they were the biggest.

I recognized the flag of Senegal, which before the Cup, I could not have done. I was moved to think that that team delighted an entire continent and for a few days, made Dakar the happiest place on earth. I am awed at the effect sports can have on people. Then there was the cross of St. George. I thought that England truly had a shot at glory. Perhaps their showing here will give them the confidence to step up and return the Cup to the land where the game began.

I saw the dark German flag and could not help but feel proud of their team. They had been maligned before the Cup and had already made it farther than most had predicted. Their team is smart, tough, and relentless. As much as I do not root for them, I fear they will reach the finals and once there, who knows?

Finally we passed the wonderful flag of South Korea. I have come to love this country; it's people, it's culture, and it's team. I say again that there could not have been a friendlier host. Everything had been wonderful. The people bent over backwards and succeeded in putting on the perfect games. It is not often that they have the world looking at them, and they stepped up. Not only their team, but their people. They should be proud of their efforts. As for their team, I will never forget them. Their spirit is second to none. They listened to their brilliant coach and ran like a team possessed. They play the game the way all games should be played, as hard as possible. Merely an afterthought before, they are now one of my favorite teams. Their players deserve much praise, particularly my favorite player, Park Ji-Sung.

Soon we had left the flags behind and moved out of the city to the rice paddies and finally to the airport.

The return flight was without incident and after nearly 20 long hours, Ivy gave me the tightest hug I have ever felt. After hugging countless strangers in moments of unbridled joy, this one was my favorite, and I was glad to be home.

Epilogue

A tournament of upsets and surprises ended with some usual suspects. Jimmy spent the first night at my house and we woke up early to watch the Reds. As I had feared, Germany beat an exhausted Korean team. The next day, Brazil ended Turkey's hopes for both revenge and a trip to the final. Although neither Germany nor Brazil were regarded as favorites entering the tournament, their pedigree cannot be questioned.

In the final, Ronaldo secured his legacy by scoring twice in leading the Samba Boys over the Germans, 2-0. For some reason, voting for the Golden Ball Award for the tournament MVP was done before the final and was given to Oliver Kahn. He certainly had an outstanding tournament, however in the final, his failure to handle a shot led to Brazil's first goal.

Despite their stellar performance, no Americans were transferred to Europe. Brian McBride had a successful loan spell with Everton, but returned to the States for the start of the 2003 MLS season. Frankie Hejduk and Joe-Max Moore both returned to MLS from Europe and Earnie Stewart moved from his team in Holland to MLS.

Ivy and I were married in November and are planning a trip to Portugal for the European Championships, though I doubt I will write a book on them.

I am still in contact with many of the friends I made in Korea. For all the wonderful times I had watching the U.S. and their stunning run to the quarterfinals, it is the people I met that I remember the most. From the group of Portuguese who predicted they would beat us 4-0, the young man from Newcastle who said he could see us in the finals, the Frenchman who has me listening to Mozart when I need a pick-me-up, John the Irish law professor drinking only from a bottle who got me a ticket for one of the best matches of the Cup, and Damian who helped me with all my computer needs in his PC Bang to Mark who survived his ungodly trip home, Mike who nearly did not survive his return to San Francisco after partying a little too much at the final, hours before his flight, Scott and Neil who have still not seen the show that featured them, Kaela who may be the perfect girl - good looking and loves soccer and beer, Big Dog who started a discussion on what was the first food each of us ate upon returning, Chuck who I have kidded about his volume but is a great guy whom the Koreans are lucky to learn from, Tonya and Doug and their baby girl, Monty who is still wondering where his U.S. flag (that he left in my hotel room) is, and Jimmy who is still playing with me for the FC Rangers in Fredericksburg and updating his site, www.onthesidelines.org. These folks, and many others, along with O'Brien's goal, which still gives me goose bumps, are my lasting memories. It truly is the people that make the event, and I found in Korea that soccer fans are, contrary to their reputation, some of the warmest people in the world. I thank everyone I came in contact with for making this experience so wonderful for me. There are many U.S. fans I met that I did not mention in this book and for that I am sorry. I would like to take a moment to name a few here. Rishi and his sister, Rupa. Marshall, Dribs,

Sean, Dave, Brock, Kevin, Will, and others whose names my small brain has been unable to retain. I hope to see you all in Germany.

Printed in the United States
By Bookmasters